NEST OF TRAITORS

Nicholas Whitlam is a professional banker. Having worked in London, New York and Hong Kong, he is presently chief executive of a large Australian bank. Mr Whitlam holds degrees from Harvard and London Universities; The Petrov Affair was the subject of his Harvard honours thesis. Born in 1945, he lives in Sydney with his wife and three children.

John Stubbs has worked as a journalist in Asia and the UK as well as Australia, and is now with the *Sunday Sun* in Brisbane. Prior to writing this book he was based in Parliament House, Canberra, first as parliamentary correspondent of the *Australian* and later as political correspondent with the *Sydney Morning Herald*. He is the author of *The Hidden People: Poverty in Australia*.

NEST OF
TRAITORS
THE PETROV AFFAIR

NICHOLAS WHITLAM
JOHN STUBBS

University of Queensland Press

ST LUCIA • LONDON • NEW YORK

First published 1974 by Jacaranda Press Pty Ltd
Published 1985 by University of Queensland Press
Box 42, St Lucia, Queensland, Australia

Printed in Australia by Dominion Press — Hedges & Bell

Distributed in the UK and Europe by University of Queensland Press,
Stockley Road, West Drayton, Middlesex UB7 9BE, England

Distributed in the USA and Canada by University of Queensland Press,
5 South Union Street, Lawrence, Mass. 01843 USA

Cataloguing in Publication Data

National Library of Australia

Whitlam, Nicholas, 1945 —
  Nest of traitors.

  Rev. ed.
  Bibliography.
  Includes index.

  1. Petrov, Vladimir Mikhailovich, 1907 — .
  2. Petrov, Evdokia, 1914 — . 3. Espionage, Russian —
  Australia. I. Stubbs, John N. II. Title. III. Title:
  The Petrov affair.

364.1'31'0994

Library of Congress

Whitlam, Nicholas.
  Nest of traitors.

  Bibliography: p.
  Includes index.
  1. Australia — Politics and government — 1945 —
2. Espionage, Russian — Australia. 3. Petrov,
Vladimir Mikhailovich, 1907 — . 4. Petrov, Evdokia.
I. Stubbs, John. II. Title.
DU117.17.W48   1985   994.06   84-28120

ISBN 0 7022 1857 X

For Alice, Edward, Peter, Sasha, Susie and Will

Contents

Preface to paperback edition

It is now thirty years since that potent brew of politics, personalities and espionage that became known as the Petrov affair erupted in a way which determined the direction of Australian political life for a generation. It took place in a world very different from the one in which Australians live today. One such change has been the continuing revolution in communications, creating a community that is better informed and somewhat more sceptical of the pronouncements of its leaders.

One result, particularly noticeable in the decade since the original publication of this book in 1974, has been that more Australians have become openly critical of some of the more outrageous activities of our Intelligence community. The debate about what constitutes a proper role for Australian security intelligence services, and what controls over these services are desirable or feasible, continues even within the Labor government elected in 1983. Characteristically, it has been accompanied by a series of revelations about bizarre incidents and questionable behaviour involving members of those services.

Yet in many respects nothing has changed since the Petrov years; if anything, there has been an increase in the tension and conflict of interests between competing powers which make such services essential.

On Monday, 24 September 1984, the Hawke Labor government released what are described as the Petrov Papers and they are now available for inspection at the Australian Archives in Canberra.

Despite the public fanfare that accompanied the opening of the archive, it was a curiously unsatisfactory exercise. Documents essential to the proof of the common theories that an elaborate conspiracy underlay the Affair — or, equally, that would have enabled those who dismiss such theories positively to refute them — were simply not released.

The first of the very sketchy Cabinet documents made available refers to the meeting of 13 April 1954 — after Petrov actually defected.

The Cabinet meeting took place only the day before parliament was to adjourn for the 1954 election, an election that was to prove one of the most crucial in Australian political history. On the evidence of that Cabinet minute, it must be accepted that most of Menzies' ministers did not know what was going on until that day. They must be absolved from participation in a conspiracy.

We now know officially, however, from the records of the head of the Australian Security Intelligence Organisation of the time, Colonel Spry, that Menzies himself knew at least as early as mid-February of the likelihood of Petrov's defection. Menzies' later claim to parliament that he had not heard the name Petrov until 10 or 11 April has long been known to be false and this is now documented.

The crucial question of whether he knew much earlier than February is not resolved; it cannot be determined without access to ASIO records and "running sheets" covering the period of the dealings between ASIO, Bialoguski and Petrov. It is only in such records that traces of the sinews which could once have connected and activated a living conspiracy might have been discovered.

There is nothing in the documents, as now available, which is in conflict with the accounts given to the authors a decade ago by Dr John Burton and Dr Michael Bialoguski. The voice of Dr Burton emerges as that of a rational, forward-looking man who has somehow managed to keep his cool in a climate of acrimony and hysteria.

The transcripts of the secret sessions of the Commission show that Burton was rewarded for his calm thoughtfulness with aggressive — some would say cowardly — insinuations about his loyalty. But he did not falter from his belief that the Royal Commission was provocatively and gratuitously sowing distrust and suspicion against people of independent or radical views, citizens who would never reveal information vital to the defence of Australia, no matter how provoked.

Burton is also firm in his statements to the Commission that most of the evidence produced by Petrov was known to British Security five years before the defection. In these statements, given in secret session, he asserts that Petrov himself was claiming a position and knowledge far in excess of a man who, as Petrov's own evidence had shown had "a purely cipher background".

There is a minor, but curious, discrepancy in the archives relating to Dr Bialoguski. The opening of our book records the unconventional method in which the colourful Australian counter-spy collected information from the drunken Petrov's pockets in Sydney on 19 June 1953, and a matching exhibit is contained in the archives.

The mildest of Petrov's examples of unconventional English (which Bialoguski saw as a preparation for defection at that early stage) recorded in the document is: "Balls to you." The exhibit is, however, a much briefer document than Bialoguski's account to the authors indicated. It records only half a dozen names and telephone numbers. And yet Michael Thwaites, the former ASIO agent, in his ASIO apologia on the affair, *Truth Will Out*, published in 1980, refers to forty or fifty names being copied on this occasion by Bialoguski, while Petrov was "sleeping heavily".

God knows what else has been flushed with the passage of time.

In retrospect the 1984 publication of Document J raises an important issue about the selective political use of secret evidence. The treatise, allegedly written by Communist journalist Rupert Lockwood who himself disputes authorship of part of its contents, indeed matches its description before the Commission as a "farrago of facts, falsity and filth". On 15 July that year, the Australian public was informed by Mr Justice Owen that two staff members of the Labor leader, Dr Evatt, (in addition to his former press secretary Fergan O'Sullivan, author of Document H) had been sources for Document J.

Evatt reacted passionately to this charge. He pointed out that Owen's statement had been made without any evidentiary support and that it caused immediate and perhaps ir-reparable harm to private citizens. It played no small part in precipitating and motivating some of Evatt's disastrous deal-ings with the Commission. These were both personally and politically destructive. Any independent observer would feel sympathy and understanding for Evatt: he was ambushed, and it was a battle he couldn't win.

And yet now, thirty years later, we find for the first time that in Document J there are grave charges of disloyalty to Australia against members of the Menzies government and its closest and most influential supporters. Neither the Menzies government, nor ASIO, nor the Royal Commission saw fit to examine, investigate or publicize these allegations against those on the conservative side of politics. They had precisely the same source as those that proved so decisively destructive-ly to Labor; they should have been examined. It is entirely possible that we were too soft on Rupert Lockwood. But if the accusations he made against Evatt's colleagues were taken seriously, why were those against Menzies not.

A chilly, acrid whiff of McCarthyism and the excesses of the Cold War arises from the documents now released. In some respects they are patently misleading. The recorded Cabinet decision to hold the Royal Commission suggests the Menzies government intended to occupy the high moral ground so that there could be no suggestion of a political smear campaign.

Yet it is a matter of record that individual Cabinet ministers, in particular Arthur Fadden, embarked on such a campaign while electioneering. It is common knowledge among journalists of the era that these tactics were reinforced in semi-official leaks and background briefings by a series of false and sweeping allegations against Labor figures.

The new documents do not resolve many of the basic questions about the conduct of Australian authorities of the period. While the central issues remain matters of individual decision, nothing has given us reason to alter the judgments we made in 1974.

Nicholas Whitlam

John Stubbs

1 The pig and the Pole

On the night of 19 June 1953, while the 'atom spies' Julius and Ethel Rosenberg awaited death within a few hours in Sing Sing's electric chair, Vladimir Mikhailovich Petrov, a diplomat with the Soviet embassy in Canberra, lay in a drunken sleep in the guest bedroom of an expensive private apartment overlooking Sydney Harbour. In the lavatory nearest the bedroom, his host, Dr Michael Bialoguski, was copying on to a roll of toilet paper the contents of documents he had filched from Petrov's coat pockets.

Earlier that evening, Bialoguski, whom Petrov probably believed to be a dedicated Communist sympathizer, had left the Soviet diplomat with several bottles of whisky. Bialoguski had set off, in his guise as a conscientious Communist, to a demonstration in favour of clemency for the Rosenbergs, but he had every confidence that Petrov would 'have a few nightcaps' while he was out. Bialoguski, an engaging, colourful character, had in fact been an agent of the Australian intelligence services for many years. He had assiduously cultivated his friendship with Petrov from the time he first met him in the Russian Social Club in Sydney nearly two years earlier.

The Australian counterspy made ten separate trips across a creaking floor into the unconscious Petrov's bedroom. His spoils included a list of more than forty names of Australian citizens, and a variety of notes including the draft of a letter to Madame Ollier, a French diplomat based in Canberra. It was almost sunrise when Bialoguski made his last notes, by this time on the cardboard at the centre of the roll. The final item was a list of misspelt expletives, swearwords and unconventional English, together with their Russian equivalents, part of Petrov's increasingly personal and basic study of the Australian way of life.

That roll of toilet paper was to be produced less than a year later, with due legal formality, before three berobed and bewigged Royal Commissioners towards the climax of the

1

'Petrov affair'.[1] For in April 1954 Vladimir Petrov defected, bringing with him papers that he alleged were secret Soviet espionage documents, and a Royal Commission was appointed to investigate the Petrov information. The leader of the Opposition, Dr Herbert Vere Evatt, members of whose staff were mentioned in the documents, challenged Petrov's story and the authenticity of this material. Evatt accused Petrov of being at the centre of a conspiracy designed to harm the Australian Labor Party. The result was 'a political battle of a fury not previously known in the country, nor ever known in [most others]'.[2]

This small episode in Bialoguski's apartment held some of the elements of tragedy and farce characterizing the Petrov affair, which was to have a profound impact on the subsequent political history of the nation and scar the lives of many individuals. It destroyed, politically at least, the ALP leader, Dr Evatt, and precipitated events that for more than the immediate future shattered his party's prospects of gaining power. The verdict of the *National Times* in 1973 was that the affair, and Petrov's defection, 'had widespread and continuing repercussions—including the near destruction of the Labor Party—and is now seen as the most significant event in Australian politics between 1949 and 1972'[3]—the years of the Cold War, Korea and Vietnam, when the Labor Party was kept in the political wilderness. Yet in early 1954 Labor had seemed certain to win the coming federal election.

Such was the setting of secrecy, distortion and hysteria in which the affair was played out that only now, twenty years later, has it become possible to look with some detachment at its roots, and the conduct and motivations of those at its centre.

The Labor government that was expected to come to power in the election of 1954 would have been a very radical one, in the view of the Australian security services. It advocated, for instance, recognition of the new Communist government in China, a pledge that was not to be carried out until Labor won office two decades later. Further, it was sympathetic to the small and the newly independent nations of the Third World, and was critical of the unquestioning dependence on 'great and powerful allies', Britain and America, that dominated the foreign policy of the conservative parties led by Robert Menzies.

The degree to which there was a conspiracy by opponents of a potential Labor government in arranging Petrov's defection has been a matter of unresolved controversy within informed political circles. This book is an attempt to tell the tangled, dramatic and emotional story in an unbiased manner, now that the passage of time enables the affair to be examined with some degree of historical perspective. But the story that emerges is disturbing. The Petrov affair was the culmination of Australia's McCarthy era, and—while the nation was spared the worst excesses of the American experience—the threat of such excesses was real; in the end, many innocent Australians suffered hardship in, and harm to, their daily lives, the lives of their families, and their careers.

Beyond the specifics of the affair itself, the Petrov experience raises a much wider issue that is still relevant in every Western democracy: the question of how security services can be established and controlled so that they are neither political tools of the existing regime, nor political forces in their own right that act covertly as a secret government. There is evidence that the Australian intelligence establishment, with assistance from the British secret service, combined both these undesirable roles during the course of the Petrov affair.

Both Petrov, then aged forty-six, and Bialoguski, thirty-six, had had a hard road from Russia to the bedroom and lavatory of Bialoguski's apartment in the exclusive 'Cliveden' block at 22 Wolseley Road, Point Piper; but they were very different from each other in character and taste—a fact that Bialoguski took great care to conceal from Petrov.

Michael Bialoguski was born of Polish parents in Kiev, the capital of the Ukraine, in 1917. Russia was in the midst of a chaotic revolution within a year of his birth. When Poland became a sovereign state, the family fled to its eastern provinces. Bialoguski went to school at Vilna, then a city of about 200 000 people. In 1935 he matriculated to the faculty of medicine, but also continued to study the violin at the Vilna conservatorium.* He was a fifth-year medical student when World War II broke out, and shortly afterwards the Soviet Union ceded Vilna to the Lithuanian Republic, which had links with Nazi Germany. At one stage Bialoguski was arrested and beaten after what he describes as 'really a piece of bad fortune', when the Lithuanian authorities searched his room and found weapons that he had been concealing overnight for a group of dissidents. While in prison he failed to be registered as a permanent resident of Vilna, so that when the Russians occupied the Baltic states in 1940 he was classified as a 'refugee', with the option of applying for Soviet citizenship or for permission to go abroad. After he had been interrogated by the secret police, the NKVD (later known as the MVD, and now the KGB), he decided to 'waste no time getting away from Soviet occupation'.

Bialoguski refers still to the 'impersonal brand of cruelty practised by the Russians' at that time. Since it was impossible to leave the occupied territories unless one could first obtain permission to enter another country, he cunningly developed a story that he had an aged and ailing aunt in Curaçao in the Dutch West Indies, for which a visa was unnecessary. Leaving his mother, and with his only asset a one-carat diamond concealed in a tube of toothpaste, he made his way by train along the Trans-Siberian Railway to Vladivostock. Moscow, which he saw in a snowfall on the way, apparently made a deep and lasting impression on him, with 'the sight of furtively and silently moving people against the background of huge heavy buildings. ... It seemed these shabbily clothed passers-by did not belong to this magnificent city, and that they could not care less about it.'

To his relief (and the subsequent suspicion of some of his critics), he then managed to board a boat to Japan in the

---

*Music has remained the major interest in his life, to the extent that he has hired the Albert Hall in London, at a cost of thousands of pounds, to conduct an orchestra, and has been responsible for the formation of a Commonwealth Orchestra.

company of other refugees. He discovered at the Polish embassy in Tokyo that he could enter Australia if he wished. Accordingly he sold the diamond to pay his fare and arrived in Sydney on 24 June 1941 with a small suitcase, a violin and £13. Upon arrival Bialoguski spent several nights sleeping on a bench in Hyde Park. He was twenty-four years old. In the same month Germany invaded the Soviet Union, and less than six months later Japan bombed Pearl Harbour.

After an initial rejection, Bialoguski managed to enlist in the Australian army in 1942. On the basis of his medical training he was sent to the massive army hospital at Concord West, Sydney, where he scrubbed floors for some time, but after complaining of this role he was released to attend Sydney University as a medical student. This episode was characteristic: Bialoguski always seems to have enjoyed a high opinion of himself, to have had a great desire for self-improvement and recognition.

Then, according to his own story, there came a critical turning point. Bialoguski had been embittered against the Russian model of authoritarian communism, specifically by the occupation of his homeland, his own experiences and those of his family. Now, in Sydney, he found the Communist Party becoming politically active, influential and prosperous in the very favourable atmosphere created by the fierce resistance of the Russian forces to the German invasion. He saw the Communist rallies in Sydney's free-speech area, the Domain, and found himself on the mailing list of the Polish Alliance, an organization that appears to have had active Communists among its leaders.

An indication of his attitude at that time emerges clearly in his book, *The Petrov Story*, published in 1955:

Throughout the ages the oppressed, underfed and barbarian people had possessed better fighting qualities and shown greater disregard for their lives than their comfortable and often better armed opponents. The Russians were no exception. They had to fight because they were confronted by an enemy who gave them no opportunity of honourable surrender, and, on the other side, they were driven into action at pistol point by the NKVD men attached

5

to each unit. The Russian man was acting like a cornered, hungry animal which has no way to escape and instinctively fights back.

His Australian acquaintances would not listen to his Russian horror stories and were enthusiastically supporting a national appeal to send sheepskins to the Soviet Union.

At the beginning of 1945, Bialoguski decided to find out for himself whether the general Australian 'attitude of complacency towards the Communist fifth column was being shared by the authorities'. In the telephone book, under Commonwealth Departments, he found the name of the Commonwealth Investigation Service and its address at 117 Pitt Street, Sydney. One day in March he set off for the address, clutching a copy of the *Slavonic Review* he had received in the morning's mail.

Bialoguski was welcomed in the small, paper-littered office of a Mr Bill Barnwell, whom he described as being in his late forties, a 'strongly built man, blue-eyed and showing the ruddiness of good health'. More important than his blue eyes was the fact that he was also 'full of vigour and enthusiasm' for Bialoguski's unsolicited approach and the material he presented. Bialoguski later wrote that Barnwell said he was personally 'struck by the analogy between the early Hitler propaganda and the Slavonic stuff'. At this first interview, Barnwell cut out an application form from the publication *Russia and Us* for Bialoguski to fill out and so obtain membership of the Australia–Soviet Friendship Society. He also instructed him to make regular visits to a club frequented by Soviet sympathizers and others, the Russian Social Club in the basement of a building at 727 George Street, near Central Railway Station. It had a strong subversive core, Barnwell told him, and ran public dances every Saturday night. The following Saturday evening, Bialoguski made his way down the dimly lit stairs to the club. And so began what must have been one of the most turbulent, erratic and significant careers in the history of Australian intelligence work.

Bialoguski continued an association with both the Commonwealth Investigation Service and the Russian Social

Club over the next few years as he moved through a number of medical jobs. After spending most of 1948 in partnership at Thirroul on the south coast of New South Wales, he moved back to Sydney to establish his own practice at the beginning of 1949. When the Australian Security Intelligence Organization was formed in that year he applied for a position to its first head, Mr Justice Reed, after consulting his CIS contact. On 11 August 1949 he was contacted by ASIO, allocated the code name 'Jack Baker', and given £4 a week to cover his out-of-pocket expenses. His ASIO superiors encouraged him to step up his participation in the activities of the Russian Social Club, where he was increasingly regarded as a strong Soviet sympathizer. It was at the club that he was introduced to Petrov on the night of 7 July 1951.

Bialoguski's opinion of Vladimir Petrov at their first meeting, as set out in his book, is a more flattering one than he now holds; 'He was a pig,' he told the authors recently in London. In *The Petrov Story*, Bialoguski describes their encounter that evening. Petrov had recently arrived in Australia, and the introduction was made by Lydia Mokras, a tall, blonde and—even to Bialoguski—mysterious Russian girl who lived with her Czech husband in a flat in Cambridge Street, Stanmore, a Sydney suburb.

'Lydia got up to dance with a shortish, stocky man with grey hair and a round face,' he wrote. Then she brought him to the table and said, 'This is Vladimir Petrov, the new Soviet consul.' Bialoguski had recently been told by his security contact that it would be of great interest if he could learn anything about Petrov, for it appeared that he had 'great say and considerable power' in the embassy, and apparently had 'come especially to pep up the embassy staff'.

Bialoguski's first impression was of Petrov's impassiveness. 'No sign of expression or emotion passed across Petrov's large face. When he laughed he sounded hearty, but the laughter never showed in his eyes. He looked at the world suspiciously and talked little. He walked with a suggestion of a rolling gait, and a tattooed anchor at the base of his left thumb confirmed the belief that he had once been a sailor. I made a snap judgement then that behind the thick frame of expressionless immobility, Petrov hid a cunning and alert mind.' Thus Bialoguski wrote in the atmosphere of that now more distant time. But today, in personal interview, his opinion is that the master-spy was not only a 'pig' but a 'peasant', and Bialoguski used the latter term with its most unfavourable connotations. He stated explicitly, however, that neither epithet detracted from his belief that Petrov was 'tough and cunning'.

Later in their relationship, when Bialoguski was cleverly and cynically encouraging Petrov, they drank heavily together. On the night of 27 November 1953, while Petrov relaxed with Bialoguski over many drinks at the doctor's Sydney flat, he gave Bialoguski a maudlin and romanticized account of his early life. Bialoguski recalls the incident, saying that at the time it seemed Petrov had forgotten there was a listener, and that his thoughts were 'far away ... in immense dark forests and snow-covered tundras; the land where time matters not, because there isn't much to remember and nothing to look forward to; where men toil like beasts and die like beasts, crowded in the suffocating stench of their wooden huts'.

This, Dr Bialoguski wrote, was Petrov's version, on that night, of his own life story:

I come from peasant stock, and my parents could neither read nor write. [Petrov was born in 1907 and was christened, in the Russian Orthodox Church, Afanasy Mikhailovich Shorokov.] I was a small boy when my father died—killed by lightning. I was only seven and the memory of my father is vague. My mother and my only two brothers—Ivan and Alexander—lived in the small village of Larikha in the Tyumen district. Larikha was no different from any other Siberian village; it was virtually cut off from the rest of the world—from its troubles and its joys—by the huge waste lands.*

Seven months in the year we had winter and the snow was waist-deep. In the spring you would fall knee-deep in the sticky

---

*It is perhaps worth noting here that this is Bialoguski's verbatim report of Petrov's monologue. Bialoguski did in fact keep a detailed diary, parts of which the authors have inspected, and with dedicated singlemindedness

mud if you tried to cross any of our village streets. Yes. The life
was hard and one had to be tough to survive. My brothers and I
slept on the floor, crowded in one room. All we had for a bed was
a bit of straw. A year after my father's death I went to the school
in the village, that was from 1915 to 1917. But the revolution
ended my school days, because all schools were closed. For the
next two years I stayed at home with my mother. I was twelve
now, and I had to take my share of the job of trying to keep us
alive. Since my father's death things had been going from bad to
worse, and our small family was now on the verge of starvation.
Luck was with me. The village blacksmith took me as an appren-
tice. The work was very hard. Some of the tools I had to use I
could hardly lift. I won't forget as long as I live those eight long
years I worked for the village blacksmith. Just imagine getting up
at five in the morning in winter when the temperature is well below
zero, and the sun doesn't rise till eight. I remember crawling off my
bed, heavy with sleep, splashing icy cold water on my face to wake
myself properly, and running for my life in fear of being late for
work. Then I toiled and strained every muscle in my body till eight
or nine in the evening; coming home physically and mentally numb
from exhaustion, and falling on my straw bed in full clothes, dead
to the world.

Petrov began to receive some schooling when, while still
working for the blacksmith, he joined the local branch of
Komsomol, the Communist youth organization. The rest of
Petrov's life can be pieced together from his book, *Empire of
Fear: The Petrovs' Own Story*, the transcript of evidence at the
Royal Commission, and the Bialoguski book.

Advancing rapidly in the youth organization, Petrov
became a full member of the Communist Party at the age of
twenty and was sent for training to Sverdlovsk, one of the lar-
gest industrial towns in Siberia. His first appointment of any
importance was in the town of Serov, beyond the Urals, where
he worked as a party organizer among the youth in the metal

---

trained himself to memorize speeches and conversations in great detail. He
was assisted in writing his book by Eric McLoughlin, a journalist with the
Sydney Morning Herald.

trades union. In 1929 he changed his name from Shorokov to the more ambitiously doctrinaire 'Proletarsky'.

Then in 1930 Petrov was called up for compulsory service in the Russian navy, trained as a cipher specialist, and posted to Kronstadt, a naval base on the Baltic Sea near Leningrad. He served both at the base and at sea in a destroyer, and was discharged with the rank of petty officer. In 1933, on completion of his military duties, he entered the cipher service of the OGPU, a predecessor of the MVD, and served at headquarters, the so-called Moscow Centre, until 1937. Then he was sent to western China for six months, where he gained the coveted Red Star.

By 1940 Petrov had reached the rank of major in the Soviet security forces, and headed a cipher section at the Moscow Centre. In 1943, he and his second wife, Evdokia, were posted to the Soviet embassy in Sweden. This was the first time, he testified, they took the name Petrov; the change was made since it was judged too militant to send overseas an embassy official named Proletarsky.

Petrov's relationship with his second wife was to play a vital part in the drama that surrounded the climax of the story. She was born in even poorer circumstances than her husband, in 1914, in the village of Lipky not far from Moscow. Ten years later the family moved to Moscow. There she, like Petrov, joined the Komsomol. After her secondary schooling, completed in 1933, she spent two years studying foreign languages. She was meanwhile employed as a cipher clerk in the RU, another section of the espionage system. Then in 1934 she was transferred to the OGPU proper. In 1937 a daughter was born by her de-facto husband, but the parents were separated soon after this when he was arrested by the police. The child died a month before she married Vladimir Petrov in 1940.

The Petrovs' Stockholm posting lasted from 1943 to 1947. He performed cipher duties for the MVD 'Resident' agent (heading the 'Legal Apparatus', an intelligence network operating under diplomatic cover), and, more important, carried out SK work, which involved checking on the conduct and political reliability of members of the staff of the Soviet embassy, trade delegations and missions, and of other Soviet citizens visiting or living in the target country. This was, necessarily, a branch of intelligence that implied Moscow's trust in the political conformity of the cadre-worker himself. While in Sweden, Petrov was promoted to the rank of lieutenant-colonel. Mrs Petrov was a typist, cipher clerk, accountant and technical assistant to the same Resident. She also performed some MVD work as an intermediary between the Resident and a number of his agents. It was Petrov's first glimpse of life in the West, and he enjoyed it. He told Bialoguski: 'You know, Michael, Sweden's a nice place too, and the life is good there. I would like to have seen more of it, but I didn't know too many people and I had to be pretty careful about what I did and where I went. I had nobody there like you— nobody I could knock round with like I can with you here.'

In late 1947 the Petrovs returned to Moscow and resumed their former name of Proletarsky. For the next three years Petrov continued to perform SK work focused on Soviet vessels and delegations visiting English-speaking countries. His wife did SK work involving a number of European countries and then, in 1948, began to concentrate on espionage in Sweden. Suddenly in 1951, with but one week's notice, the Petrovs were posted to Australia.

Petrov was overtly sent as a referent, a simple clerk. After arriving in Australia he was promoted to the vacant position of third secretary, while also serving as consul and representative of Voks, the Soviet cultural organization. The Voks position brought him into contact with two important bodies, Australia–Soviet House in Melbourne, and the Russian Social Club in Sydney. But Petrov's principal duties appear to have been based on his covert MVD positions in the line of SK and EM work, the latter dealing with the infiltration and observation of émigré organizations from the Soviet Union and other Communist states. Mrs Petrov, meanwhile, served as the ambassador's secretary and the embassy bookkeeper. She was, it appears, covertly an MVD cadre-worker, with the rank of captain. As such she was a cipher clerk and, in all likelihood, eventually Petrov's cipher clerk as temporary MVD Resident.

There is dispute about Petrov's seniority and his importance at the Russian embassy in Canberra. Opinions range from the view that he was a bumbling, drunken cipher clerk, with an exaggerated sense of his own importance, to the claim maintained by the Menzies government, the Australian security chiefs of the time, and Petrov himself, that he was the head of the MVD in Australia. As MVD Resident, he would have been the most significant and sinister force in the Soviet embassy, not excluding the ambassador. He would also have been the most valuable potential source of security information. If Petrov were MVD Resident in Canberra, he was at a comparable level in the power structure to his contemporary in New York, the disciplined and brilliantly successful 'Illegal Resident' Colonel Rudolf Abel.

2 The Gnomes of Melbourne

In February 1949, an adviser to the Labor prime minister, Ben Chifley, found him chuckling to himself in his office in Parliament House, Canberra. 'I've just traded three boilers with Tom Playford for two judges,' Chifley explained.[1] To start a development project in his state, Playford, conservative premier of South Australia and a tough horse-trader, wanted three large steam boilers from an Australian government munitions plant that had been run down after the war. Chifley required the temporary services of one judge for a Royal Commission; the intended role of the second judge was to be more significant.

On 24 February 1949, Chifley formally concluded this arrangement in a letter to Playford requesting the services for twelve months of Mr Justice Reed of the South Australian Supreme Court, to found a permanent Australian security service. In justifying his choice, Chifley stated: 'In order to carry the fullest public confidence I am convinced ... that the new service should be organized under the leadership of a man of high standing and wide experience of affairs.' Justice Reed was accordingly released by Playford and began the formation of the Australian Security Intelligence Organization.

There were two significant strands in the background to Chifley's decision to set up an internal security service. First, his government was becoming increasingly embroiled in industrial conflict with unions in which Communist officials played an influential part. Second, a private but bitter battle was being waged within the ranks of the government's advisers over whether a security service should be established. This conflict had led, shortly before Chifley made his decision, to a weird cloak-and-dagger operation, details of which have not previously been fully revealed.

In June 1940, during his short initial term as conservative prime minister, Robert Menzies had banned the Communist

Party for alleged anti-war activities in the context of the Russo-German non-aggression pact. By 1942, after the German invasion, the Soviet Union had been accepted as a key member of the Allies, and the new Labor government of John Curtin lifted the ban in December of that year. When Chifley became prime minister in July 1945, the Australian Communist Party had more influence in the trade union movement than it had ever enjoyed before. Between September 1945 and December 1947, it has been estimated that nine Communist-controlled unions, representing only 26 per cent of unionists, were responsible for 84 per cent of the time lost in strikes.[2] Assisted by the favourable view of Soviet Russia and its heroic war effort held by the Australian community, the Communists had captured or consolidated control of the leadership of key unions, those vital in an economy suffering from shortages of labour and basic materials. Thus, by 1949, major strikes were having damaging effects on the government's popularity and its ability to carry out its pledges.

Chifley, a former railway engine-driver, was a moderate with sound experience in a skilled craft union. He had a highly realistic understanding of the operations of the Communist union leaders, and was aware of their industry and integrity in trade union affairs—in this respect it is interesting to note that Australia saw the emergence of the incorruptible Communist trade union leader, who enjoyed the respect of his fellows largely because he worked hard for them, long before many other Western democracies. But, beyond this, Chifley had a deep respect for political freedoms.

He put the onus for ending Communist domination of key unions on the unionists themselves. In 1946 he wrote: 'While we often disagree entirely with the views held by other people, freedom of speech and freedom of the press are cardinal features in a real democracy and are part of the policy of the Australian Labor Party.'[3] In 1948, as troubles continued, he said: 'The overthrow of Communist leadership in trade union circles is a matter for the workers themselves.'[4] In the wider context of the struggle against communism that was increasingly engaging the attention of the world, Chifley told

Parliament:

The great struggle that democracy is having today to combat the inroads of Communism is due to the fact that the conservative interests of the world have fertilised the soil in which Communism has grown. It is the fruit of hundreds of years in which 80 per cent of the people have lived in the direst poverty. ... The soil in which Communism has flourished was fertilised by people without any idea of democracy. ... Communism can be beaten only by improving the conditions of the people, because bad conditions are the soil in which it thrives. I have often expressed the opinion that the Government regards the banning of Communism as futile. ... If a ban is imposed on the Communist Party, it will merely change its name as it did in Canada. We are going to fight Communism in the open.[5]

The foreign (as opposed to the domestic) aspect of the concern about communism in Australia was a complex one, and was to prove critical in the decision to establish the Australian Security Intelligence Organization.

From 1941 to 1949, Dr Evatt was minister for external affairs in the Labor government. There is little doubt that Evatt's foreign policy, particularly in the postwar years 1945–48, when the nations of Asia were emerging into independence, was one of the factors that led to great pressure being put on Chifley to establish ASIO, thus setting the stage for the Petrov drama.

Evatt had created a strong and identifiable Australian foreign policy. He was more sympathetic to the aspirations of the indigenous leaders of the countries in Australia's region than to the colonial powers that had dominated them. These views, illustrated by his lack of sympathy for Dutch attempts to maintain a colonial empire in Indonesia, and his similar attitude to the Chiang Kai-shek cause in China, were opposed with secret horror by a clandestine group of Australian military intelligence figures, some of whom played dubious but important roles in the Petrov affair.

The 'Gnomes of Melbourne', as this group has been called, revolved around Colonel Charles Chambers Fowell Spry, director of military intelligence from 1946 to 1950. In 1950, after the defeat of the Chifley government, the new prime minister, Robert Menzies, promptly replaced the civilian head of the Australian Security Intelligence Organization, Mr Justice Reed, with the same Colonel (later Brigadier Sir) Charles Spry. He was to play a shadowy and suspicious role in the Petrov defection. Spry's group were dubbed the 'Gnomes of Melbourne' by Dr J. W. Burton. The name, Burton explained to the authors recently, was appropriate because 'Spry was a small man, and he was surrounded by this staff which was full of very short people who crept around in the background like gnomes. As in all security operations at that time, the operations of the group were based in Melbourne.'

Before becoming an incidental victim of the Petrov affair, John Burton had one of the most meteoric careers in the Australian public service. He joined the Department of External Affairs at the age of twenty-six in 1941, and was seconded as private secretary to Dr Evatt the following year, returning to the department in 1943, where he was acting secretary (or head) at various times until 1947. In that year he became 'permanent head' of the department. He was thirty-two, a remarkably early age for a public servant to reach such an exalted position.

Almost immediately, Burton became aware of the existence of the 'Gnomes' and their activities, and soon thereafter he came into conflict with them. On taking up occupation of his new office, he found in the most secure safe a list of members of a secret organization. The External Affairs Department had belonged to this organization, which Burton claims had been operating at least as early as the period of the Menzies–Fadden government of 1939–41, until a year or so before he became head of the department.

In September 1955, after the Royal Commission into the Petrov affair made its report, Dr Burton issued a public statement that was distributed to, but not reported in, the Australian press. His statement, referring specifically to the period between 1945 and 1948, revealed conflicts between the Department of Defence, influenced strongly by Colonel Spry, and the External Affairs Department, then under the ministerial control of Dr Evatt. It reflected clearly one of the opposed views amid the domestic and international tensions of that time:

It was a period of relatively open diplomacy in which Western powers generally stated their view, and in which Australia in particular spoke openly and freely. Suggestions ... that attempts were being made to find out about Western policies from the Australian Foreign Office are unreal in this context.

There was, however, a 'serious situation' arising out of the relationships between the Department of External Affairs and the Department of Defence. ...

Australia, under strong Ministerial leadership, was an active member of the Security Council. Australia followed policies based on United Nations principles and the settlement of differences by negotiation and conciliation. It had regard for fact and principle, and not strategic groupings. Defence was effectively pushed out of the field of foreign policy and was forced to confine itself to its proper functions. In short, for the first time Australia had a foreign policy, and Defence feared the new situation. Other governments, with whose intelligence services Defence co-operates, used this link to hinder Australian policies.

From 1946 there were persistent attempts to regain lost ground, especially when the Minister, Dr Evatt, was out of the country. For example, during his absence the Secretary of Defence [Sir Frederick Shedden] sponsored an enquiry into leakages from government departments, a Defence man making the enquiry.

The report was never shown to External Affairs, and the episode led to bitter exchanges and relationships between the departments.

Subsequently many attempts were made by the Secretary of Defence to smear senior officers of the Department of External Affairs, as, for example, when the Prime Minister, Mr Chifley, was advised on one occasion not to include me, the Secretary of the Department, in an Imperial Conference delegation.

The Prime Minister was not impressed, and in his own way showed his position by taking to a subsequent conference the Secretary of External Affairs, but not the Secretary of Defence.

The position was aggravated by conflict with the Defence intelligence services. Under previous administration External Affairs was a member of a secret society composed of intelligence officers who had taken special oaths of secrecy, which society in Australia was closely connected with the Intelligence Services of another country. Information conveyed to this group could not be passed on to any other person not a member of it.

As Secretary of External Affairs, I refused to be associated with it, stating that I would not receive information which could not be conveyed to the Minister and the Prime Minister.

I had seen at close quarters during the war the Defence tactic of dazzling Governments with science, and forcing through policy decisions without Governments being fully aware of all relevant facts. I would not be a party to any attempt to take policy responsibility, in practice if not in form, out of the hands of the elected government. The Prime Minister was informed of the position, and External Affairs advised Defence it would pass to Defence Intelligence Services any information relevant to Defence, and expected it would receive in return any information, secret or otherwise, and regardless of source, relevant to Foreign Affairs.

More than twenty-five years later, Dr Burton, now reader in international relations at University College, London, has given the authors the most complete details so far revealed of the identity of the members, and of the struggles he waged with what he then described as a 'secret society'. This is the same group that, in 1973, the *National Times* called a 'clique of intelligence officers operating outside government control as the self-appointed guardians of Australian democracy'.

Unless they were given specific permission, their oath forbade them to pass on information they learned at meetings of the group to any outsiders. These outsiders, of course, included the ministers of the elected government. Dr Burton's immediate response on discovering, in the departmental head's safe, evidence of the existence of the group was to report it to the prime minister. Burton then appointed Colin Moodie, an officer of his department, as the External Affairs representative on the secretive body. 'I told him that, whatever oath he took, he had to pass on relevant information to the Department and the Government.'

By 1973, Moodie was Australian ambassador to South Africa. When, that year, the *National Times* representative attempted to obtain details of events subsequent to his appointment to the group, he wished the paper success in its project and added: 'I shall be most interested to read the final product.'

Dr Burton has told the authors that the 'Gnomes' were a fluctuating group of between ten and fifteen individuals, admitted to membership because of the positions they held at the time. Among those entitled to join were the heads of naval, army and air force intelligence, nominees of the Defence Department, and someone from the Commonwealth Investigation Service (with which Dr Bialoguski was associated from 1945 to 1949).

3 The British connection

The Russian government, apparently by an ironic accident, helped to tip the scales in favour of the secret forces led by Colonel Spry that succeeded in convincing Prime Minister Chifley of the necessity to establish the Australian Security Intelligence Organization. Chifley made this decision reluctantly and with the expressed wish that the security service should function under the control of a man outside the world of military intelligence, 'of high standing and wide experience of affairs'. It was, as it turned out, a naive hope that did not long outlive Chifley's political demise. The behind-the-scenes intrigues that preceded his decision have not previously been revealed in detail.*

In 1948, a group of British intelligence officers led by Roger Hollis, who was later to become head of MI5, the British equivalent of ASIO, visited Australia. Hollis conferred with Dr Burton, newly appointed as head of the External Affairs Department, and discussed suspected security leaks in the Australian public service. An obvious reason for British interest in Australian security was the atomic weapon research being conducted by Britain in this country. The MI5 agent stationed in Australia at that time was a Mr Hembly-Scales, overtly a liaison officer at the British High Commission. He was also a member of the 'Gnomes', which Burton had refused to join.†

After consultation with Spry, Hollis had, through Hembly-Scales, given Burton a list of security 'suspects'. These

---

*This chapter draws on evidence Dr Burton gave privately to the Petrov Royal Commission, but which was not published in the transcript. He has released a copy to the authors, and revealed additional details in interviews with them. (See Appendix 1.)

†In 1973, during the course of the *National Times* investigation, John Stubbs spoke to Sir Roger Hollis, who was living in retirement in Somerset.

individuals, in Burton's view at the time, were sometimes at such a low level that they did not have access to secret information, were people in whom he had justifiable faith, or made no secret that their political allegiance lay with the Communist Party. All were 'very Australian types' and neither secretive nor criminal in the way they led their lives; they were a part of the society that then existed in Australia, in which Chifley wished the debate on communism to be fought in the open. But this was not, according to Burton, the last time he was to hear of the people on the MI5 list. On the next occasion he was confronted with these names, they were in the G Series documents said to have been stolen by the defecting Petrov from the safe of the Russian embassy.

The Hollis mission to Australia seemed to be making little headway in convincing the government that it should establish a fully fledged secret service, even though Hollis used the telling argument that Australia would, by doing this (and by no other means), get access to high-level intelligence information from the United States. There would also, he implied, be wider advantages. He acknowledged the existing cooperation between British and Australian military intelligence services, but claimed that some American intelligence authorities were reluctant to give Britain access to high-level information that it was thought might fall into insecure hands in Australia. The British security establishment, for its part, wanted to continue its liaison with Australia—but it was not prepared to jeopardize its access to American sources by doing so while there were doubts about the safety of the information relayed to Australia. Australia, with an acceptable security service, could be a member of the club, with benefits to itself and the British Commonwealth.

He confirmed that he had visited Australia and held discussions on security matters with Australian officials during 1948. He died later in 1973. The Ministry of Defence, which has the War Office records of that period, confirmed in answer to Stubbs' inquiries that the junior MI5 official named by Burton, Hembly-Scales, was 'in government service in the late 1940s, and was in Australia in 1948'.

As the private debate was continuing, a Russian official decided that an unusually large Soviet delegation should be sent to an international conference to be held at the Lapstone Hotel in the Blue Mountains west of Sydney. Spry and Hollis immediately pounced on this as justification for the establishment of a security service, believing, or at least arguing, that the disproportionate Russian presence must have a sinister purpose: it showed conclusively the espionage threat to which Australia was exposed.

Burton, in discussion with both Chifley and Spry, made an ingenious—but, in the end, ineffective—counterproposal. He later outlined this proposal and its consequences in written evidence he was to submit to the Royal Commission. This statement was dictated under security conditions in a room supplied by ASIO through Kenneth Bailey, the solicitor-general, and typed by a typist from the security organization. It has never been published. The following is an extract from another version of this evidence compiled by Dr Burton immediately after its submission, using the notes from which he had dictated to the ASIO typist.

The history of the establishment of the security organisation is of both interest and relevance.

During the visit of the British Intelligence Officers in 1948, a large Russian delegation came to a conference held at the Lapstone Hotel.

After consultation with one of these officers [Hollis], I made the suggestion to the Prime Minister that in view of the allegations of an espionage network in Australia it would be useful to employ existing facilities to screen the Russian delegation, and to ascertain their contacts in Australia.

I argued further, to the Prime Minister, that even though there were no outcome of such an investigation, it would be useful to demonstrate to the British authorities that the Australian Government was able to safeguard the security of the country without a special security organisation with wide executive powers, thus introducing for a first time in Australia the European secret police institution.

Mr Chifley was most reluctant to give approval for the extraordinary measures—or so it seemed then—which were to be taken, including phone-tapping, the wiring of hotel rooms, reporting by drivers and External Affairs officers attached to delegations, and so on.

He finally agreed, placed one of the British officers [Hembly-Scales] in charge of the operation, and State police and Commonwealth officers, including Spry, were called in.

It was during this exercise, Dr Burton recalls, that he had a series of long and sometimes rather philosophical conversations with Colonel Spry, who was involved in the operation, although he had declined Burton's invitation to take charge of it on the creditable grounds that it was civil and not military. Burton's version of the heart of these discussions was given in a radio interview with a representative of the Australian Broadcasting Commission, broadcast in April 1973. 'We had a lot of opportunity of talking in depth about the problems of democracy,' Burton said. 'It was [Spry's] view that a secret service—a group of people communicating together who undertook not to communicate to their own government—was essential. Indeed, you couldn't have a democracy with its changes of policies and its changes of parties working efficiently unless there was this kind of reserve power, this reserve group, that would try to control things in certain circumstances.' It is Dr Burton's contention that this philosophy was put into operation by the group around Spry during the Petrov affair, and that they succeeded in distorting the way in which democratic processes, in their own clumsy fashion, normally decided who would govern Australia.

Burton has repeated his broadcast statement to the authors and described the atmosphere in which the conversations took place. Both men, he says, spent long hours in Burton's office at the External Affairs Department waiting for the various post-office technicians, government car drivers and External Affairs officers to report on any suspicious actions by the Russian delegation. Only once was there an alarm. During a monitored and taped telephone conversation, in Russian, between a member of the visiting delegation and an official of the Russian embassy in Australia the name 'Dalziel' had been clearly mentioned. Allan Dalziel was a member of the personal staff of the minister for external affairs, Dr Evatt. There was a flurry of activity as the tape was brought to an official Australian translator, and then anticlimax when he later revealed the contents at a hurried meeting in Solicitor-General Bailey's office. The conversation consisted of the delegation member complaining about transport arrangements, and the embassy staff-man making various suggestions and then finding and reading the instructions for the conference issued by the Australian government, which included Dalziel's name as the person to be contacted about complaints.

In August 1973 the editor of the *National Times*, Max Suich, asked Spry (by then both knighted and retired) to comment on Burton's claim during the ABC broadcast that Spry had believed democracy could not work without a secret (and undemocratic) reserve power exercised by a reserve group. Sir Charles replied: 'In my capacity as Director of Military Intelligence I was a member of the Joint Intelligence Committee, a sub-committee of the Defence Committee.' (This was, at least, an acknowledgment that the nucleus of the 'Gnomes' had official existence.) 'Mostly my meetings in Canberra with Dr Burton were of a courtesy nature. I found him to be an intelligent person who possessed very firm political views. However, I considered that his assessment of contemporaneous international affairs was not always correct.* I cannot support what you quote [Burton]

---

*Sir Charles does not go on to say, though he obviously implies, that his own interpretations of contemporaneous events were correct. For an outline of Burton's views of the period, see his book *The Alternative: A Dynamic Approach to Our Relations with Asia* (Sydney: Morgan's Publications, 1954). Burton was strongly influential in the formation of Labor's progressive foreign policies. This rare correspondence between Sir Charles and Mr Suich was published (in full at Sir Charles' direction) in the *National Times*, 3–8 September 1973.

as saying—"It was [Spry's] view that a secret service—a group of people communicating together who undertook not to communicate to their own government—was essential." This would ignore political realities. Any person', Sir Charles went on to say, 'who controls a security intelligence organisation knows that this cannot be done, nor would it be, in the interests of democracy.' He stated that he did not apply such a policy as director-general of ASIO 'as such an attitude would have been in direct contradiction of the functions of the organisation' as defined in legislation passed in 1956 and the government directive under which it operated before then.

This is not a comprehensive or (some may think) convincing rebuttal of Burton's original statement. Spry makes no reference to the matter of the 'reserve group, that would try to control things in certain circumstances', specifically put to him in the same question by Suich. He does not deny having had conversations with Burton.

In the event, Dr Burton was able to report, in his evidence to the Royal Commission six years later, that the Lapstone Hotel 'experiment had no results which were helpful in counter-espionage; the Russians appeared to make no attempt to contact Australians, and Australians no attempt to contact them'. He claimed that the experiment

nevertheless demonstrated the extent to which a permanent organisation engaged in counter-espionage and using these techniques would quickly spread distrust and suspicion throughout the community, and ... indeed could create the conditions such an organisation is designed to avoid.

G.P.O. technicians were amazed at their instructions, and in fact questioned them. Car drivers and departmental officers and many others, who for the first time saw in operation phone-tapping, reporting on guests of the Government and other such measures, realised that Australia was capable of the same techniques as totalitarian states.

It was an unpleasant experience from this point of view, and while such procedures might be advisable in a particular situation, under the specific direction of the Prime Minister as was so in this case, their continuation on a permanent basis, by persons with a long-term interest in finding evidence of espionage, and without any possibility of detailed control, appeared to be introducing the devices of the enemy as a means of combatting him.

I wrote a report on this experiment, which I sent to the Solicitor-General, in which I strongly urged the greatest possible caution in the establishment of any new organisation.

In fact Burton wrote the report for Evatt, who was overseas, and in accordance with bureaucratic niceties sent it via Bailey, so that the solicitor-general would be aware of his recommendations. But Evatt never received the report. He heard of its existence, and of the Lapstone Hotel incident itself, for the first time in July 1954, when it became clear to Burton, from Evatt's antics, that he was acting in the dark.

Burton lost the argument with the British, Bailey and Spry. As he went on to tell the Royal Commission: 'In the light of information given by British officers, and as a result of strong appeals at a high level from the British Government, in relation to information to be obtained from the United States, a Security Organisation was established.' It was not the first time, according to Burton, that British security services, in liaison with Australian military intelligence contacts, had attempted to further their own ends without the knowledge of the government and to the disadvantage of its declared policies. In another section of his evidence Burton related:

Some time ago the Australian staff at Moscow was in difficulties because of the lack of an officer who knew the Russian language well. Day-by-day living in Moscow, as well as the work of the Embassy, required the services of a good linguist.

No one being readily available in the [External Affairs] Department, a search was made outside. A recommendation was in due course made to the Department from an Australian intelligence organisation, through the defence liaison officer of the Department. The person recommended, an Englishman, was duly appointed, and to save delay was sent immediately to London even before receipt of a Soviet visa.

Official visas were not normally delayed, but this one never arrived. The officer was held in London for a time, where he resigned without asking to be returned to Australia.

It was some time later that it was learned by the Department that the person in question was an experienced intelligence officer who had operated against the Russians in the Middle East, and was apparently known to them.

Only passing reference was made to the matter by Soviet officials in Canberra, but from that time onwards it was quite impossible for the Department to make any useful contacts with the Soviet Ambassador or his First Secretary. Social entertainments of senior officers, which had been regular though not frequent, were terminated. Attempts which I had previously made to discuss regularly proposals before the United Nations, and policies Australia was promoting, had to be discontinued.

Informal explanations that an error was made and that External Affairs would not knowingly take part in attempted espionage were not believed or accepted. The records will show, also, that the work of the Embassy at Moscow from that time became more difficult and less useful, until, in fact, I as Secretary of the Department had no option but to recommend a severe curtailment of the mission, if not its withdrawal.

Dr Burton's claim that the decision to establish ASIO was reached in the light of information given by British officers, led by Hollis, and that this was reinforced by strong appeals at a high level from the British government, is echoed in Chifley's letter to Playford in February 1949, in which the prime minister referred to the persuasive influence of 'consultation with other Governments of the British Commonwealth'.

The decision, says Burton, was made by Chifley, Evatt and Senator McKenna as acting attorney-general: 'Being aware of the dangers, the organisation was placed under a member of the judiciary. Its executive powers were meant to be limited, and it was intended that it should be kept strictly within the bounds of essential counter-espionage. Every step was taken to ensure against the development of a situation in which there would be throughout the community "spies, pimps and informers". The fears which Mr Chifley had then, and which led him to place the organisation under a member of the judiciary, have proved to be well-founded.'

Mr Justice Reed, traded to the Commonwealth government by the premier of South Australia for one and a half steam boilers, began to lay the foundations of ASIO early in 1949, becoming its first director-general. In December of that year, Chifley led the Labor Party to defeat in the federal election and Menzies became prime minister in a conservative coalition government. The extended dispute over foreign policy and domestic security questions between the Defence Department and Dr Burton's Department of External Affairs was over. Defence had won. In 1955, in an understandably bitter analysis of the situation, Dr Burton said: 'There has been no foreign policy since, the foreign policy of Australia being entirely based on two defence pacts [SEATO and ANZUS] which lack any positive aspects.'

Mr Justice Reed returned to legal duties in South Australia in July 1950, and Colonel Spry was appointed head of ASIO. Burton commented: 'By placing a Military Intelligence officer in charge of civilian security the Government gave the intelligence services unlimited opportunity not merely to control policy decisions, but more especially to interfere with the political life of the community. It is axiomatic that intelligence officers who seek to determine long-term defence and foreign policy may also use their best endeavours, and the machinery at their disposal, to ensure that any Government elected will be the Government which pursues policies they favour.'

In 1950, Burton dutifully accepted a posting as high commissioner to Ceylon, instead of the position he had held as permanent head of the External Affairs Department. He resigned from the public service the following year, aged just thirty-six, to contest—unsuccessfully—a seat as Labor candidate in the federal election that year.

4 A tale of two leaders

It was the best of times, it was the worst of times,
It was the age of wisdom, it was the age of foolishness,
It was the epoch of belief, it was the epoch of incredulity,
It was the season of light, it was the season of darkness,
It was the spring of hope, it was the winter of despair ...

Charles Dickens: A Tale of Two Cities

For two men the Petrov case was to prove decisive. It climaxed a long political fight to the death between Evatt and Menzies, overtly centred on what the latter described as the 'red menace'. This conflict began its advance to the forefront of the political stage early in 1950, soon after Menzies became prime minister for the second time.

Their public performances aside, the historical record shows a number of parallels between the careers of Menzies and Evatt. Robert Gordon Menzies and Herbert Vere Evatt were born in the same year, 1894; Menzies' father was a storekeeper in the tiny Victorian town of Jeparit, Evatt's a publican in working-class East Maitland on the New South Wales coalfields. When Evatt was a child, his father died; Menzies' father held the seat of Lowan in the Victorian Legislative Assembly from 1911 to 1920.

Both attended secondary schools in their respective state capitals, Menzies a private school and Evatt a state one. Menzies graduated from Melbourne University, where he headed the student government organization, with first-class honours in law, and began a successful barrister's practice at the Victorian Bar. Meanwhile, at the University of Sydney, Evatt was collecting a string of degrees: a B.A. with triple first-class honours, an M.A. with first-class honours, an LL.B. with the University Medal, and finally, in 1924, an LL.D. He capped this with an Oxford LL.D., and then became a lecturer at Sydney University.

Both Menzies and Evatt were appointed King's Counsel in

the same year, 1929. Evatt was already representing a breakaway Labor group in the New South Wales state legislature. Menzies, after entering the Victorian Legislative Council in 1928, transferred to the Legislative Assembly in the following year, and by 1932 had risen to the position of deputy premier. In 1934 he won election to the Federal Parliament, and was immediately appointed attorney-general in the conservative United Australia Party government. Rising rapidly, in 1939, aged just forty-five, he became the youngest prime minister in Australia's history. Evatt, meanwhile, had been appointed in 1930 by the Scullin Labor government to the country's supreme court, the High Court. At thirty-six, he was the youngest High Court judge in the nation's history, and over the next ten years earned a solid reputation as a jurist. In 1940, he resigned from the bench to enter Federal Parliament. The following year, a crisis in the traditional conservative coalition with the Country Party first felled Menzies from the premiership, and then destroyed the coalition government itself. In October 1941, Evatt was awarded the attorney-general's portfolio in the wartime Labor government of John Curtin.

Evatt was also minister for external affairs, and as such he fought for representation of the small nations in the drafting of the United Nations Charter, signed in June 1945. As a result of this, while deputy prime minister under the new Labor leader, Ben Chifley, Evatt was elected president of the General Assembly for the 1948–49 session. In the United Nations he fought against the Soviet veto, and at home he supported the use of troops to work open-cut mines to break the Communist-led coal strike in the election year of 1949.

Despite careers that seem similar in the chronology of their progress, from ordinary beginnings, through brilliant academic achievements, to the Bar and domestic political successes, then brief but significant appearances on the international stage, Menzies and Evatt were not at all alike.

There was nothing subtle about the differences between them. Menzies was massively erect and outwardly dignified, immaculately attired in double-breasted suit, and with eyebrows combed; he relished nothing more than making an after-dinner speech in his cultivated accent, ideally in the presence of British royalty. On the other hand, Evatt was an extraordinarily untidy man, dishevelled to the point of eccentricity. A former assistant recalls his amusement when, during a UN mission to the Middle East in the late 1940s, Evatt decided to line his shirt and shoes with pages from an airmail edition of *The Times* as insulation against the desert heat. After the aircraft landed, Evatt was greeted by a queue of international diplomats. He kept his insulation in place as he moved along the receiving line, but his progress was accompanied by strange crackling sounds. Speculative comment was rife among the dignitaries.

The apparent parallels between the two men extended to their mutual interest in cricket, yet at the same time this common factor spells out some pertinent differences between them. Evatt was a mediocre cricketer in his youth, but he really knew the game and loved it, and for years was the official scorer for North Sydney Cricket Club.* There is no evidence that Menzies ever played cricket or any other sport. As his political career matured, however, the pull of the game's association with all things British seems to have exerted a powerful influence. Menzies became a Lords Taverner, and he adopted the English, as opposed to Australian, cricket expression 'afternoon light' as the title for his first volume of memoirs.

Both leaders were given to passing their cricketing knowledge on to others. Keith Miller, the Australian all-rounder, who had been having great success with the bat at the time, recalls being greeted by Evatt one Sunday morning in 1952 or 1953. Miller was flattered to be engaged in conversation by Evatt, especially as they were directly in front of the main entrance of the New South Wales Leagues Club in Phillip Street, Sydney, and members were filing in and out. His

---

*He was a better rugby player, having founded the University of Sydney Rugby League Club, which flourished in the 1920s. However, he was never accused of having taken too many knocks to the head during an active youth.

pleasure soon turned to embarrassment, however, as Evatt, in broad-brimmed felt hat and cumbersome suit, launched into a full-scale demonstration, before a growing crowd, of how Miller should be correcting his cover-drive.

Equally, Jack Fingleton, a distinguished cricketer of the 1930s, and now a cricket correspondent for *The Times* and the *Sunday Times,* and a member of the Canberra press gallery, had always been secretly proud of his relationship with Menzies. During the early 1950s, the prime minister often consulted him on some of the technical points of the game, and he frequently invited Fingleton to comment on individual players' idiosyncrasies and faults. Fingleton recalls explaining to Menzies how one prominent batsman seemed, to him, to hold a hand too high on his bat. Not long afterwards Fingleton heard that Menzies had held forth on the topic, at some length, in an exclusive Melbourne club. On fuller investigation he found that there was, in fact, a unique congruence between their views. Fingleton's job was to comment on cricket, and Menzies' wasn't; thereafter, according to a friend, Fingleton was more cautious in his private comments to the prime minister about the game.

There was a strong verbal contrast between Menzies and Evatt. The former spoke in cultivated tones; he was proud to sound like an Englishman, and he used his oratorical skill to great effect. Evatt, for his part, had clearly had no elocution lessons. His voice was rough and he spoke in a monotone. His accent was almost aggressively nasal in the Australian style, but not particularly appealing, even to Australians.

Menzies' character is not too difficult to analyse. Modern history is studded with examples of talented people born in poor or ordinary circumstances, who have enjoyed and excelled in a fortunately privileged education, prospered in their chosen profession, welcomed the establishment's embrace, and finally become pillars of that very establishment. But nobody ever 'duchessed' Evatt. He was a much more complex character than Menzies, and it is essential to come to grips with his personality for an understanding of his part in the Petrov affair.

Despite his immense abilities. Evatt had tragic weaknesses. His personality, and the interaction between him and Menzies. became a critical factor as the affair unfolded. The two sides of Evatt were illustrated in an intimate, though sympathetic, way by Dr Burton in a long tape-recorded interview he gave nearly ten years ago, after Dr Evatt's death. The quotation from Dickens at the beginning of this chapter is the one that springs to Burton's mind, even today, whenever he reflects on his days with 'the Doc', the name by which almost everyone knew Evatt.

It is interesting to note the manner of their meeting. It is of relevance because of the political significance and impact of allegations made later about the conduct of members of Evatt's personal staff, the method of their recruitment, and their relationships with him.

I first encountered [Evatt] when I was a junior officer in External Affairs. The government had just changed and he had been appointed minister. There was a call on the phone and without ado he asked me to come over to his office. It was rather an extra-ordinary situation for a minister to ring through to a junior officer—I didn't know him. I asked him why and he said he wasn't to be cross-examined on the phone.

I went over to the office, I think it was perhaps a Friday, and the next thing I knew I was dispatched to Sydney for the weekend. He always went to Sydney for the weekend, and apparently my duties were to make sure that he was in touch with cables and what was going on generally. [It was to be] only for the weekend: some two or three years later I extracted myself from this general duty!

I can see now in retrospect what had happened. He had taken office, and he perceived External Affairs as something hostile, something created by the previous government. [It] was a crisis situation, he wanted to handle this crisis situation himself. His personal private secretary happened to know me, or have met me, or we talked on the same platform or something. Apparently he mentioned this [to Evatt]. This was typical of Evatt, grasping at a friend of a friend: [it] offset some of his suspicions. ·

Evatt wanted a small staff around him, so that they could determine foreign policy independently of the External Affairs officers he distrusted.

Dr Burton is by no means uncritical of Evatt:

He has been criticized for being somewhat irresponsible at times. In fact, one of his former colleagues referred to the 'larrikin strain' in External Affairs. It was known that he liked to have around him people who were almost acting as court-jesters. He needed this recreation, he needed the praise they would give. Frequently in the conduct and handling of negotiations this so-called larrikin strain came out. It's hard really to explain this aspect of his behaviour, except in terms of this tremendous ability on the one side, and on the other side the tremendous need to relax, to have people around him with whom he could relax, and to a degree that made him appear to others, who didn't understand, as though he was behaving as a larrikin.

One of the worst examples of this, perhaps, was the Paris Peace Conference in 1946. Again the delegation was well prepared for this conference. It had attached a great deal of importance to the conference of the satellite powers being a success. Attempts were made to draft up proposals which would cover the requirements of Europe in the future. He agreed with all these when they were put to him, and we looked forward to this conference because it looked as though, after all the years of war, something constructive could be done. But this larrikin strain came out. It wasn't introduced by him initially. He had with him Mr Beasley, who was known for his violent anti-Communist viewpoints, and within a day or so of this conference we had the spectacle of Mr Beasley making a speech in answer to Mr Gromyko, when he said, 'We know who you are, we call you "Commies" in Australia.' And this set the tone of the conference, which got worse and worse. Dr Evatt did nothing to pull Mr Beasley back, on the contrary seemed to be encouraging him ... thinking that this was the kind of thing which would go down well in Australia. It was not the normal means of conducting peace conferences, and those around him could have no influence at all on him in circumstances such as this. He finally left the conference earlier than was required, and it was to everyone's benefit.

It is hard to summarize the behaviour or character or nature of such a man. In a sense he is Australia's greatest political tragedy. There was tragedy because of the times. He was an idealist operating in the worst phase of Australian and world politics. There was McCarthyism at home, no less than abroad. ... Failure to recognize China is a case in point. This was a period in which an idealist was forced to be on the defensive, and it brought out the worst because there was little opportunity for the best. Those who saw the potentialities thwarted by circumstances over which he had no control had a great affection for him. Those that did not see his idealism, or did not share it, could not understand the ways in which he was being frustrated and couldn't understand the willingness of others to give him support despite the negative characteristics—they had no affection for him. Not only was he a person of extremes, but he created all around him people of extreme opinions.

Dr Burton described Evatt's actions over the recognition of China as an example of 'extreme realism'; others would see it as more like political cynicism:

He was always very keen on the recognition of China—he thought it was the proper thing to do and in some circumstances pressed for it. But then he was faced with an election in 1949. The United Kingdom government, having recognized China, sent out a senior official to persuade the Australian government to follow suit. And to make this possible, to make it clear that a well-considered decision was being taken, all officers from the whole of South-east Asia were recalled for a conference to Canberra.

They duly met and discussed the matter, and unanimously agreed there should be immediate recognition. No one had any doubts about it whatsoever. Sir Keith Officer was there. He was perhaps the most senior member of the permanent diplomatic service. After the deliberations, Dr Evatt walked in and said: 'Well, Sir Keith, what do you think?' And Sir Keith said: 'We are quite unanimous, there is no doubt in our minds at all, there should be recognition of China.' And Doc Evatt's response was: 'Keith, you're a Red!' ... and Evatt walked out.

And Australia didn't recognize China. Everyone in that room knew that he'd wanted to, but this was being politically realist in the extreme—it didn't make any difference to the election, of course, and everyone knew it wouldn't.

It also postponed the Doc's confrontation with Labor's right wing.

Dr Burton believes that any final understanding of Evatt would have to be within a 'kind of framework of extremes':

He was brilliant, there is no doubt about this. His school and university records show this. Of course, I know little of these early days, except what one sees in printed reports. But his grasp of essentials was—well, I have to go and use superlatives too—it was completely fantastic. In subject matters in which one thought one was fully familiar, with which one was working all day, he could always get to the essentials much more rapidly. I suppose it was a lawyer's brilliance and a lawyer's training, but there was something a lot more than this. Well, this side of his character is well known— his worst critics never denied his brilliance.

Evatt's brilliance was questioned at least once. The story goes that he took a taxi in New York during one of his visits to the United Nations, and upon arriving at his destination found himself shuffling through the greenbacks in his wallet, trying to find the correct denominations. With typical impatience he flashed at the driver: 'In my country we use different colours to indicate different values.' Without hesitation the driver retorted: 'Listen, fella, in my country we expect people to be able to read!'

Dr Burton continues his framework of extremes:

Then on one extreme he was an idealist. He would sacrifice himself, as is well known, for an ideal, usually for human rights of one kind or another, for individual rights. These things he really understood; this was what he valued more than anything else. He would sacrifice himself physically and even politically without hesitation. Evatt expected others to do the same, of course; anyone around him was expected to sacrifice himself for these ideals. But *he* had to decide the ideals. ...

I can recall one occasion during the great coal strike, during the Chifley regime. This was an unfortunate episode, and many suspect that maybe if it wasn't for political reasons the strike wouldn't have occurred, or that Mr Chifley wouldn't have been so adamant. Dr Evatt sensed this. A phone call came to me on one occasion from the well-known Communist leader, Ernie Thornton. He phoned from Sydney, I was in Canberra. Thornton recalled that he had met me on one occasion, though I didn't recall it, and he asked point-blank whether I could arrange for him to see Dr Evatt. ... At the time I had a farm ten miles out of Canberra and Dr Evatt suggested that he might meet Thornton out there on the Sunday and they'd discuss the strike. This was fine, but it meant that I had to accommodate Thornton and party. ... The same thing happened a few weeks later, and Dr Evatt thought that he could see the end of this strike. He was then faced with the problem of having to tell Mr Chifley that he had met Thornton and had negotiated with him, really against Mr Chifley's desires. Well, there was no worry to him at all. He merely said: 'I can tell Mr Chifley that Thornton is a personal friend of yours and was staying with you, and I happened to call out and I met him.'

The Doc was very loyal to his colleagues and vested great trust in them. Indeed, it has been said that he was trusting to a fault. Burton recalls his support:

I was at an ILO conference in Philadelphia in 1944, and one of the main purposes of going was to see if we could write a full employment obligation into the ILO Charter. This led to serious conflict with the US State Department. I was chopping and changing texts almost hourly, sending messages back and obviously confusing everyone in Canberra. Equally obviously, I needed some instruction of some kind. What I got was a short telegram saying: 'You have to break eggs before you can scramble them.' Dr Evatt was saying over the head of the department: 'Do your best, it's up to you.'

He was a tremendously sympathetic and generous and sentimental person. If one was sick, he would always be in attention. He was tremendously sentimental about his children and family and close friends. He always had a tremendous sympathy for the underdog; his legal career shows this. His generosity to his friends was always—almost extreme. On the other side he was ruthless, merciless and inconsiderate frequently. He would drive people, even his closest associates and his family, as required in the fulfilment of some objective with which he was concerned. ...

He was quite merciless in respect to officials whom he didn't think were sympathetic toward him, and to petty opposition. He was inconsiderate in the extreme of both staff and, I suspect, his family at times. When there was some project that had to be pursued, we frequently had all-night sessions preparing speeches, which could have been prepared ten days in advance. We wouldn't start until midnight, and one frequently went home for a shower and started work again. This was so unnecessary with a bit of organization, but these things weren't important to him. He regarded people as expendable in terms of the objectives he was pursuing.

Government chauffeurs could attest this aspect, as could many a passenger on a flight between Sydney and Canberra in those days. Evatt never allowed enough time to travel between home or office and the airport. He expected super-human efforts from his drivers, and whenever they were running late he required them to radio ahead to delay the scheduled flights. The strain was too much for the drivers, and in the end none would work for him. Fellow airline passengers were usually unaware of the reason for the delays, although on more than one occasion the Doc's arrival was greeted with a round of boos. Burton recalled:

He was courageous physically—he hated flying. He had to force himself into some of the Liberators, and it was clear, when one was travelling with him, that he was under tremendous mental stress all the time. He took all kinds of precautions, and one had to talk to pilots and make quite sure they were on the right track and they were well trained and so on. He was never satisfied with the assurance that the pilots valued their life as well as his.

When flying from Honolulu to San Francisco in the Liberator, there was a point of no return—the point at which the pilot had to decide whether to come back or to go on after having made an assessment of the headwinds and so on. Having had one experience of this kind, Evatt always insisted that at Honolulu an extra petrol tank be put on board. This was a fire hazard—the fumes came in the cabin and the crew never liked it—but he wouldn't travel without it. I recall one dramatic little episode where we took off with these fumes in the cabin. In the morning Mrs Evatt straightened herself up, and combing her hair she created flashes of sparks. Dr Evatt immediately pounced on these and almost on her, with his great sixteen stone or so. But this was an indication of the tremendous nervous energy that went into flying, and yet he never hesitated on any occasion to take whatever plane was required.

He was the most charming person and he was a delight to be with on occasions. Yet he was about the rudest person you could come across. All of these qualities in extremes, and there would be a quick switch: one never knew what to expect. Hence there was tremendous tension, tremendous nervous tension right throughout his departments—and, I suspect, throughout Parliament House, because his colleagues were experiencing the same nervous tension. One would meet someone and say, 'Well, I wonder what the mood is today?' This duality, these extremes, and the quick switch from one to another, is to my mind the secret to understanding his whole personality, and indeed his whole political career.

All his close friends and, I'm quite sure, his wife saw this kind of duality and each one of us made up our own minds whether the positive side made the negative side worthwhile. ... In later days this duality in character became accentuated. It was almost a split personality; you had to remember which Evatt you spoke to last time—whether it was the office Evatt or the home Evatt.

I suspect that in his life there were symbols which were important to him. Security symbols—even his well-known grey cardigan, which always had to be with him, in hot weather as well as cold. Sometimes he regarded people as kind of symbols. On quite a number of occasions one felt that one had to be with him, not to help him in any way, but to be there as almost a mascot or goodluck symbol. He showed many signs of this extraordinary superstition, and yet he was about the most rational person that you could have a conversation with. There were many other extremes like this. He could rough it like anyone. He went in the most horrible wartime aircraft and we stopped at all kinds of army stop-off points across the Pacific, and it never seemed really to disturb him ... and yet when comforts were available he demanded only the best, and sometimes at great inconvenience. One of the great trials of his staff, when the War Cabinet used to meet in Melbourne once a week, was to get [him] from Canberra to Melbourne, by train, in a good frame of mind, and the frame of mind depended almost entirely on whether he got a reserved seat for breakfast at Albury.

The two leaders, Menzies and Evatt, were closely observed by John Douglas Pringle, who left *The Times* in London to become editor of the *Sydney Morning Herald* in the early 1950s. Pringle published a book, *Have Pen Will Travel*, drawn from his diaries.[1] His observations, those of an independent foreigner, give an interesting view of the two leaders at that time.

Pringle first saw Menzies at a dinner of the Manufacturers

Association at which he was subjected to four hours of Australian oratory. 'All except Menzies were appalling,' Pringle wrote in his diary on 19 September 1952. 'But Menzies was brilliant—easy, amusing, the accomplished artist. Before I left England I had been told that he was the best after-dinner speaker in the English-speaking world and I am now ready to believe it. He is a fascinating personality. Handsome though fleshy; like one of the better Roman Emperors. His obvious intellectual brilliance makes him outstanding in this country of second-rate minds and also unpopular. I do not yet know whether he is a real statesman or not. The *Herald* people say no.' Pringle added that he had just read a character-sketch of Menzies written by the *Herald*'s proprietor, Warwick Fairfax, comparing him with Hamlet.

A few days later Pringle met both Prime Minister Menzies and Evatt, then leader of the Opposition, separately in Canberra. Menzies retailed a number of 'good stories about Churchill who, he said, now treats him very nearly as an equal and allows him to have about 45 per cent of the conversation'. He told Pringle that Churchill said: 'You seem to conduct your affairs in Australia with a fine eighteenth-century gusto!' Pringle added in his diary: 'This seems very true. One might also add, from what I hear, with a fine eighteenth-century dishonesty and corruption, everything, in fact, except grace and elegance!'

The next day he met Evatt, whom he described in his diary entry as 'an impressive figure. ... slow, kindly, very intelligent, with much less of the smart lawyer than I had expected. I should guess that his socialism does not go very deep but he seemed remarkably sensible on many points.' He observed that Evatt was 'none the less cordially disliked and distrusted by everyone, including his own party, so I expect I have seen only one side'.

Pringle commented in his diary that day, 25 September 1952: 'I could not help thinking that a country that had Menzies for its Prime Minister and Evatt for the Leader of its Opposition was not doing too badly.'

5 Traitors in our midst

In the period between Petrov's arrival in Australia in February 1951 and the point at which Pringle recorded his impressions of Evatt and Menzies at the end of 1952, there were several important developments on the international and domestic political scene. These events were to make significant contributions to the foundations and framework of the Petrov affair.

In March 1951, the Australian High Court ruled that legislation passed by the Menzies government to ban the Communist Party was constitutionally invalid. The Communist Party Dissolution Bill had been introduced in April of the previous year. Besides declaring the Communist Party illegal, the legislation gave the executive power to name Communists, required the onus of proof of innocence to be on the accused, barred Communists from official positions in the unions, and banned them from the public service. Evatt, of course, led the fight against this proposed infringement of traditional civil liberties. A former High Court judge himself, he appeared before the Full Court, on behalf of the Waterside Workers' Federation, to challenge the legality of the Act. He, and many others, saw the inherent threat posed by the legislation to the rights and liberties of all minority groups. Menzies had made no secret of the fact that he had personally supervised the drafting of the Act, which had been based on the American Smith Act. Accordingly, he did not conceal his anger when, by six votes to one, the Full Court held that it was invalid. 'In spite of the Chifley–Evatt section of the Labor Party at Canberra, the community must either have, or get, the power,' he told reporters.[1]

In April 1951, in the federal election arising from a double dissolution of the House of Representatives and the Senate, the Menzies government gained control of both Houses. Then, in June, Ben Chifley died, and Evatt succeeded him as parliamentary leader of the Labor Party and leader of the Opposition. In the same month Menzies pressed on with another attempt to ban the Communist Party: he called a special conference of all state premiers, asking them to sign over to him the necessary power to carry out his plans. The Labor premiers of New South Wales and Queensland refused.

Only one course was left open to Menzies—to submit the issue to a referendum of the Australian electorate, in which the approval of a majority of electors and a majority of states would be required for the desired changes in the Australian constitution to be effected. Evatt, in a whirlwind campaign, led the Labor Party's efforts to persuade the country to reject Menzies' proposal. It was a bitter and emotional struggle, which as a by-product further strained relations between Evatt and the right wing of the Labor Party. But Evatt won. On 22 September 1951, by a narrow margin, three states—New South Wales, Victoria and South Australia—as well as an outright majority of Australians voted no to the proposition that the Menzies government should be given power to ban a political party of which it disapproved.

'Democrats throughout the world will be proud of Australia,' Dr Evatt proclaimed. 'The Australian people have rejected the Menzies government's attempt to seize totalitarian power.'[2]

'I intend to keep on fighting,' Menzies trumpeted.[3]

After the referendum rebuff, the 'fight' being waged by Menzies and his supporters against the Communist Party moved from the public stage of Parliament, the courts and the hustings to the shadowy byways of the security services. On the fringes of the diplomatic and political world there was intensive security activity, not at this stage directly related to Petrov, but later to be drawn in to bolster shaky allegations that some sort of spy network had been in operation.

Early in 1952, however, there was a public manifestation of this underground activity, an episode that mirrors in all its sordid aspects the malignity of the Petrov affair and its persistent effects. It was a textbook Australian example of

McCarthyite smear tactics, in this case directed against a Communist journalist, Rex Chiplin, and Dr John Burton, by extension.

In the House of Representatives on 27 May 1952, a Liberal MP, W. C. Wentworth, put a 'question without notice' to the minister for external affairs, R. G. Casey:

I ask the Minister for External Affairs whether certain negotiations for an economic agreement between Australia and the United States of America took place over a period of years from about 1947 onwards. Was a draft summary of the results of those agreements to date made early in 1950, shortly after this [Liberal–Country Party coalition] Government took office? Was that draft considered to be a highly confidential document, which was available only to top-ranking officials of the Department of External Affairs and certain other departments?

Was there a leakage of that document to the Communist Party? Did the Communist Party allege that the draft had been betrayed to it by a highly placed Government official? Did the version of the draft that was published in the Communist newspaper *Tribune* of November 14, 1951, contain details which proved that the Communist Party had had access to the confidential draft? Is the Minister aware of the identity of the official who betrayed the draft to the Communist Party? What action did the Government take, and what further action does it propose to take in relation to this incident?[4]

It was no secret who had written the *Tribune* article, or that the paper was the official organ of the Communist Party. Chiplin's signed column had begun appearing, under the heading 'Rex Chiplin Says', in 1948. His name appeared on the story to which Wentworth referred in his question. It was published less than two months after the failure of Menzies' referendum, and discussed a 'traitor treaty'. Chiplin, besides revealing for the first time the existence of the treaty, took a political stance in relation to its contents and likely effects. His view was that many of its provisions, including the sections that eliminated the liability of American corporations establishing enterprises in Australia to taxation in both Australia and America, would lead to foreign domination of important sectors of the Australian economy.

Today, concern about the social effects of the sort of economic colonialism practised by so-called multinational corporations, many of them based in the United States, is not, of course, the exclusive preserve of the Communist Party. It is one of the most serious questions facing governments, workers and smaller businesses in virtually every country. There is little doubt that, in those Cold War days, Chiplin's attitude on this matter would have been influenced by an intractable opposition to the policies of any Washington administration, implicit in his sympathy for the Soviet regime. Nevertheless, in retrospect, Chiplin showed great perspicacity in the essence of his article, despite the ideological bias reflected in the way he presented his information.

But this incident does not involve any need to make a political or even moral judgment on the beliefs or character of Chiplin. If he had been guilty of a criminal offence, the authorities and the courts had ample opportunity to act on that offence, to prosecute and to judge. Six months had passed between the publication of the article and the day when Wentworth rose in Parliament and asked his question.

It is a technical offence for a public servant to give to an outsider, without authorization, information gained in the course of his employment. But this is a rule honoured only in the breach. Every competent journalist covering the political scene aids and abets public servants in breaking these regulations, simply by asking them about the background to various major public issues. This is done in the quite legitimate belief that in a democracy there is a right to public knowledge of the information on which politicians are making decisions. There is no evidence, nor any reason to believe, that Chiplin's story affected the security of Australia in any way.

Normally, when a question as detailed as that asked by Wentworth is put, without notice, to a minister, he directs that it be 'placed on notice'. He later supplies a written answer that is published in Hansard and, like an oral and impromptu answer, is covered by parliamentary privilege against any legal redress. Casey, however, replied immediately. His department, he said, had begun an investigation into the 'very grievous' situation revealed by the leakage of information to the Communist newspaper. The statements in Wentworth's question were 'all substantially true'. The investigation was proceeding with some success. Clearly the leakage had emanated from a 'reasonably senior officer', but Casey said he was convinced that it had not come from 'any officer of the Department of External Affairs who is now in the department'. This, of course, was pointing the finger straight at Dr John Burton.

Wentworth lost no time in spelling out for the public record the implication left by Casey's answer. At 11.20 that night, in the debate on the adjournment, during which Members can raise any matter that concerns them, he specifically suggested that Dr Burton could be involved in the leakage. Casey, replying to Wentworth in Parliament, made what became known as his 'nest of traitors' speech. He stated that the draft 'treaty of commerce, friendship and navigation' between the United States and Australia published in *Tribune* in November 1951 had in fact been prepared about February 1950, when Dr Burton was still head of the Department of External Affairs. He said that he thought it improbable that Burton had been responsible for the leakage, but went on to emphasize that some senior public servant had been treacherous. 'There are traitors in our midst,' Casey told Parliament. But the government was 'doing its utmost to uncover the nest of traitors that exists somewhere or other in the Public Service'.[5]

On 29 May 1952 the *Sydney Morning Herald* said in an editorial: 'Mr Casey's revelations that a senior government official had passed on important secret information to a Communist newspaper and that there was a "nest of traitors" in the public service must cause serious disquiet at home and damage to Australia's reputation abroad. That a situation has developed where adherents of a party pledged to destroy the State and giving allegiance to an unfriendly alien power have been able to worm their way into the Government service with access to confidential information, provides the completest vindication of the Administration's policy on Communism and its efforts to outlaw the Communist Party.' As it turned out, this was going a bit far.

It was established beyond doubt at the Petrov Commission that the leak had actually come from the Department of National Development, almost certainly during the period that Casey was the minister in charge, and not from the Department of External Affairs, either before or after Dr Burton had gone to Ceylon. This was accepted by the Commissioners after evidence had been given that a typing error occurring only in the Department of National Development, where the word 'immigration' was wrongly used instead of 'navigation', had been perpetuated in Chiplin's story. It was also established, beyond what seems reasonable doubt, that Chiplin had been provided with the document by a female security agent who had been the personal secretary of a Commander Jackson, director of the Department of National Development during the period Casey was minister. It appears highly likely that the Commonwealth Investigation Service had instructed her to pass the document to Chiplin as an *agent provocateur* immediately after the failure of September's referendum. Chiplin published his 'traitor treaty' article less than two months after the vote, and had obviously been handed the information sometime during the intervening period.

The evidence to support this belief did not emerge, even for Chiplin himself, until a dramatic series of secret sessions at the Petrov hearings in February and March 1955, three years later. Yet it is clear that Casey and other members of the government became aware of the true situation in the meantime and did nothing to remove what Dr Evatt later described as the 'grievous slur' under which Burton and senior officers of External Affairs remained. They, and particularly Casey, had ample opportunity in the intervening years to clear Burton's name, as they were asked countless questions on the subject by Eddie Ward and other Labor MPs.

The partial resolution of the Chiplin story obliges us to abandon our rough chronology of events and go forward those three years to the Petrov Commission. The Chiplin story was, however, in no way essential to the resolution of the Petrov story. Always, at best, a sad side-issue, it illustrates what had been going on behind the performance of Casey and Wentworth on the public stage in 1952, as the Petrov affair was gradually built to its climax.

Under cross-examination at the Petrov Commission, and despite threats of severe penalties, Chiplin refused to disclose the name of the person who had provided him with the document. Then, on 18 February 1955, his evidence was interrupted while the Commission went into secret session and a woman, to be known only as 'Mrs A', was called as a witness. She said that during the war she had worked with naval intelligence (one of the paid-up subscribers to the 'Gnomes'—they supplied drivers for the Russian delegation in the Lapstone exercise), and since 1947 had been in touch first with the Commonwealth Investigation Service, and then ASIO.

This came as a shock to Chiplin. The woman and her daughter had been close family friends of Chiplin, his wife and young daughter for nearly five years. They had first met when Mrs A was working in Canberra as a journalist in 1949. She was now a widow living in Warrandyte, twenty miles from Melbourne, and they had remained in reasonably close contact. After less than half an hour in the Royal Commission's witness box, she collapsed in a state of emotional distress. Chiplin had refused to tell even his own counsel the identity of the person who had supplied him with the draft treaty, but in the interval caused by her breakdown, aware for the first time that she was a security agent, he revealed that it was none other than Mrs A. He also said that she had regularly supplied him with material from the Department of National Development.

W. J. V. Windeyer, counsel 'assisting the Commission', explained: 'The witness is in an emotional state and not fit to give evidence this afternoon, due, I gather, to the stress of having to give evidence about a long and extraordinary course of events.' Later Mrs A was to give some indication of the sources of that stress. Asked by Chiplin's counsel whether she had 'visited Chiplin's home a good deal' with her 'own little girl', she answered: 'That is so, happily so.' Of Chiplin she said: 'He has always been a most sympathetic person. Mr Chiplin has been a very honest person to deal with. I have no wish to do Mr Chiplin any harm. This is not easy for me ... none of it. I have lost everything in coming here— everything I had up till Monday. I have lost my friends—my close friends over the years—and my association with the Left Wing; I have now lost my Left Wing friends.'[6]

Mrs A, who broke down twice more, told the Commission that about the time Chiplin's article appeared she had, under instructions from R. W. Whitrod of the Commonwealth Investigation Service, given Chiplin a confidential list of American companies that had invested in Australia. She denied that she had given him the copy of the draft treaty, which had come from the department in which she had been working at the time. But she went on to say that six months later, under instructions from security, she had rung Chiplin after Casey's 'nest of traitors' outburst in May 1952, and had asked him to come to see her in Melbourne. She was worried about being implicated. By what was described at the Commission as 'sheer accident', the deputy director-general of ASIO, G. R. Richards, was sitting beside Chiplin on the return flight to Sydney, and shared a bottle of beer with him.

Dr Evatt was later to say: 'It is a fair inference from the "nest of traitors" episode and from the evidence before the Commission that the Menzies Government had some prior knowledge, not merely of Petrov's probable defection, but of the nature of the evidence of leakages which might appear from his documents.' By this time Evatt had not only heard the evidence of Chiplin and Mrs A, but had been informed by Burton of the Lapstone Hotel exercise, and the surprising resemblance between the list of security suspects then supplied by MI5 and the names in Petrov's G Series documents. Evatt also made the point: 'Mr Casey, particularly, must have known of Dr Burton's innocence, yet he remained silent in Parliament, although question after question was raised, in reply to which he blustered and evaded the direct requests of Opposition members that the matter must be cleared up.'

There was only one light side to this sorry episode. It was claimed that, in the Petrov documents, Chiplin was known to Moscow by the code name 'Charlie'. This obvious play on the name Charlie Chaplin was, as several people observed, much more likely to have been a creation of the schoolboy talents of the Australian security services than of the grey-faced men of the MVD.

At this time, the Australian Security Intelligence Organization was not the only secretive body that combined a zealous opposition to communism with a dislike for the left wing of the Australian Labor Party and the foreign policies of Dr Evatt. J. D. Pringle, through his links with Catholic intellectuals, became an authority on the Catholic Social Studies Movement, known simply as the 'Movement', formed in Victoria in 1942 by B. A. Santamaria, a young Catholic lawyer of Italian parentage, with the permission of Melbourne's Archbishop Mannix. Its objective was to fight the influence of Communists in the trade unions, although its existence was kept a strict secret until its formal establishment as a national organization was approved by the Catholic bishops in 1945. In that same year the 'Industrial Groups', another anti-Communist force, were set up in Sydney by officials of the New South Wales Trades and Labor Council. Although the Industrial Groups were non-sectarian, they had the same aims as the Movement, and about a third of the 'Groupers' were also members of the Movement. By 1952 the Industrial Groups had, after a long struggle, gained considerable power in both the unions and the Labor Party in New South Wales and Victoria. 'The extraordinary feature of the situation was that this whole curious relationship was quite unknown to the Australian public [or] to the rank and file of the Labor Party,' Pringle says. 'It was a conspiracy of silence.'[7]

On 28 January 1953, in *News Weekly*, a newspaper published by the Movement, there appeared an article that was to prove strangely prophetic. It reinforces Evatt's argument that the timing of Petrov's defection more than a year later was the result of a conspiracy to damage the Labor Party's electoral prospects.

Startling repercussions are expected to follow the disclosures soon to be made on the activities of certain members of the Russian diplomatic staff in Australia.

As a sample of what will be revealed in the anticipated disclosure, take the case of the Third Secretary attached to the Russian Legation in Canberra.

It would appear that the Third Secretary's job has very little to do with diplomatic relations between Russia and Australia, but is concentrated mainly in the accumulation, assessment, and compilation of material on the Australian industrial position. Regular reports from the Third Secretary are forwarded to Moscow, enabling the Commissars to check on the accuracy of other reports reaching them from Australia.

Given the Movement's preoccupation with communism and industrial relations, it is not improbable that this information was passed on by the similarly preoccupied ASIO and CIS, some of whose agents may have been Movement people.

The security services of Western countries regularly share information on Soviet espionage agents or suspected agents. Igor Gouzenko's documents led to the arrest of Alan Nunn May, the Canadian security service ensuring that Scotland Yard's Special Branch were acquainted with the relevant information. We have already seen how Roger Hollis, a future head of MI5, made a special visit to Australia in 1948 to explore British security's suspicions about the External Affairs Department. As all Soviet diplomats are possible MVD agents, there is little doubt that the Petrovs were kept under surveillance by Swedish, British and American security when they served in Stockholm from 1943 to 1947. MI5 and the CIA would certainly have passed on to ASIO whatever they knew of Petrov when he arrived in Australia in 1951.

Sharing information at a top level is well known, but it seems likely that this *News Weekly* article was a case of sharing information at an operational, almost public, level. The publishers of *News Weekly* certainly did not come to their conclusions through original research. Somebody told them.*

---

*In July 1974, Gough Whitlam, the first Labor prime minister of Australia since the Petrov affair, released a list of titles of more than fifty articles prepared by ASIO for distribution to 'selected journalists'.

6 Booze, brothels and Beria

Dressed as Arab potentates, and both wearing fezes borrowed from J. C. Williamson's theatre wardrobe, Bialoguski and Petrov had a wild night out in Sydney early in 1953. Petrov had introduced Bialoguski to Alan Clarke, a Sydney dentist said to be a secret Communist, but overtly a member of the Liberal Party. According to Petrov, Clarke was even friendly with Labor state cabinet ministers.

'"You must meet my harem," Clarke often said to both Petrov and myself,' recalls Bialoguski. Clarke had travelled widely; he always 'referred to his women friends as "my harem", and frequently interlarded his conversations about them with references to his experiences "during my travels through Egypt"'. Bialoguski wrote:

Both Petrov and I believed he was a mere boaster, so we decided to put him in an awkward position by taking him up. We proposed that a 'harem night' should be held in his flat, that I should come as an Egyptian, Prince Ali Mohammed, and that Petrov should be a pasha who belonged to my entourage. To give the whole thing an air of veracity, I wrote a letter to Clarke recalling a friendship with him in Egypt, and announcing that I hoped to be in touch with him soon during an incognito visit to Australia.

To our astonishment Clarke made no attempt to back out. He arranged that on a specific evening three young women should be 'presented' to the visiting prince. ... I am dark, wear a beard, and with a fez could pass as an Egyptian in the eyes of the uninformed. Petrov, with a fez on his head, needed no further embellishment; he looked every inch the Eastern potentate.*

After arriving at Clarke's flat in Macleay Street, Potts Point, and referring to his thirty-eight wives, Bialoguski let it be known that he would grant each of the three girls a

---

*Long interviews with Bialoguski in 1973 and 1974 and his book *The Petrov Story* are the main sources for this and other chapters.

ten-minute audience. He invited them to his country as his guests. but warned that, by tradition, any woman who visited the palace of his ancestors was required to join the harem during her period of residence and accept all the obligations, as well as the favours. of its permanent members. ```That, of course, might be an obstacle which ... what, no obstacle at all! How sweet of you. I'm sure you will never regret the decision.``` he wrote later.

Petrov. said Bialoguski. soon 'began a performance that made my "audiences" look like a schoolboy's prank. ... Uninhibited by the limitations my high rank imposed on me, Petrov bestowed boisterous favours in all directions. He pinched one young woman here. another there, but all in a place which I'm sure made sitting for all a painful process for days to come. I had never seen Petrov more cheerful.'

On other occasions Bialoguski took Petrov to brothels in Kings Cross, presumably in the seedy Chapel Street area. But if Bialoguski and Petrov were happy in each other's company, neither had successful working relationships with his own security contacts.

The beginning of 1953 was a crucial time in my relationship with Petrov; despite his high position in the Russian Embassy he was not happy, and there were obvious signs of friction. I could see what was going on; Petrov and his wife obviously did not get on well with the Ambassador, Lifanov. Petrov's main complaint was that both he and his wife were not fully appreciated by the Ambassador, who, he said, never ceased to try to thwart them. 'Here we are,' he would say to me, 'Dusya [Mrs Petrov] and I working day and night, and what do we get for it in return? Nothing but complaints. According to Lifanov nothing we do is right. He is always criticising and finding fault. Dusya is a nervous wreck. He is nothing but a big bully.'

Was this the head of the dreaded MVD talking? There is ample evidence that Petrov was afraid of his overt superiors: this leads one to believe that they may have been his covert superiors as well.

Bialoguski says that Petrov apologized for not taking him

more often into the company of other Soviet officials: 'These people are perpetually spying on each other, and if they can do anything to trip each other up they'll do it. If they see us together they will say, "Here is Petrov and Bialoguski drinking again!" As though it would matter if we were.' But it was not just a taste for alcohol and high living that was causing Petrov problems with his Russian colleagues. On 5 March 1953, Stalin died. Petrov's ultimate superior, Lavrenti Beria, almost immediately found himself in political difficulties, and Petrov was accused within the Soviet embassy in Canberra of attempting to form a Beria faction. In July, Beria was arrested, and by Christmas he had been tried and executed.

Bialoguski was reporting regularly on Petrov to ASIO. When, on 28 January 1953, *News Weekly* reported 'disclosures soon to be made' about Petrov, more than a year before his defection, Bialoguski was telling ASIO about 'changes taking place in his mental outlook and personality'. 'There was', says Bialoguski, 'a marked division between the two Petrov personalities, and in it lay the secret of his dissatisfaction.' The two personalities were the playboy who, in company with Bialoguski, 'liked good food, good drink, a good joke, a bit of high life and a pleasant and relaxed social atmosphere', and the suspicious Soviet official, 'the martinet who must see to it, as part of his duties, that every other member of the staff, including the Ambassador, never ceased to be official automatons always ready to sink their individualities in the interests of the supreme Soviet State'. Petrov, in Bialoguski's view, was like a man who, already in satisfactory employment, reads the 'positions vacant' column and speculates on the worth of each job should he be in need of one.

One day before May 1953, while they were passing a block of flats in Sydney that was up for sale, Petrov looked at the building and remarked to Bialoguski: 'Something like that would be good for you and me, Michael.' Bialoguski decided to test him soon afterwards, and an ideal opportunity arose. They both frequented a Kings Cross café, the Adria, run by a Pole named George Chomentowski 'in the manner of a Soho eating place'. When dining there Petrov posed as a visiting

Melbourne retailer of women's ware. It was a measure of his attraction to the commercial sphere that he went out of his way to talk to anybody who would listen—George, the waiters and the waitresses—about his dress shops.

Chomentowski indicated to Bialoguski early in 1953 that he was anxious to find someone willing to become a partner in his restaurant. Bialoguski went to Petrov and said that he had been offered a half share for £1000, but could not raise the money. He was prepared to give Petrov half of his share, under a separate private agreement, without informing Chomentowski. Petrov agreed, subject to Bialoguski carrying out a check on the restaurant proprietor's background.

Then, in May 1953, Petrov and his wife were given notice of their recall to Russia, on leave, for three to six months. Petrov indicated that he feared it was to be a permanent recall and, before the time of his departure was due, appeared in Bialoguski's surgery in Sydney 'with a dramatic air, looking drawn and depressed'. 'I've had a dreadful time with my eyes,' Petrov complained. 'I'm practically blind in my right eye, and the left one is not much good either. I can see black spots floating about all the time.' Bialoguski believed then that Petrov was exaggerating his problem as an excuse to postpone his return; he did, however, arrange an appointment for Petrov with a Dr H. C. Beckett, an ophthalmic surgeon with whom he shared waiting rooms in Macquarie Street.

This incident coincided with one of the periodic crises between Bialoguski and ASIO. When he was asked in 1973, 'Are you able to give any rational explanation for the apparent imbecility of ASIO in its dealings with you?' Bialoguski replied:

I think ASIO strongly suspected me—on both a personal and a security basis—to the end. There was my appearance. I wore a beret and a beard, and this was at the height of the Cold War. If there had been an un-Australian activities committee, I had the sort of appearance that would have qualified me to appear before it. It wasn't only that I looked awkward—I *was* awkward and a bit on the bumptious side. I had a very deep belief in individual freedom and I was dealing with a formal and inflexible branch of the public service. I quite often told people to get stuffed. They simply didn't have any experience of dealing with me or people like me, or with the intelligence situation they found themselves in. I was an 'amateur' and they thought they were professionals. They resented my teaching them their job and criticizing their performance. I am not referring here to the people I was in touch with. I refer to the mythical 'control figure'. I take it this was Spry, whom I never met.*

Early in May 1953, when he was more than ever convinced that Petrov was a potential defector (and was on the verge of entering a business deal with Petrov, and helping him delay his return to Moscow), Bialoguski sent his resignation from ASIO to the 'mythical "control figure"':

The Director General, Security.
Dear Sir,

I wish to submit my resignation as from a date to be mutually agreed upon.

The day of the presumable departure of Petrov would be convenient to me.

The reasons for my resignation, which I submit with regret, are as follows:

(1) I feel that the manner in which a contribution towards the rental of my flat was refused by you was unfair and discourteous, especially as I had submitted a request for possible financial assistance some months ago (to which I received no reply).

In connection with the above I wish to point out that in obtaining

---

*Although Bialoguski has to be seen as a key figure in the Petrov defection, Spry never introduced himself to Bialoguski either before or after the event. They did, however, have what might be called a 'nodding acquaintance'.

Once Bialoguski was exposed at the Royal Commission as an ASIO agent, he went regularly to listen to the proceedings and, of course, to give evidence on more than one occasion. Spry was at the sittings virtually every day; both knew who the other was, but they never went further than nodding to each other as a sort of partial acknowledgment.

The closest Bialoguski ever got to full recognition as part of the security service came one day when Spry testified. After a long, boring cross-examination by Windeyer, Spry returned to the bench he shared with Solicitor-General Bailey and various security people including Bialoguski; flushed with the excitement of his performance, he asked them all: 'How did I go?'

the flat I was moved to a great extent by certain advantages in my dealings with Petrov—advantages which, I feel, were proved subsequently—and also by the fact that possession of a flat would cut down expenses in other directions. [This was the luxury apartment at Point Piper, where Petrov was increasingly staying on his visits to Sydney, and where Bialoguski was to rifle his pockets while he lay drunk and asleep.]

(2) The delay in considering my application (those recently and in the past) has proved a frequent embarrassment to me because most of the time I am compelled to make instantaneous decisions in the best interests of my employment with you.

Needless to say, if I were to wait for a word from you before deciding on a course of action my competence would suffer.

(3) Your insistence on inspecting my flat in my absence I could interpret only as an indication that you haven't sufficient trust in me.

It seemed also to lack a practical point of view of the subsequent refusal to grant the assistance [*sic*].

(4) It has been my impression over a long period that my telephones have been tapped.

As much as I would like to believe that this was a measure (if I am correct in my assumption) to protect me, I feel I could have been told about it.

The above are the things that make the difference between happy team work and a poorly paid duty.

I feel that my continuing the work I was doing for you in the past is in the public interest, and that a considerable amount of money (public money) has been spent on my activities, which only recently began to bear fruit.

Therefore, I shall be happy to reconsider my resignation if I can be convinced by you that my doubts and grievances are without foundation.

The simple fact is that ASIO, partly for the reasons he later explained to the authors—that he was foreign and an 'amateur'—did not trust Bialoguski. He had found evidence that his flat had been searched without his permission.

On 10 July 1956, another Polish immigrant, George Marue, appeared in Sydney Central Criminal Court charged with having passed valueless cheques. The prosecuting policeman, Detective Sergeant G. Golding, told the court that Marue had, when arrested, claimed to have been employed secretly to spy on Bialoguski, while Bialoguski spied on Petrov. According to Golding, he had said: 'I will upset the Menzies government. I will tell people what went on in the Petrov inquiry.' Golding also claimed that Marue had told him he had bought liquor through the Soviet embassy at duty-free prices and then sold it to Chequers, the Sydney nightclub.

Marue was a well-known member of the rather flashy coterie of refugees, émigrés and others who loosely centred their activities around Sydney's Kings Cross area. Many of them seem to have been in touch with the security services, presumably to spy on one another. Bialoguski believes Marue was engaged to watch him by either the CIS or the New South Wales Special Branch. In the House of Représentatives on 22 February 1956, Eddie Ward had alleged that an unnamed New Australian working for ASIO had 'joined with Dr Bialoguski in the distribution of liquor which was obtained improperly through diplomatic channels. On one occasion when Dr Bialoguski was asked where he was obtaining these supplies of liquor, he said he was getting them through diplomatic channels with the aid of "that thief Petrov".'[1] But Bialoguski has flatly denied any dealings in Soviet duty-free liquor in his conversations with the authors.

Bialoguski's suspicions about ASIO's distrust of him were well founded. They are also an indication of the atmosphere enveloping many of the activities of ASIO at the time. There was, for example, as Bialoguski's experiences and the fact that Richards was on the plane beside Chiplin indicate, widespread phone-tapping and interception of private telegrams. Dr Burton was later to discover, at the time of the Petrov Commission, that his private telephone in Canberra was tapped.

Writing about his letter of resignation, Bialoguski made the point that it had been phrased in such a way as to leave ASIO the option to 'iron out the differences', if it wanted to. But despite the fact that he seemed to be on the verge of bringing Petrov over the wire, he was in for a shock. He had handed his resignation to his immediate ASIO contact. The following day this man rang him at his Macquarie Street surgery and told him to cease activities immediately.

Bialoguski had been through all this before. He first resigned in September 1951, very soon after he had been introduced to Petrov. He was then given a more flexible expense account, and immediately re-established contact with Petrov. The next month, October, after a second threat to resign, his salary was increased from £2 to £10 per week in addition to the new expense account.

Now, in May 1953, Bialoguski was not to be dismissed so lightly. He knew the American vice-consul in Sydney, Harry Mullin, socially. Bialoguski says that he has never known whether Mullin had any direct link with CIA work. At any event, he went straight to Mullin's home in the Sydney north-shore suburb of Killara and told him what had happened. The meeting took place on 16 May. 'When I suggested that if there were a US intelligence service here that might be prepared to interest itself, I specified two conditions on which I might be prepared to cooperate'—Bialoguski would not divulge any details of the workings of ASIO, and permission would have to be obtained from the Australian government for him to work with any 'US service'. Mullin said he would have to consult the American consul-general.

Without waiting for a reply, Bialoguski then made another effort to force ASIO to rescind his dismissal. The next day he went in search of Bill Barnwell, the man who had originally assisted him in joining the old Commonwealth Investigation Service, which still employed Barnwell, although Bialoguski had moved on to ASIO. Explaining why he went to Barnwell, Bialoguski later stated: 'The CIS is the older body, and its members, though they may deny it, are somewhat jealous of the newer, more glamorous organization. One of the sore points with the CIS is that most of the glamour work has been taken from them by the Security Organization. ... I felt that the CIS might seize the chance to "cash in" on work as "spectacular" as that on which I was engaged.'

The circumstances of their meeting give a wry indication of the overt political affiliations of the run of Australian security men in that era. On Saturday 17 May, Bialoguski found Barnwell actively canvassing for the Labor Party in his home area, Manly, a northern beach suburb of Sydney. It was voting day in the 1953 Senate election. Barnwell was apparently surprised to be told by Bialoguski that he had not, as the CIS suspected, joined the other side. 'Since my link with him had been broken I had played the part to which I had assigned myself so efficiently that Bill was convinced his "promising pupil" had gone "commo". He was greatly relieved to know that his original trust had not been misplaced,' Bialoguski wrote.

This initiative was partly successful. Barnwell told him that he could do nothing without consulting the 'old man', Brigadier F. G. ('Black Jack') Galleghan, who ran the CIS; then, two days later, he informed Bialoguski that Galleghan said they could 'not interfere in any circumstances'. But the wheels had begun to turn. A few hours later his ASIO supervisor, who had relayed the information that he was to cease activities, was on the phone again asking Bialoguski to continue with Petrov until the diplomat left for Russia—just as Bialoguski had suggested in his letter of resignation. ASIO had not bitten at his request for more money, but he had been reinstated.

That same day, 19 May 1953, Petrov arrived in Sydney for his appointment with the eye specialist. In Bialoguski's presence as referring doctor, Beckett advised Petrov that it would be unwise for him to travel to Moscow then because of his eye condition. Bialoguski continued to suspect Petrov of exaggerating his complaint to avoid being recalled, and judged that he was ripe for defection.

He officially communicated this opinion to ASIO, and then raised what, in retrospect, appears one of the central issues of the Petrov affair: the timing of the defection. 'It was up to Security to decide whether it was worthwhile to try to bring about [Petrov's defection],' Bialoguski said he told ASIO at this time.

'It is not a thing that can be decided offhand,' I warned them.

'There are important factors to be taken into consideration. It could be argued, for instance, that from a long-range point of view it might be a distinct disadvantage.' We had to weigh the propaganda value of the defection of a man like Petrov. I emphasised this point because, strictly from an espionage point of view, it actually did not matter much whether he defected or not, so deeply had I penetrated into his activities. In fact, from that point of view, I have often thought since that it would have been better if Petrov had never defected. If he had not, we would still be in the position to play our opponents along without them being aware of it, and in the event of war, or some such crisis, I would have been in a position to emasculate the whole Soviet espionage system in Australia without its controllers knowing what had happened.

In May 1953 he does not seem to have been alone in this view. ASIO, still penny-pinching over Bialoguski's expenses and ever ready to sack him, apparently did not place high importance on encouraging Petrov's defection. But as the inevitable 1954 national election approached, and as the electoral prospects of Menzies' coalition government foundered, ASIO's view of the importance of a Petrov defection underwent a strange metamorphosis.

7 Money is no object

'Well, we've got a new star on the horizon!' Bialoguski was to shout angrily at his ASIO supervisor on the evening of 23 July, the year before Petrov defected. When the man looked straight ahead as if he didn't understand, Bialoguski continued: '... A brilliant new agent, Dr Beckett.'

'Whenever I think of this incident, my blood still boils,' Bialoguski says. 'I never learned the reason for these childish antics.' His reconciliation with ASIO in May had proved to be a temporary one. He was not, however, the only person having trouble with ASIO in mid-1953. Dr Evatt was later to claim that 'Operation Petrov' had its beginnings at about this time, and that ASIO was, by a series of raids, interviews, and nefarious and secret activities, starting to update the dossiers it had been given by the British security men in 1948. Burton believes these formed the basis of the papers Petrov was to 'produce' when he defected.

The proprietor of the Adria, George Chomentowski, had told Bialoguski that the price of partnership in the restaurant had risen to £2000, and that he wanted an early decision. Meanwhile, ASIO also wanted Petrov to answer a series of questions that Bialoguski described as 'both clumsy and unnecessary', designed to discover his intentions and future movements—one that Bialoguski found less than subtle was whether Petrov preferred Australian hospitals to those in his own country. Bialoguski went to Canberra and saw Petrov, who told him to 'keep in touch with George [about the Adria deal] ... it is too good a chance to miss'. He managed to elicit responses to most of the questions posed by his superiors; Petrov preferred Russian hospitals.

The incident in July that so disturbed Bialoguski occurred after Dr Beckett had arranged for Petrov's eye complaint to be treated in Canberra hospital by a local doctor. Petrov arrived in Sydney on 23 July and was accompanied by

Bialoguski when he kept an appointment with Beckett to have his condition checked. 'Beckett suggested, to my surprise, that if I had business elsewhere there was no reason why I should stay during Petrov's examination,' Bialoguski later wrote. When he returned after about forty-five minutes, Petrov was standing on the footpath outside. It was the first time, Bialoguski says, that he had ever seen Petrov ruffled. As soon as he got into Bialoguski's car, Petrov spat: 'That fellow is a bastard. We must be very careful of him. He's got something to do with Security.' When Bialoguski asked what had happened, Petrov went on: 'He examined me as usual, then he asked me how I liked being in Australia. I said it was a nice country—plenty of food, good drinks. Then he said he believed I'd be leaving for Moscow shortly. If I liked the country, why shouldn't I stay here. A former Czech consul had stayed and was doing all right. He said he knew a Security man who would help me if I wanted to stay.'

Apart from the lack of consultation, there were two reasons for Bialoguski's rage at Beckett's overture to Petrov. First, he argued, it endangered him personally. 'The way they had acted introduced a serious element of risk that I would become suspect in Petrov's eyes. They had jeopardised all I had been working for, and exposed me to danger, because retribution was almost certain if Petrov came to the conclusion that I was an agent.' This may seem a little extreme, but his second ground for complaint had more substance: Beckett's advances were naive and clumsy, and could not have succeeded. 'I wondered wryly why Security had not chosen a new Boy Scout as a person likely to handle the job satisfactorily. They could not have bungled things more had they done so,' he wrote later. The man to approach Petrov should, he had advised ASIO, be someone with high standing in the community, and the contact should be made in a social atmosphere in surroundings of wealth and importance. It is clear that there was no love lost between Beckett, who was not short of money, and Bialoguski who was.

Bialoguski, no matter how disillusioned he had become with ASIO, continued working on Petrov. But no attempt was made to fulfil an earlier undertaking given by ASIO that an appointment would be arranged for him with Richards, deputy director-general of the security organization, to iron out his problems about expenses. Petrov, meanwhile, was making a series of moves that do not appear to have resulted in any espionage gains for the Soviet Union, but were to injure innocent individuals when the names of the people he approached were disclosed at the Royal Commission. His manoeuvres look alarmingly like those of an *agent provocateur*.

At this stage, Bialoguski's relations with security and Petrov's relations with his embassy went into an abrupt and parallel decline. In July 1953 the Russian ambassador, Lifanov, began making a series of critical reports to Moscow about both the Petrovs, accusing them of a number of offences and alleging that they were trying to form a pro-Beria group in the embassy. At the same time, Kovaliev, a commercial attaché and the representative in the embassy of the Central Committee of the Soviet Communist Party, made similar reports to the committee in Moscow. Petrov learned secretly of these communications from Prudnikov, the embassy cipher clerk. The accusations were to come to a head later in the year under the new Soviet ambassador, Generalov, when he succeeded Lifanov.

The clashes within the Soviet embassy, despite the seriousness of the pro-Beria allegations, were to have a burlesque character on occasions. Early in November 1953, Bialoguski had a private meeting with the Petrovs in Canberra, after attending the Soviet National Day celebrations on 7 November. 'Throughout the meal Mrs Petrov complained about the Embassy staff, especially Generalov,' Bialoguski reported. 'She thought the other wives were jealous of her better dress and superior taste, and the fact that she had more spending money. I was surprised when she enquired about business openings in Sydney. She kept nagging Petrov about buying her a £200 fur coat. He looked as all husbands do in similar circumstances, and on this occasion at least I felt sympathy for poor old Vlad.'

A fortnight later, in late November, Petrov stayed with Bialoguski in Sydney. 'I was still fogged with sleep when he awakened me early the following morning, but that was not the only reason I couldn't fully grasp what he was talking about. Petrov, early as it was, had been drinking. ... As he talked I could see what had happened; he had been brooding on his wrongs, taken a drink to cheer himself, taken another and then sufficient to put him in a mood to air his troubles to somebody he could trust. As I awakened, Petrov was directing a stream of abuse against the [new] Ambassador. Finally he ran out of invective and speaking directly to me said, "This man can't stand the truth. Do you know what's happened now—Dusya's got the sack."'

At recent embassy staff meetings in Canberra, Petrov told Bialoguski, Mrs Petrov had been attacked by the ambassador for her attitude to his wife. Bialoguski's report of one of Petrov's statements sounds more like an incident in a slapstick movie than a rigid staff meeting at a Russian embassy, which should have been designed to increase efficiency and enthusiasm, and to encourage self-criticism: 'One thing the Ambassador found hard to pardon was an incident in which Mrs Petrov expressed her disapproval of [Generalov's] wife by throwing some confection at her—a pie, he believed, but what kind of pie he did not know.'

Another source of conflict was Petrov's Alsatian, Jack. He was so strongly attached to the dog that, when he came close to defection and it became apparent that he might have to leave both Jack and Dusya behind, he seemed, to Bialoguski, to be more concerned about the Alsatian's future than that of his wife; not surprisingly, even Dusya resented Petrov's relationship with the dog, which would growl fiercely if she tried to separate them. In the incident that Petrov recounted to Bialoguski, Jack had installed himself in Petrov's embassy office one day, and growled when anyone tried to coax him out. To Petrov's disgust, the ambassador finally intervened. According to Bialoguski, Petrov spoke 'like a man who has taken up the cudgels on behalf of a socially-affronted friend'.

While Mrs Petrov was clashing with the ambassador's wife,

Bialoguski, for his part, had his most serious crisis to date with ASIO. This resulted in a series of events throwing some light on the involvement of Menzies in Petrov's defection. By late August 1953, Bialoguski's impatience at the failure of Richards to honour the undertaking for an interview, at which his problems with the security service could be ironed out, was such that he asked for leave without pay. This was granted, although he continued to associate with Petrov and kept the same detailed notes as before. 'The leave had a meaning for me,' Bialoguski says. 'I was able to take certain steps which I felt would not have been available to me if I had been officially on duty. I had decided that my position had to be completely revised. Richards would not see me. I looked around to see where I must go.'

Believing that Richards' attitude to him had the approval of Spry, Bialoguski decided to see Menzies on the reasonable grounds that the security service and its head were answerable only to the prime minister. On 2 September he telephoned the prime minister's private secretary, Geoff Yeend, who agreed to try to arrange an appointment for the following morning. Bialoguski's account of this episode in *The Petrov Story* was compiled from his contemporaneous notes. He is unshakeable in maintaining its accuracy.

Next day, on meeting Yeend, I handed him a sealed envelope addressed to the Prime Minister. In the accompanying letter I explained that I was an agent, gave my code name of Jack Baker, and asked to see him on a matter of urgent importance. Yeend arranged that I should come back later. Upon my return he told me that he had been deputed by the Prime Minister to act on the latter's behalf, and as proof my letter to Mr Menzies lay open in front of him.

When I parked my car at Parliament House on this second call, I found myself within twenty yards of a Soviet Embassy car, just as the Ambassador, Lifanov, emerged from it. He was on his way, I discovered later, to pay his farewell official visit to the Prime Minister before his departure from Australia. All the time I sat in Yeend's office I could hear Lifanov's voice as he talked to Mr Menzies in the adjoining suite. ...

When Yeend told me he was acting for the Prime Minister, I put my case exactly as I would have done to Mr Menzies himself. In fact I assumed that Yeend would relay exactly what I had to say to his chief. Yeend seemed surprised by what I had to tell him. He said he found it hard to believe that the treatment I had received had been directed by the heads of the organisation. One would have expected, he said, that Security would know how to win friends and influence people.

The interview finished on an agreeable note. Yeend said that the next time he saw Spry, probably the following week, he would mention the matter to him and tell him that the Prime Minister was interested.

It was in a sanguine mood that I left Canberra for Sydney. In my own mind I had taken my dispute with Security to an arbiter—the only arbiter possible in this case—and there was now every prospect that my difficulties would be smoothed and that relations would be happier in future.

Bialoguski stated to the authors in 1974: 'I told Yeend about Petrov. I named Petrov, and I told him about the importance of the work.' Bialoguski said that he had made it quite clear to Yeend that Menzies must authorize their conversation before it could take place. Yeend assured Bialoguski that he had obtained that authorization from the prime minister. Bialoguski had naturally been unwilling to speak without this assurance, for otherwise it would have been an offence for him to discuss security matters.

In 1973, Yeend told Evan Whitton of the *National Times* that he gave Menzies no information on the Bialoguski visit until some months after the Royal Commission began its hearings, when, from a newspaper photograph of Bialoguski, he recognized the 'Jack Baker' who had visited him. 'A lot of people sought interviews with the Prime Minister. Some said they were important ASIO agents; some said they were being persecuted by radio waves—that sort of thing. I undertook to take Baker's complaint to the correct quarter. I rang up the local ASIO man, Max Phillips, and asked him first if he had an agent named Jack Baker, and if so would he pass on his complaint to Colonel Spry.'

Menzies was later to make false claims about the date on

which he first became aware of Petrov's plans to defect. On 12 August 1954, he told Parliament:

I know it is one of [Evatt's] theories that the whole of this matter was cunningly concealed so that it might be used for the purposes of winning an election. Therefore I say to the House and to the country that the name of Petrov became known to me for the first time on Sunday night, 11 April, I think, or the preceding Saturday night. It was one of those nights, when the head of the Australian Security Service came to see me at the Lodge in Canberra with the first two or three literally translated documents that Petrov had handed over. By 13 April, after consultation with the Cabinet, I was announcing the position in this House, and on the following day we established a Royal Commission. Therefore, the whole idea that there was some cunning concealment falls to the ground. Now, since we are forced to discuss these matters, may I say that when I was told of these things on the Saturday or Sunday night at my house in Canberra, oddly enough I referred to the Zinoviff [*sic*] letter. I said, 'I wish this could not have happened just now, because the last thing I want to have happen is something that may look like an election stunt.'[1]

Spry, in the *National Times* in 1973, stated categorically that he told Menzies Petrov's name on 10 February 1954. We also know that the security service, through Dr Beckett, had made a direct approach to Petrov to defect on 23 July 1953, and that Bialoguski had gone to Menzies' office on 3 September 1953. Bialoguski said in early 1974: 'There is a direct parallel with Nixon's relationship to Watergate. If Menzies did not know what was going on, he should have known. I believe he knew.' (Today, of course, it is obvious that Nixon knew all about Watergate.) Menzies' claim that he did not know about Petrov until the eve of the defection (on the eve of the federal election) serves one prime purpose. It is his answer to charges that Petrov's defection was designed and timed to preserve his government.

Whether Menzies heard of Bialoguski's visit to his office or not, Spry certainly did. Bialoguski said in his book: 'My feelings of satisfaction with the Canberra interview continued for some days, but when a week had passed without any word,

I telephoned Yeend again. Yeend said he had spoken to Spry, and I could rest assured matters would be adjusted soon. They were adjusted all right! Two or three days later North [the fictional name he gives to his security contact] summoned me, and grimly announced that I had been fired.'

Bialoguski refused to believe this because of what Yeend had said to him. He was then summoned to the office of a security man named McDermott, who put him straight: 'I have a message for you from Colonel Spry. He wished me to tell you that your services with the department have been terminated and that you are to cease your activities forthwith. He also told me to tell you that he is in charge of Security— not the Prime Minister.' McDermott went on to inform Bialoguski that ASIO was aware that he had contacted the Americans. Bialoguski then asked whether Spry's decision was irrevocable. 'Quite irrevocable,' was the answer.

Bialoguski's diary entry for the next day, which the authors have inspected, begins: 'I am on my own now.' Forthwith he wrote a letter to Spry:

To the Director General,
Security.
Dear Sir,
I have been informed that my services with your Department have been terminated. I feel that in doing so you have put the Departmental pride well above the interests of the Commonwealth and the principles of fair play. This, however, is now entirely a matter for your conscience.

In view of my long and varied experience in under-cover work and the first-hand knowledge of the Soviet methods and mentality, I wish to make a few points of constructive criticism which, I sincerely hope, will be accepted by you in the same spirit in which they are submitted.

Re:—

1. Teamwork! This expression I heard very often from your contacts, and indeed, in the course of my duties I have come to realize the importance of it so much more because it was so obviously missing.

As pointed out in my resignation of May last, I was unnecessarily hampered in my work and repeatedly irritated by the delay with which my inquiries were answered. You were in a habit of not answering hypothetical questions although they could not possibly involve the internal security of your Department. Your attitude caused me a great deal of personal and financial embarrassment as I often had to make instantaneous decisions and enter into obligations (e.g. my flat) without knowing whether they would meet with your approval.

'Red tape' hampers the teamwork and the initiative of your Department, and many an agent, I feel, would after a while adopt the line of least resistance, thus failing to exploit many opportunities presenting themselves in his work.

Any 'advanced' agent has to play his part around-the-clock. But what happens during the week-ends and outside working hours (9 a.m. to 5 p.m.)?

I could not speak to my usual contact [Mr North] unless I left a telephone number for him to ring up.

In most cases this is impracticable. In most cases the more important part of my activities was confined to the evenings and week-ends, and I was still not given the private telephone of my contact, and was very often left in need of advice.

Teamwork? Well, what about Dr Beckett's case? As a result of my hard work an approach to Petrov appeared likely to succeed. Without any consultation with me an approach was made through Dr Beckett. A most unsuitable man was selected who, due to his clumsy action, has ruined every chance of success that was there. Had you availed yourself of my knowledge of the Soviet mentality, and of Petrov's in particular, before instructing Dr Beckett, a better outcome would have ensued.

And all that was needed was about an hour's discussion with a person responsible for the assessment of the pros and cons of the contemplated action.

That's for the 'teamwork'.

Re:—

2. Atmosphere of suspicion; courtesy.

I believe that undercover work on the highest level in fighting Soviet Communism could best be done by scientists and artists of no political affiliations as both these groups are held in great esteem in the Soviet Union and are greatly sought after by the Soviet agents in this country.

If you have an artist or a scientist of note employed as an agent, and you give him the credit for intelligent and skilful dealings with the potential enemy's agents you should, by the same token, give him the same credit in dealings with your own Department.

You will probably agree that every 'advanced' agent becomes of necessity a 'double agent' in the technical sense of this word as he endeavours to be of some service to the enemy in order to gain his confidence. His loyalty, however, remains on one side, and he does not dare to swerve from the road to the ultimate aim. All the above, nevertheless, does not, I agree, mean that the guard should be let down and that the possibility of an agent being in fact a 'double agent' should not be entertained. Such a possibility, however, should in no circumstances create an atmosphere of suspicion. An agent should never be made to realize that he is also a suspect, and, therefore, in dealings with what I call an 'advanced agent' less apparent suspicion and greater courtesy is needed.

I wish to conclude in expressing my appreciation of the efficiency and courtesy shown to me by your Mr North; Messrs Barnwell, Galleghan, Brownley, East, Scott and others have also in the past greatly assisted me through their friendly and practical attitude towards me personally and to my problems.

Petrov, unaware of Bialoguski's dilemma, continued to visit him and drink his whisky. Then came the morning towards the end of November 1953 when he was awakened by Petrov's drunken ravings about the new ambassador, Generalov, and the revelation that his wife, Dusya, had been sacked. 'Ever since she has been sacked she has been crying,' Petrov told Bialoguski. 'Look, it has come to a point where we both think the best way out is to put a bullet through our heads.' Bialoguski soothed Petrov and sent him back to Canberra. But he now knew that Petrov would defect.

After briefly wondering whether to seek the backing and cooperation of the *Sydney Morning Herald*, where he had contacts, or 'just to produce Petrov out of the hat as a fait accompli', Bialoguski decided to alert ASIO to the situation. He rang his contact. 'Security did not exactly roll out the red carpet,' he says, but four days after his phone call 'Jack Baker was back on the job with official blessing'.

Bialoguski was at last taken to see Richards. 'You must realize how important this is,' was Richards' opening remark.

'It is imperative that we should see Petrov as soon as possible after he has decided to defect. We will expect a clear indication of his good faith. I have been on to Colonel Spry and this comes directly from him. The whole affair must be conducted through us.' Bialoguski then asked about expenses and the basis on which he was to resume his work as an agent. Richards replied without hesitation: 'Don't worry about expense. Money is no object.'

Vladimir Petrov (NEWS LTD)   Evdokia Petrov (HERALD & WEEKLY TIMES LTD)

Early days: the Petrovs outside the Soviet embassy in Canberra, with Ambassador and Mrs Lifanov (far right) and other staff members. In 1953, Lifanov was to accuse Petrov of attempting to form a pro-Beria faction within the embassy. (NEWS LTD)

Petrov indulges his taste for high living away from the embassy. On his right, Alan Clarke, and at left, Mrs Joan Clarke and Dr Michael Bialoguski. (SYDNEY MORNING HERALD)

'Cliveden', where Bialoguski entertained Petrov during his Sydney visits — still an exclusive address (FRANCES KELLY)

8 A rabbit out of the hat

Australia was uncommonly festive in February and March 1954, on the occasion of Queen Elizabeth II's royal tour—the first visit of a reigning monarch to Australian soil. Her subjects showed unusual interest; expressions of loyalty and goodwill were rife. But when the royal party left on 1 April the country settled back to its familiar, and perhaps unique, urban parochialism.[1] There was the usual round of sporting contests. The private secondary schools staged their then-important annual regatta in each state capital, with Shore the victors in Sydney. Clive Churchill's Australian Rugby League team was preparing to win the Ashes at home against England. Freddie Dawson, the popular visiting American boxer, was troubled by an eye injury. The autumn racing carnivals were continuing (with Karendi about to score an upset win over Carioca in the Doncaster). In Sydney, the Royal Easter Show was beginning.

Meanwhile, the Liberal–Country Party coalition, having bathed luxuriously in the Queen's reflected glory, now had to face political reality. With its three-year mandate running out, the government decided to hold a short session before facing the electorate again. Polling day was set for 29 May, and Parliament could not sit beyond 14 April.* For the most part the session was dull. Several minor bills were debated, and Parliament learned that Casey, the minister for external affairs, would visit Geneva for the forthcoming conference on Indochina. Debating was a little more active than in December, but that was only to be expected in the final session before an election.

---

*The previous federal election, following the double dissolution called by Menzies after the High Court had ruled his Communist Party Dissolution Act invalid, was held on 29 April 1951. The Australian constitution demands that Parliament rise to face the electorate at least two weeks less than three years after an election.

On Tuesday 13 April, the last day before Parliament was to rise, the House of Representatives resumed debate after the weekend break. Just before six o'clock it rose for dinner, and reconvened as usual at eight for the evening session, which is always broadcast by the Australian Broadcasting Commission. Before normal debate was resumed, Prime Minister Menzies asked leave of the Speaker to make a statement.[2]

It is my unpleasant duty to convey to the House some information which I this morning laid before Cabinet, for the first time, and which we decided should be dealt with as soon as possible.

Some days ago Mr Vladimir Mikhailovich Petrov, who has been Third Secretary and Consul in the Soviet Embassy in Australia since February 1951, voluntarily left his diplomatic employment and made to the Australian Government through the Australian Security Intelligence Organization a request for political asylum. The Director-General of the A.S.I.O., acting with the authority of myself, the Attorney-General, and the Department of External Affairs, received this request. The request has been granted and following on established diplomatic practice protection has been provided for Mr Petrov.

The Members, after sitting in stunned silence, broke into loud 'Hear, hears!' Menzies then read Petrov's application for asylum, and his renunciation of communism.

Mr Petrov, who has been carrying out in Australia the functions of the Russian Ministry of State Security—the M.V.D.—has disclosed complete willingness and capacity to convey to our own security people a great number of documents and what may turn out to be much oral information and explanation. In the examination of this material, involving as it does a great deal of translation and comparative research to establish the meaning of particular expressions and code names, much time will necessarily be spent. I am therefore not in a position to make a full statement. But, in the comparatively few days since Mr Petrov came to our security people enough matter has been examined, though only a small fraction of the whole, to show there are matters affecting Australian security which call for judicial investigation. These matters concern not only the activities of the M.V.D. agents in Australia, but also the position of some Australian citizens named in the documents under 'cover' or 'code' names or otherwise, as contacts or co-operators.

As would be expected, I do not propose to mention the names of the people until the investigation is so far proceeded with that a coherent case of proper probative value can be prepared.

There will be, of course, continued surveillance of persons named, most of whom, incidentally, had already come under the notice of the security service. The Government, therefore, proposes to set up a Royal Commission of investigation into what I may call espionage activity in Australia.

Menzies pointed out that much of the material needed further analysis before the Royal Commission could proceed. His announcement then concluded:

While I would have been agreeable for all of us to defer an appointment of such importance until after the new Parliament had been appointed, there should be no unavoidable delay of investigation of what are already beginning to emerge as the outlines of systematic espionage and at least attempted subversion.

Legal investigation shows that the Royal Commission Act needs amendment in order to authorise a Royal Commission and to compel the giving of evidence by witnesses. I will give at once notice of the amending bill and invite the House to pass it tomorrow.

Conspicuously absent from the chamber, at the time of the announcement and in the confusion that followed it, was the leader of the Opposition, Dr Evatt. His deputy, Arthur Calwell, was present but felt either unqualified or unable to reply for the Opposition. And so, after seven shattering minutes, debate continued on a public service superannuation bill. The Labor Party had made no comment in reply to the prime minister.

Calwell immediately telephoned Evatt, who was in Sydney, to tell him of the surprise announcement. Later that night, Evatt issued a statement:

The Federal Parliamentary Labor Party will support the fullest inquiry into all the circumstances connected with the statement made by Mr Menzies tonight and the matters contained in or relevant to that statement. If any person in Australia has been guilty of espionage or seditious activities, a Labor Government will see that he is prosecuted according to Law.

That has not only been our established policy, but we have acted in strict accordance with it. In short, we shall see to it that no guilty person is condemned, and that the whole matter is dealt with free from all questions of party politics and on the basis of the established principles of British justice.[3]

Given their public statements, both Menzies and Evatt apparently intended approaching this important event on similar legal lines. Menzies' announcement to the House and Evatt's press release indicated a unity of purpose, directed towards a thorough examination of Petrov's evidence and legal action upon that evidence. Both leaders seemed anxious to avoid unnecessary sensation and speculation.

But Menzies soon lost sight of this. His publicly expressed caution was rapidly forgotten, for that same Tuesday night, in Canberra, he held a news conference for all the political correspondents in the capital, though Peter Thomas of the Communist *Tribune* was barred from entry. At this conference Menzies enlarged on his announcement to the House. This amplification could only encourage sensation, and it contradicted his public pledges of just a few hours earlier.

The prime minister's remarks at this conference shared front-page headlines the next day with the security investigation of the US nuclear physicist, Dr Robert Oppenheimer. The prestigious *Sydney Morning Herald*,* quoting Menzies, said 'Petrov had given the Australian Government a "safe full of files—the really secret safe from the Russian Embassy" ', and these files were 'voluminous'. Adding drama, the paper reported that the Petrov house, situated near the Russian embassy, was clothed in darkness. It stated that Mrs Petrov was not going to seek asylum in Australia, that 'she elected to remain with the Russian Embassy' and 'she [would] return to Russia soon'. Further, it seemed 'Australian security

---

*All press quotations in this chapter are drawn from various articles in the *Sydney Morning Herald*, Wednesday 14 April 1954.

authorities [had] known since he arrived that [Petrov] was a secret police official'.

Another story that day, echoed elsewhere in the press, said: 'Petrov's request for political asylum was made about ten days ago. That was the day on which his term of duty with the Russian Embassy in Canberra expired.' This meant that the prime minister had had ten days in which to make the announcement of the defection. But Menzies later denied that he knew of Petrov's defection so early in April, although all evidence disagrees with him.

Further information obtained in Canberra was that Menzies had already begun the task of finding a Royal Commissioner. Also, the Commission was expected to meet immediately after its appointment to receive a broad outline of submissions from counsel whom the government would appoint to assist it. The reports went on to say it was expected that the Commission would then have to rise for some weeks while all evidence was prepared, and would thereafter sit continuously. This meant that the Royal Commission would meet during the forthcoming election campaign—hardly a time for sober judgment.

By 1953, it had appeared that Evatt was leading the ALP back to power. The Senate election of that year saw Labor increase its share of the vote from 45·9 per cent in 1951 to 50·6 per cent.[4] 'The A.L.P. was actually well on the way to recovery by 1954. They made five gains at the expense of the Liberals in Federal by-elections and were enjoying their only absolute majority in the history of Victoria. Industrial peace and the end of the Korean War reduced the importance of Communism as a domestic issue, especially as most branches of the A.L.P. and virtually all unions were now under anti-Communist control.'[5]

The royal visit in 1954 had helped the conservative government to some extent, but as late as 6 April the *Sydney Morning Herald* had to admit the coalition was trailing: 'It looks as if [Menzies] will have to "pull a couple of rabbits out of the top hat he wore with such assurance during the Royal tour" if his Government is to survive the election in May.' There was a 'decline in the Government's standing', so much so that it was likely to be defeated. Perhaps Petrov provided a way out.

Twice before, in 1949 and 1951, Menzies had won elections when communism was an issue. Was he introducing the Petrov Royal Commission to run another election campaign on an anti-Communist platform? No voter could forget that Dr Evatt in late 1951 had successfully fought the Menzies referendum designed to ban the Communist Party in Australia. Petrov's documents showed 'the outlines of systematic espionage and at least attempted subversion' by Communist Russia and its agents. Doubtless this new information would help the government in the forthcoming May election. The prime minister's 'unpleasant duty' may well have been his private relish.

9 Bringing the Petrov case into party politics

Menzies' statement to Parliament brought about an overnight transformation in the political climate; instead of favouring Labor, it now became potentially hostile to that party's electoral prospects. The House of Representatives reassembled on Wednesday 14 April for the last day of sitting before the election. As he rose to speak, Dr Evatt had good reason to be angry with Menzies, who had not warned him of the previous night's announcement. On Tuesday, at the usual morning meeting to discuss arrangements for the day's business, Evatt had told Harold Holt, the leader of the House, that he would be leaving Canberra at five o'clock that afternoon.[1] Yet, though Holt went directly to the cabinet meeting at which Petrov's defection and the forthcoming announcement were raised, there was no effort to contact Evatt until after he had left Canberra. The Labor leader could reasonably have suspected that the delay was intentional.

Nor could Evatt have been happy about developments since the announcement. At his news conference on Tuesday night, Menzies told reporters that he had been forced to go ahead with the announcement, even when he 'learned' of Evatt's absence, because the standing orders required a day's notice before voting on a bill. This, the reporters knew, was specious. All that was needed was a suspension of standing orders for the bill to be voted on the same day it was proposed. Even if Labor had opposed this, the government could have approved the suspension with their majority.*

---

*Even the well-known right-wing journalist Alan Reid admitted that reporters were dumbfounded when Menzies made this statement; see the *Sun-Herald*, 25 April 1954. At this time, Reid was less sympathetic to the government than usual; he suggested that, before flying to Sydney, Evatt had in fact checked personally with Menzies to ascertain whether any

Finally, Evatt was disturbed by Menzies' about-face from his publicly stated 'unpleasant duty': at his Tuesday night news conference, the prime minister had flamboyantly and sensationally discussed the Petrov defection.

Evatt's speech that Wednesday reflected the disappointment and suspicion that the Labor Party felt about the defection and Menzies' handling of the matter. In his speech, Evatt re-read and enlarged his statement issued in Sydney the night before. He criticized the prime minister for not warning him of the impending announcement, and added that, when Menzies was leader of the Opposition, the Labor government had always kept him 'generally informed of the activities' of the security service.[2] Evatt emphasized that he would have cancelled his trip to Sydney if he had been given an 'inkling' that there would be an important announcement.[3] And fiery Eddie Ward, an old Labor infighter, anticipated later developments when he interrupted to ask about the dormant 'nest of traitors' accusation that Casey had made about the External Affairs Department in May 1952.[4] Casey had never enlarged on that statement, despite repeated questioning.

Evatt emphasized the need for prosecution of any guilty parties disclosed in the evidence before the proposed Royal Commission. He also asked that the Opposition have a say in the formation of the Royal Commission, the selection of Commissioners and the setting of its terms of reference, because the coalition was in every sense, after that Wednesday, a 'caretaker government'.[5] In spite of Menzies' rejection of the Opposition requests, however, the House voted unanimously in favour of the Royal Commission on Espionage Bill.

On Thursday 15 April, the *Sydney Morning Herald* reported that 'many Federal members' felt that the political impact of

---

matters of importance would come before Parliament that night. Reid now tells the authors that the prime minister subsequently wrote a three-page letter to the *Sydney Morning Herald* management in an attempt to have him sacked. For once Menzies was unsuccessful. Reid says that Evatt remained convinced to his death that Menzies had misled him, and that if he had been in Parliament when the announcement was made he would have been able to defuse the whole affair.

Petrov's defection had benefited the government.[6] The Liberal and Country Parties had always been anti-Communist, and this latest event, with all its immediate implications, was seen as proof that they had not overemphasized the Communist threat. Besides inducing confidence, in some quarters, in a government that could root out such evil, the sensation of the defection also tended to obscure more mundane political issues.

The Petrov case came to dominate the daily press. There were comparisons with the defection in Canada, in 1945, of Igor Gouzenko, a cipher clerk in the Soviet embassy. The *Sydney Morning Herald* found 'that at least so far, it forms a close parallel'.[7] Gouzenko had defected with espionage papers from the files of the Russian military attaché's office in Ottawa. Investigation based on these documents, which were examined in a closed Royal Commission, had eventually uncovered the famous Soviet atomic spy ring. In the Petrov case, later evidence destroyed the initial similarities. But the fact that both Gouzenko and Petrov were nearing the end of their tenure in the country to which they defected, and that both brought documents reputedly the product of Russian espionage activity, was enough for even the Opposition to concede the similarities; Dr Evatt alluded to them in his speech to the House on 14 April.

In the days after that final Wednesday sitting of Parliament, Menzies (or, certainly, people very close to him) systematically released more and more information about the Petrov case. These revelations can be divided into two separate categories: details of the documents Petrov handed over, and background on Petrov and his daily routine after defection. In retrospect, the two categories apparently had a single goal—that of arousing interest in and speculation on the crisis so that the conservative government would reap a bumper political harvest.

A startling series of articles appeared in the newspapers on Thursday 15 April, the day after Parliament rose. The *Sydney Morning Herald* reported: 'Some Canberra sources forecast Wednesday that people closely associated with politicians would be named in the Petrov case. There is speculation that some members of Parliament may have to give evidence at the inquiry following the disclosure of these names.' 'M.P.s' were convinced that some people named were 'prominent'. By the following Sunday, sources close to Menzies had told the *Sun-Herald* that the information in the Petrov documents could 'blast the Opposition from its benches ... very important figures are involved ... they would occupy, if Labor was returned to power, posts from which they would have access to vital information'.* In the minds of Labor politicians there was no doubt about the ultimate source of these damaging insinuations. Only the prime minister and the security service had access to the documents. Everything pointed to Menzies as the originator of the leakage.

Other disclosures snapped up by the press caused further speculation: 'Legal opinion in Canberra is that the choice of a Royal Commission as a means of investigation suggests that most of the Communist activities revealed will not be of a kind susceptible to legal prosecution.'[8] 'Canberra officials' were expecting evidence at the Commission to show 'sabotage in unions rather than treasonable disclosures'.[9] At a news conference on 15 April, Menzies outlined the work of the security service since 1950, when he had replaced Mr Justice Reed, the original director-general of ASIO, with the head of military intelligence, Colonel Spry. The organization's operations since 1950 had been aimed at communism, and it had been allocated a vast increase in funds for such investigation. As a result of this, Menzies emphasized, the 'names in Petrov's documents are not new to security'.[10] The Labor Opposition was beginning to fear that the Royal Commission would become a witch-hunt.

Stories about the Petrovs had also begun to appear. Mrs Petrov, it was alleged, did not believe that her husband had

---

*Senior journalists in the Canberra press gallery at the time have told the authors that Sir Arthur Fadden, then treasurer and deputy prime minister in the coalition government, was mainly responsible for conveying the inspired stories and leaks about Petrov and such tantalizing unattributed statements.

defected, but thought he had been kidnapped.[11] She had remained in the Russian embassy ever since Petrov was first missed on 6 April. Meanwhile, the Soviet ambassador said that Petrov's story was 'nonsense from beginning to end'. The newspapers described Petrov as about forty-five, short and thickly built, and stated, incorrectly, that he had been a senior MVD official in the Russian navy before coming to Australia. They surmised that he must have occupied a special position at the embassy since he had been given so much freedom to mix with Australians. He trout-fished, and 'drank in hotel bars' where he was 'convivial'. Petrov was a 'Beria man', the papers alleged, and since the MVD chief had been deposed in mid-1953 Petrov was afraid to go home.

During the press conference of Thursday 15 April, Menzies gave more data on Petrov: he was well, and had even listened to the dramatic announcement of the defection.[12] Somebody had apparently taken the time to warn Petrov, but not the leader of the Opposition, that Menzies would make his statement to Parliament that evening. No doubt this news conference was intended to help along the many stories about Petrov, to keep the public controversy moving.

By Friday, Menzies was making predictions—carrying his own name—on the Royal Commission's activities. There would be a preliminary sitting of the Commission, and it 'would probably take place even before the documents were completely scrutinized'. Common law privileges would apply: 'A witness can refuse to answer questions that may incriminate him.' Parliamentary privilege would prevail.[13] This was too much for Evatt—Menzies was overpublicizing the Petrov affair. Not a great politician, but a man of unquestioned legal brilliance and achievement, Evatt felt that he must protest at the prime minister's handling of the case. On the night of Good Friday, 16 April, he made a statement:

Mr Menzies' day-to-day commentaries referring to the investigation of the Petrov affair call for very close attention.

In some respects they amount to an unjustified interference with the procedures of just investigation which should always be committed to an impartial tribunal and never determined by the political head of what is a 'caretaker' government.

... Mr Menzies has actually published information as to the extent of the previous knowledge of Security Intelligence.

... He even anticipates the decisions as to procedure which the tribunal alone could be called upon to make.

... It is obvious that Mr Menzies is over-eager to exploit the present situation. He has actually suggested that there would not be criminal prosecutions for sedition or treason.

As I pointed out in the House, what is needed in every case of espionage is a prompt application of the criminal law, so that any person guilty shall be prosecuted and convicted according to the law.*

Menzies labelled these criticisms 'curious and hysterical',[14] and editorial reaction to Evatt's protest was harsh. The *Sydney Morning Herald* editorial the following Monday was headed 'Bringing the Petrov Case into Party Politics'.[15] It charged Evatt, not Menzies, with creating a political issue. The editorial considered Evatt's Good Friday statement intemperate, concluding that the prime minister had acted soberly, and Evatt unwisely. But the editorial did positively identify Menzies as the source of most, if not all, the information that had been published about Petrov and the Commission. It referred to 'the Prime Minister's extra-parliamentary "commentaries" that Dr Evatt bitterly found fault [with]'.

In retrospect, Evatt's statement was a political disaster.† He had fallen into Menzies' trap and helped bring the Petrov question into the centre of the political arena. Menzies had tempted him to do so with his daily hints and speculations.

---

*The *Sydney Morning Herald* commented, on 20 April 1954: 'Mr Menzies and Dr Evatt make no secret of their dislike for each other, although each has until now been restrained in public.'

† The previous few weeks had not been very pleasant for the Evatts. Dr Evatt's younger brother, Clive, had been forced to resign from the New South Wales Labor cabinet in the last days of March. Clive Evatt was near the end of a colourful political career that had begun in 1939 and met with early success. His presidency of the Australia–Russian Society in 1948 was not a popular move within his party, which believed this body to be Communist controlled.

The conflicting statements about the case, as well as the general dislike for Evatt's intervention, helped precipitate a popular wish that the Royal Commission would meet and resolve the confusion before the election. As early as Monday 19 April, the same day as the *Sydney Morning Herald* 'party politics' editorial, the Melbourne *Age* called for a sitting of the Royal Commission before the election campaign started:

Accusations by Dr Evatt and rejoinders by Mr Menzies make it clear that unless a halt is called the Petrov affair is certain to be bandied about in the election. Short of agreement to abstain from further controversy, the best thing would be to remove as soon as possible the doubts and misgivings beginning to arise in the public mind. It would be desirable that the Royal Commission sat before the campaign starts. ... There is already a tangle of assertion, denial, mystification and conjecture. ...

Dr Evatt, meanwhile, was joined in his attack on the government's activities by two of his Labor lieutenants. On Sunday, in Adelaide, Clyde Cameron called for action under the Crimes Act.[16] He advocated immediate arrests, pointing out that the government had given 'collaborators' enough warning to destroy documents and perhaps go into hiding. Similarly, on the following day, the leader of the Opposition in the Upper House, Senator McKenna, criticized the 'mishandling' of the case.[17] He said the government had been 'too hasty'; by its own admission evidence had not been sifted, yet forecasts of its conclusions were made. Criticizing the alert thus given, Senator McKenna felt that nothing should have been said by the government until it knew the full position; then prosecutions should have been the first move.* But these rational criticisms were too subtle for the Australian electorate, which was not only preoccupied with the

---

*At about this time there was a practical example of this procedure. In West Germany, a Russian MVD captain, Nikolai Khokhlov, defected and a 'wave of arrests' followed (*Sydney Morning Herald*, 23 April 1954). For his story, see Nikolai Khokhlov, *In the Name of Conscience* (New York: David McKay, 1959).

Easter holidays, but was also alarmed at the suggestion of Soviet espionage. Criticism of the handling of the Petrov case was interpreted by many as support for Communists and communism.

10 Thirteen minutes that shook the Kremlin

In the midst of this political crossfire, the most sensational events of the Petrov affair were taking place. The setting for a crucial scene of this drama, when Mrs Petrov gave the first indication of a desire to remain in Australia, was the lavatory of the aircraft carrying her back to Russia, during the flight between Sydney and her only Australian touch-down point, Darwin. Her rendezvous there with an airline stewardess acting for ASIO was trenchantly described by the magazine *A.M.* as the 'thirteen minutes that shook the Kremlin'.[1]

Petrov had not told his wife of his decision to defect, and there had been no communication between them since he crossed over. Bialoguski records that ASIO brought Petrov to visit him on several occasions immediately after his defection, and that he was in 'no state of mind to face his problems alone'. He talked almost interminably about his wife and was sure that she would go back to Russia. On one visit in the company of Richards, on a Saturday evening two weeks after his defection, Petrov said: 'If only I could speak to her, I could persuade her to stay.'

'Well,' replied Richards, 'we are making arrangements for you to talk to her.'

When asked by Bialoguski how he could do this, Richards said: 'We'll see that Vladimir meets her when she's about to leave Sydney.'[2]

Bialoguski says that on later reflection he came to the conclusion that Richards' plan was bound to fail. Mrs Petrov would be in a highly emotional state, under the close supervision of Soviet officials, and on being suddenly con-fronted with her husband would be likely to 'see him merely as the person who was the cause of it all, and burst out with some irrevocable attack before she had time to think'. The advice Bialoguski claims to have given ASIO at the time was to postpone the approach until she was aboard the ship or plane taking her back to Russia, reflecting on her future there and the possibility of punishment—'Keep Petrov away and let her go. There will be other opportunities before she is outside British jurisdiction.'

In the *Sydney Morning Herald* on Saturday 17 April, 'a Canberra source' said Petrov had spent Good Friday in traditional Russian festive fashion. Records of Russian Easter music had been sent to him. Meanwhile Mrs Petrov was sequestered in the Soviet embassy in Canberra. On the Wednesday after the announcement of her husband's defection, she gave an interview to the press in the embassy. She said she was sure her husband had been kidnapped, and that he would not leave her because he was married to her. She believed that if he had not been kidnapped he would attempt to contact her. As a result of this, the External Affairs Department persuaded Petrov to write her a letter. Mrs Petrov rejected this, her husband's plea to see her.[3]

By Easter Sunday the press was carrying long stories about Mrs Petrov's plight. She was 'under heavy guard' and was due to leave for Russia in the next few days. The following morning, 19 April, the *Sydney Morning Herald* claimed she would be leaving from Sydney airport that very night. Apart from Sydney, she would have a last opportunity to defect in Darwin, where the aircraft was scheduled to refuel. On the editorial page, the right-wing Liberal politician W. C. Wentworth told how '[Mrs Petrov] had committed a crime in the eyes of the state', and was probably going back to her death in Russia.

The Russians now made their own contribution to the atmosphere of melodrama and hysteria that Menzies had hitherto stage managed with consummate flair. As Bialoguski commented in his book:

The Russians, with astounding ineptitude, had thrust Mrs Petrov into the world spotlight and kept her there for days. If public

Bialoguski charms Mrs Petrov and Lydia Mokras (right), who introduced the ASIO counterspy to Petrov at the Russian Social Club in 1951 (COURIER-MAIL)

Petrov and his Alsatian, Jack. The dog was the subject of complaints by Petrov's embassy colleagues, but its future welfare appears to have been one of his main worries while reaching the decision to defect. (NEWS LTD)

3 April 1954: Petrov steps into the waiting car of G. R. Richards, deputy director-general of ASIO, after conducting an incoming group of Soviet diplomats from their ship to Mascot airport for the flight to Canberra. Petrov and Richards then finalized arrangements for the defection and at eight o'clock that evening the espionage documents were handed to Colonel Spry. A photograph released to the press by the Royal Commission. (SYDNEY MORNING HERALD)

A distressed Mrs Petrov is escorted by Zharkov and Karpinsky across the Mascot tarmac on the evening of 19 April 1954. Sydney radio personality Gary O'Callaghan (far left), then a cub reporter, tries to interview Zharkov. (NEWS LTD)

Airline staff help Mrs Petrov up the steps to board the waiting BOAC
Constellation (NEWS LTD)

One of the crowd of demonstrators grapples with Mrs Petrov's escorts as she
boards the aircraft (SYDNEY MORNING HERALD)

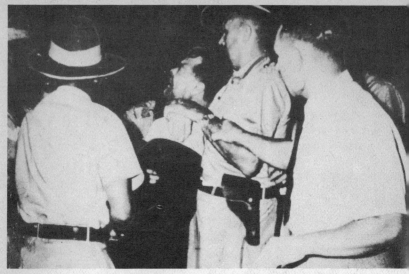

Darwin, 5.15 a.m. on 20 April 1954 — police disarm Karpinsky after the aircraft touches down for refuelling (HERALD & WEEKLY TIMES LTD)

Separated from her escorts, and now carrying her jacket, Mrs Petrov accompanies R. S. Leydin, acting administrator of the Northern Territory, and Qantas representative Frank Angel to the Darwin air terminal. She was soon to receive the telephone call from her husband that precipitated her request for asylum. (NEWS LTD)

interest showed any sign of slackening, they immediately revived it by some clumsy manoeuvre which restored her to the centre of the stage.

Instead of travelling to Sydney openly, they attempted to shroud Mrs Petrov's movements in mystery in so obvious a manner that even a 'hick' reporter could not have failed to be on their heels. Just as in a dime detective story, the sleek, powerful black limousine [the *Sydney Morning Herald* described it as a 'huge black Cadillac'] moved off from the Embassy at high speed, with all the appearance of a gangster car taking the victim 'for a ride' [this scene was played out in 1954 when Albert Anastasia was driving round New York in a similar vehicle].

Reporters excitedly noted that in the front seats were the driver and Second Secretary Kislytsin, while in the back a shrouded female figure—presumably Mrs Petrov—sat between two powerful diplomatic couriers—Zharkov and Karpinsky, who, whatever their personal qualities, had the appearance of a couple of mobsters from a third-rate gangster film.

The authors, who were children at the time—one the son of a rising Labor politician in Sydney and the other at the geographical extreme of Australian life, in the outback Queensland township of Cunnamulla in a non-political household—both have the most vivid memories of this incident and the subsequent drama. There was no television in Australia then, but there were dramatic radio broadcasts, and newsreels and newspapers had an importance and impact that they lack in the television age. These memories, and another look at the photographs today, confirm that Bialoguski's description was no exaggeration. 'The Russians could hardly have found two more provocative-looking characters for the job,' he wrote.

In those days, Australia was still, despite the efforts of people like Evatt and Burton, a backwater of international events. Until Petrov's defection, conservative politicians had difficulty in selling Russian communism to the Australian electorate as a serious and menacing issue in the abstract. It was most successful when allied to racism and the 'yellow peril', as in the Korean War, which—unfortunately for those politicians like Wentworth who liked to 'kick the Communist can'—was now over. But the fact that Russia and the United States were in bitter, if non-military conflict, with its general undertone of hysteria (reinforced by the McCarthy hearings, the execution of the Rosenbergs in 1953, and the Russians exploding their own atomic bomb in late 1949), made Soviet communism a potentially dominant domestic political issue.

Nevertheless, until the Petrov affair, the Australian electorate was most strongly motivated by what Chifley memorably described as the 'hip-pocket nerve'. These days, when Australian men no longer characteristically carry their pay envelopes or wallets in their 'hip-pocket' and pay for most things in cash, the literal significance of Chifley's phrase may not be instantly appreciated. The political common sense of it will, however, be understood by most voters. Australia's hip-pocket nerve, in the period immediately before Petrov's defection—and leading up to the election campaign—had been in a sensitive state. Because of an unprecedented boom during the Korean War in the price of Australia's major export, wool, there had been record inflation. The Menzies government had made a highly unpopular attempt to combat this with what was bitterly termed the 'horror budget' of August 1952. Now the demand for wool was declining. Economic matters, rather than those of personality or international affairs, were prominent in the mind of the public. A Gallup Poll in March 1954 indicated that 52 per cent of the electorate supported Labor. The Petrov affair—and particularly the drama centred on Mrs Petrov—was to change that.

After the 200-mile drive to Sydney the black Cadillac arrived at Mascot airport only minutes before the aircraft was to leave at 10 p.m. There, awaiting Mrs Petrov's arrival, was an angry crowd of at least 500 people, mainly immigrants from Eastern European countries.[4] The Australian Communist W. J. Brown claimed the demonstration had been organized by Wentworth and a 'group of pro-fascist migrants led by N. P. Harkoff of Redfern, Sydney'. Harkoff, Brown said, later 'boasted to Sydney newspapers how he arranged the Mascot riot and revealed that security had been aware of the plan'.[5] Bialoguski's view was less conspiratorial:

One glance at Zharkov and Karpinsky was quite enough to provoke the mob assembled at Mascot to wild excitement and mad rage. The two men looked bad, and when they laid hands on Mrs Petrov, the demonstrators were convinced they were bad. Mrs Petrov immediately became the world's sweetheart in the grip of evil, an image that was confirmed in the fairy-tale tradition when, bustled by her two oafish escorts, she lost a shoe.

As Mrs Petrov, confused and bewildered, uncertain whether the crowd was hostile to her, or to her escorts, was dragged up the gang-way to the plane by the now panic-stricken Russians, groups of people rushed forward menacingly, aiming blows at the party. Throughout this wild scene, in which violence repeatedly seemed imminent, Security men on the spot remained inactive.[6]

What neither Bialoguski nor Brown knew when they wrote their accounts was that ASIO had elaborately arranged, in consultation with Menzies, to keep its options open. Petrov was at the airport 'lying on an innerspring mattress under a cover in the back of a utility truck' close by the plane.[7]

The security people swore Mrs Petrov was not forced on board the aircraft, but Wentworth busied himself collecting statutory declarations from witnesses who claimed to have heard her cry out in Russian, 'Help me!' and 'I don't want to go!'. According to Brown's account in *The Petrov Conspiracy Unmasked*, Mrs Petrov later said about the events at Sydney airport: 'I did not speak. I did not ask for help from anyone.'

The aircraft, a Constellation, was due to touch down for refuelling at Darwin at 5.15 on Tuesday morning. Menzies was reported in the Sydney *Sun* of 20 April as saying: 'With prudent forethought, we already had security people at Darwin who were to meet the plane.'

Mrs Petrov, according to a *Sydney Morning Herald* reporter travelling on board, appeared pale and exhausted. She burst into tears, her face glistening with perspiration and her makeup smudged. She asked a steward for permission to smoke, and although this was refused she lit a cigarette and nobody made any attempt to intervene. Mrs Petrov was seated beside Kislytsin, and the two grim-looking couriers, Karpinsky and Zharkov, were in the seats immediately behind. There was also an ASIO man on board. Meanwhile the stewardess, Miss Joyce Bull, had been deputed by security, through a radio message to the plane's captain, J. Davys, to attempt to put two questions to Mrs Petrov: was she in any danger, and did she want to seek political asylum alongside her husband in Australia?[8]

Joyce Bull put the questions to Mrs Petrov when she went to the lavatory. The first visit, which took those famous thirteen minutes, was at 10.30 p.m.; there were three other visits, diligently logged by the *Sydney Morning Herald* man at 1.10 a.m., 1.20 a.m. and finally 2.45 a.m. Mrs Petrov told the hostess, in answer to the first question, that the couriers were armed, and in answer to the second, that she did not believe her husband had defected. Miss Bull got the clear impression that Mrs Petrov would stay in Australia if she was satisfied that her husband had indeed defected voluntarily. The pilot relayed this information to security in Darwin.

When Mrs Petrov and her escort left the aircraft at Darwin at 5.15 a.m. on Tuesday 20 April, the security service went into action. The couriers were immediately separated from Kislytsin and Mrs Petrov, and six policemen demanded that they surrender their weapons in accordance with airport regulations. Zharkov and Karpinsky refused and were disarmed in a public struggle. Karpinsky had a ·32 Walther automatic on his hip, and Zharkov carried a similar weapon in a shoulder holster. 'We can be tough, too!' bragged one of the newspaper headlines carried over a photograph of Karpinsky being disarmed.

Menzies' 'prudent forethought' had extended to giving special directions to the deputy administrator of the Northern Territory, R. S. Leydin, about the conduct of the operation. In the absence of the administrator, he was in charge of the Territory, under the direct control of the Menzies government in Canberra. Leydin asked Mrs Petrov, who had meanwhile been separated from Kislytsin, whether he might talk to her. He had been authorized, if she wished to stay in Australia, to grant her political asylum on behalf of the Australian government. But, even after their first conversation, the drama continued. She was still, according to security officials later, not convinced of her husband's well-being, or that she could be guaranteed safety.

There was also a suggestion that Mrs Petrov at that stage believed her husband was dead. Two hours later the drama was pitched up yet another key when she was called to the customs office, where Leydin told her that her husband wanted to speak to her on the phone to make a final appeal to her to stay in Australia with him. Mrs Petrov spoke in Russian, with Kislytsin and security and police officials standing close to her, but making no attempt to intervene. She spoke quietly at first, but at one stage raised her voice, shouting, 'Nyet, nyet!'

When the call, which lasted about four minutes, finished, she shook her head and shrugged as Leydin attempted to speak to her. But shortly afterwards, and only twenty minutes before the aircraft was due to leave, Leydin came forward again; despite an attempt at intervention by Kislytsin, she said in English: 'I go with him.' Leydin and Mrs Petrov walked into the airport office and security men and police closed and guarded the door. A little later the Australian government law officer in Darwin, K. Edmunds, approached Kislytsin and told him Mrs Petrov had gone to Government House by car because she 'wanted to have a rest in Australia'. Thus, when the plane had been refuelled, the three remaining Russians continued their flight, protesting about their treatment. The last recorded words of Kislytsin on Australian soil were: 'She's been kidnapped.'

'She stays!' screamed the first newspaper poster Bialoguski saw. He later wrote: '[The headlines] were to the public as a match to a powder keg. Astonishing scenes of excitement occurred all over Sydney.'

These events took place in the early morning of Tuesday 20 April, exactly a week after Menzies' initial announcement of Petrov's defection. Many things had happened in that time, and their cumulative effect was a complete reversal of the drift of public opinion. Before, the Labor Party had every chance of forming a new government; as noted earlier, the last published opinion sample had shown the Opposition party commanding 52 per cent of the vote. Now a Gallup Poll published in the *Sydney Morning Herald* on 23 May showed a remarkable switch in popular sentiment. The survey, which had been completed on 1 May, indicated that the Menzies government had the support of 57 per cent of the voters.

The conservative government had superbly stage managed the Petrovs' defection as a Cold War extravaganza. They had succeeded in reintroducing the 'Communist menace' to the Australian political scene; they had made Dr Evatt and his party look, at best, like dangerous political opportunists. Although Evatt, and Chifley before him, had a consistent record of fighting authoritarian regimes and their supporters, including Russian ministers in international forums and their minor followers in the Australian trade unions, Labor was now identified with two armed foreign thugs who had tried to kidnap a defenceless woman. Those thirteen minutes had shaken Labor, too.

11 All the Ming's men . . .

Despite the immediate political benefits it gained from the Petrovs' defection, the Menzies government soon encountered some difficulties, especially in the appointment of Royal Commissioners to investigate Soviet espionage activity in Australia.

A Royal Commission has extraordinary powers; it is not a court of law, and it can be particularly dangerous when it interferes in political matters. For these reasons a Royal Commissioner must be a person of great discretion. He can do much good, but his mistakes can be just as harmful. The Australian Royal Commissions Act of 1923 says that as institutions they are designed to 'merely investigate and report ... they are not courts of justice: there are no parties before them, no one is tried for an offence'.[1] But the way in which a Royal Commission is conducted can gravely affect the life of a citizen. The Commission's report, even if it is pigeonholed after publication, by its references to particular people can shatter their reputations and livelihoods. Even if an individual is not reported upon adversely, an unbridled remark about him during the proceedings may produce the same effect.

Unlike a court of law, counsel's right to appear at a Royal Commission is enjoyed only by counsel appointed by the Crown, whose duty it is to assemble and submit all relevant evidence. Permission for an individual to appear before the Royal Commission, and the right to counsel appointed by the Crown, can be granted only at the discretion of the Commission, and that permission to appear may be withdrawn at any time by the Commissioners. The Act lays down that a witness may appear before the Commission because something has been said about him, but the witness cannot call others to support his stand unless the Commission itself rules that such evidence is relevant. The Royal Commissioner's powers over a witness are much more extensive than those of a judge sitting in a court of law. The role of Royal Commissioner thus demands a careful combination of ability, integrity, patience, and, perhaps above all, courtesy to witnesses.

As early as the day after his initial dramatic announcement, Menzies raised the possibility that a two-man tribunal would investigate the Petrov affair.[2] In Canada, the Gouzenko Royal Commission had comprised only two judges. There were, nevertheless, important differences between the two cases: Gouzenko defected in September 1945, yet the Royal Commission did not meet until February 1946, and then only in secret session;[3] in contrast to this, Menzies wanted a public sitting within the very month of Petrov's defection.

A week after Mrs Petrov was granted asylum, it was reported that there would be three Royal Commissioners, and that Mr Justice Owen of the New South Wales Supreme Court was thought to have been appointed chairman.[4] The article also anticipated that there would be a judge from the Supreme Courts of both Victoria and South Australia.

When a prime minister desires to appoint a judge of a state court as an Australian Royal Commissioner, he approaches the premier of that state, who in turn approaches the chief justice of the court. The first hitch came in Victoria. Aware of the internal difficulties suffered by the Labor Party, Menzies attempted to get Mr Justice O'Brien, a Roman Catholic, to join the Royal Commission. But the chief justice and his fellow Supreme Court judges were unanimous in telling John Cain, the Victorian Labor premier, that they would not make a judge available to the Australian government. Recognizing the political overtones of the Petrov affair, they chose to restrict their activities to the due process of law; they said that 'in British countries', except in rare cases, judges 'retain the confidence of the people' because they adhere to interpreting the relationship between the law and the Queen's subjects. Then, in a pointed attack on the handling of the Petrov affair, the Victorian judges declared: 'Parliament, supported by a wise public opinion, has jealously guarded the Bench from the danger of being drawn into the region of political controversy.'* If added support were needed for this opinion, it was provided three days later when the Victorian Bar Council backed the Supreme Court on its stand.† Thus Victoria was counted out.

The South Australian judge was expected to be either Mr Justice Ligertwood or Mr Justice Reed, the first director-general of ASIO. Rumour had it that Mr Justice Philp of the Queensland Bench had already been decided upon, following the Victorian refusal.[5] The prime minister did not approach the highest court in the land, because, as the *Sydney Morning Herald* reported, 'The High Court has a long-standing rule against participation of its Justices in Royal Commissions. This objection is based on the fact that such enquiries are frequently of a political or semi-political character.'[6]

Finally on 1 May, a Saturday, Menzies announced the Royal Commissioners. Owen and Philp were there as rumoured, and Ligertwood was the third Commissioner. The man who would present the evidence to the Royal Commission was the chief counsel, W. J. V. Windeyer, Q.C. There had been a battle over the appointment of Philp. Originally, the Queensland chief justice had recommended Mr Justice Townley to the Labor premier, Vince Gair. The prime minister then told Gair that he wanted Philp instead, and asked the premier to be allowed to contact both the chief justice and Mr Justice Townley to 'iron the matter out'.[7] Menzies then arranged for the release of Mr Justice Philp. Gair was reported to be angry at Menzies' request.[8] The Sydney *Daily Mirror* said at the time: 'Observers are speculating how, in view of his insistence upon selecting his own Royal Commissioners from the State judiciaries, Mr Menzies will

---

Sydney Morning Herald, 29 April 1954. Sir Edmund Herring, C.J., was quoting from statements made in 1953 by Sir Charles Lowe, who was then acting chief justice.

†*Sun-Herald*, 2 April 1954. The prime minister's cousin, D. I. Menzies, Q.C. (now Mr Justice Sir Ian Menzies of the High Court), spoke against the Supreme Court's decision.

be able to sustain his claim that he is approaching the Petrov inquiry in a non-political manner.'[9]

It can be seen that Menzies had hand-picked his three-man Royal Commission. He obviously decided on Owen soon after announcing that a Commission would be appointed; he turned down a respected member of the Queensland Bench to select his own man from that state, and then he preferred Ligertwood to Mr Justice Reed, who, because of his experience as director-general of ASIO, must have been the best-equipped jurist for the Royal Commission in the whole country. Evatt had requested that the Labor Party should have a say in the formation of the Royal Commission. He was apprehensive that Menzies would hand-pick his Commission, and this fear was justified. In no way could any of the four figures—the Commissioners and Windeyer —be seen as political liberals; they were all conservatives in a conservative profession.

On 4 May the newspapers announced that the Royal Commission would hold its opening session on Monday 17 May in Canberra's Albert Hall. At the same time the terms of reference of the Commission were released. They fell into four areas:

- Inquiry into the documentary information Petrov had given the government, and also his oral and written testimony;
- Inquiry into espionage or attempted espionage by agents or representatives of the USSR in Australia, and identification of those people;
- Determination of whether 'any persons or organizations in Australia' had communicated information or documents to those agents;
- Determination of whether any Australian individuals or organizations had 'aided or abetted' espionage.[10]

12 The most sordid campaign in history

'The most worried people in Australia last week were the local Communists,' the *Sydney Morning Herald*'s industrial correspondent told his readers as the Petrov affair continued to dominate the newspapers.[1] He asserted that many of them had, in the past, made trips to Moscow and Peking, and they now feared exposure following Petrov's defection. Then on Thursday 22 April, once Mrs Petrov, too, had defected, the Soviet embassy accused Petrov of stealing state funds and demanded that he be returned to them as a criminal.* The request was refused. On the following Saturday, the Russian embassy was more specific in its charges. Petrov had been responsible for the purchase of embassy stores, a spokesman said, and had inflated furniture prices so that he could skim off a personal gain.[2]

At the same time, some startling facts about Petrov were being released to the press. Petrov, it seemed, had spoken to ASIO in late February, more than a month before his defection, and had showed officers some of his secret MVD documents.[3] But he did not give any material to security then. Petrov had removed the documents 'one by one', over a period of time, and built up the 'voluminous' body of papers he handed over at the start of April. Although heightening the sense of intrigue—much to the government's taste— the releases also helped fire the Opposition's conviction that

---

Sydney Morning Herald, 22 April 1954. The accusation was in keeping with the normal Russian reaction in such cases. The Soviet embassy in Ottawa accused Gouzenko of stealing state funds, so in a sense this charge adds credence to Petrov's story.

Menzies' announcement had been timed for the utmost political impact.

As a result of Petrov's defection, the handling of Mrs Petrov and her couriers, and the prime minister's remarks, the Soviet government informed the Australian chargé d'affaires in Moscow that he and his staff were *persona non grata*. Diplomatic ties between the two countries were broken.* After some harassment over exit passes, the Australian contingent left Moscow on 29 April. The following day, the Australian government, observing strict protocol, provided handsomely for the withdrawal of the Russian embassy staff; this was the government's most honourable act in the Petrov affair.

It had been reported that, as early as 19 April, the prime minister had warned government Members to 'lay off' the political side of the Petrov affair in the coming election.[4] But the same report expected a 'silent campaign' from these Members. It was none too silent on the night of Tuesday 4 May, when the election campaign officially opened with Menzies' policy speech in Melbourne, broadcast by all radio stations. Outlining his party's platform, the prime minister talked of a tax cut, a more liberal interpretation of the means test on old-age pensions, and more government loans for housing. He made an 'oblique' reference to the Petrov case.[5] On the issue of communism, he asked: 'Where do the Labor leaders stand? ... If they say that they are now enemies of communism, will you accept this repentance, or will you conclude that they are now trimming their sails to the prevailing winds of public opinion?' Menzies then outlined the government's record on communism: how it had tried to legislate for the banning of the Communist Party, how Dr Evatt had frustrated the legislation in the courts, and finally how the Labor Party and the Communist Party had defeated the 1951 referendum. The prime minister concluded: 'We

---

*Diplomatic relations between Australia and the Soviet Union were re-established in 1959.

will continue to fight the Communists with whatever weapons we have.'

This mild effort to push the Communist issue to the forefront in the official campaign received robust assistance from Sir Arthur Fadden. As deputy prime minister and head of the Country Party, the minor partner in the coalition government, Fadden spoke after the prime minister at the policy speech meeting. 'If there were no other issue,' he asked, '... in whose hands would you place [the Royal Commission] results—R. G. Menzies, with his splendid record, or H. V. Evatt, with his?'[6] Two days later, the *Sydney Morning Herald* remarked: 'Petrov cannot be kept out of the election campaign.' Of course, the government did not want the Petrov affair kept out; indeed they introduced it, not only through Menzies' original sensational announcement, but in the official opening of the election campaign itself.

Menzies' request to 'lay off' the Petrov affair was disobeyed on another front as well. In New South Wales the highest-ranking Liberal, Eric Harrison, the day after Menzies' policy speech, criticized Evatt for representing Communist trade-union leaders in court 'on a number of occasions'.[7] 'This man with his record now asks you to let him take charge of the Royal Commission into Communist espionage.'

The next day, a Thursday, Evatt opened his official campaign in Sydney. At first he tried to fight on economic issues. He advocated a massive programme of social benefits: abolition of the means test, higher old-age pension payments, more generous child-endowment and increased loans for housing. He also reiterated his promise to give increased depreciation allowances to selected industries.[8] Immediately the government's economists labelled this programme 'too extravagant' and 'inflationary'.[9]

These attacks on Evatt formed the crux of the government's election strategy. The campaign had two sides: one was designed to make the Labor leader appear an irrational and untrained economist, who would point the country towards inflation and depression if he were to become prime minister; the other side of the campaign was designed to show Evatt and his party as Communist sympathizers, at a crucial time when communism was a proven menace. It was not difficult to achieve results on the economic front. Editorials blasted 'Dr Evatt's inflationary bid for votes'.[10] At first the press assessed the cost of Labor's programme at £100 million, but by the end of the campaign the estimates had reached £300 million. Throughout, political cartoons ridiculed the Labor leader. Even before Evatt's policy speech, the papers were 'setting Dr Evatt's promises against Mr Menzies' record of sober achievement', and they maintained that theme throughout the campaign.[11]

The potency of the two-pronged attack on the Labor Party cannot be overestimated. Menzies and Fadden constituted a most effective campaign partnership. The prime minister's rational approach demonstrated the 'manners' and 'finesse' necessary in a national leader.[12] Sir Arthur provided a contrast to Menzies' mildness with his own Queensland school-of-hard-knocks brand of politics. In times of crisis, such as the Petrov affair, Fadden was the perfect hatchet-man. Menzies would never go further than coolly accusing the Labor Party of 'opposing every measure against Communism the Government had ever introduced'.[13] Yet Sir Arthur branded Evatt as a man who was embracing aims 'on all fours with the Communist manifesto'.[14] On 10 May he officially opened his election campaign, as leader of the Country Party, in his home state of Queensland. There, a week before the opening of the Royal Commission, he spread the doctrine of Labor sympathy with communism.[15] He attacked Evatt and questioned his policy towards Communists during the 1940s. Then he blasted him for accepting a brief to oppose the Communist Party Dissolution Act, and for his part in the campaign against the referendum.

Each time Evatt tried to defend himself he lost ground. The more angry he became, the more he appeared unreasonable.[16] Here it can be seen that the two sides of the government's attack were also interrelated. By provoking Evatt on the Communist issue, the coalition hoped to add an element of personal irrationality to an image already impaired by criticism of the economic proposals in his policy speech. Articles described Evatt as 'emotional' and said that 'the first view of him [is] somewhat disconcerting'.[17] Thus, on 11 May, when Evatt attempted to answer Fadden by documenting his opposition to communism both at home and abroad during the 1940s, the newspapers paid more attention to his 'emotion' than to his line of reasoning.

The final stages of the election campaign included the opening of the Royal Commission. It was maintained that the disclosures would be 'as sensational ... as anything ever uncovered in Australia'.[18] MI5 was interested, and had questioned Petrov about Guy Burgess and Donald Maclean.[19] The US State Department* had also made inquiries.[20] By the second week in May, Harold Holt, the minister for immigration, had refused passports to several Communists.† All these developments were fully integrated into the government's election campaign. The Saturday before the opening of the Commission, Liberal–Country Party 'spokesmen' said they expected the peak of the election campaign to be reached 'just after the Royal Commission's sitting'.[21] And on that same day, Sir Arthur Fadden announced that the full extent of the 'Communist menace' would be seen 'next week'. The government was preparing itself for an electoral triumph based on the Royal Commission sitting.[22]

The Albert Hall, then Canberra's main meeting hall, was to be the venue for the first sitting. To many, this choice was rather ludicrous—the hall was normally used for concerts and dances. But, specially for the occasion, a bench, a witness box, a counsels' table, press tables and rows of chairs were chosen to 'give the hall the dignity of a courtroom'.[23] By

---

*In 1945, a US Senate subcommittee had demanded to speak to Gouzenko, an action that angered the Canadian government. In Petrov's case the State Department had asked to speak to him—a more polite approach.

†'The Petrov affair took a dramatic turn yesterday. ...' It was understood that seventeen people were involved in the ban, according to the *Sun-Herald* of 9 May 1954.

Saturday 15 May, all Canberra's hotel accommodation had been booked for the sitting.

The Royal Commission held its opening session on Monday 17 May.* Punctually at ten o'clock the Royal Commissioners entered the hall, dressed in morning suits. Windeyer, the chief counsel, then addressed the tribunal. He gave a brief and incomplete description of Petrov's defection and the events leading up to it, and listed the documents Petrov had brought with him. These were two typewritten documents in English, Documents H and J, and seven documents, Documents A to G, written in Russian; five of these were alleged to have emanated from the headquarters of the MVD in Moscow. Windeyer then read the correspondence between the External Affairs Department and the Soviet embassy, as well as correspondence between Petrov and his wife after his defection, but before she joined him. Just two witnesses were called during the three days of the sitting, officials who merely reinforced information that had already been given by Windeyer. Press releases at the end of April had said that evidence would not reveal the 'equivalent' of Gouzenko's atomic spy ring,[24] and further, that military espionage was not included in Petrov's activities.[25] Windeyer restated this information in his address. Headlines followed the sittings: 'Hostile Soviet activity to be revealed', and 'Some Australians aided red agents'.[26] Then on the third day the Royal Commission rose. It appeared it could not proceed until the documents had been examined more closely; the official interpreter had not even arrived from England before this opening session. Thus the Royal Commissioners decided to postpone further meetings.

The Opposition was outraged. Nothing new or of any importance had been disclosed at the Commission session; the already damaging material had simply been restated. Yet the Royal Commissioners saw fit to adjourn their sitting just ten days before the election. The Labor Party could see

---

*For the complete proceedings of the three-day sitting, see *Commonwealth of Australia: Royal Commission on Espionage, Transcript of Proceedings* (hereafter cited as *Transcript*), pp. 1–43.

Outside the Albert Hall in Canberra on 18 May 1954, G. R. Richards, deputy director-general of ASIO, ostentatiously guards the Petrov papers, apparently housed in the large suitcase. The Royal Commission was in its second day of sitting, with the federal election little more than a week away. (NEWS LTD)

Colonel Charles Spry,
September 1954
(SYDNEY MORNING HERALD)

Mr Justice Philp
(COURIER-MAIL)

Mr Justice Ligertwood
(COURIER-MAIL)

no reason why these 'appearances' had to be made, and considered the entire Commission a political stunt designed to damage its electoral prospects. This first sitting of the Royal Commission, from 17 to 19 May, was in fact a most important element in the outcome of the 1954 election.

Crowds at election meetings were estimated to be three to four times larger than those in 1951.[27] The conservative press asked if Dr Evatt's promises were 'honest and practical';[28] the *Sydney Morning Herald* carried a series of harsh articles on 'election issues'. Eric Harrison emphasized: 'The greatest single factor in promoting and encouraging Communism in Australia has been the stimulus given it by the Labor Party and Labor Governments.'[29] The *Sydney Morning Herald* began, in this week, an espionage series called 'The Web Around the World', asking: 'Which security service is most effective in fighting Communism?' Bitter broadcasts by the leaders concluded the campaign on the Thursday—Menzies called Labor's campaign the 'most sordid in history', while Evatt called Menzies and Fadden the 'vilest slanderers and smearers' for implying that the Labor Party had Communist sympathies and tendencies.[30]

Still, when the votes were cast on 29 May, the Liberal–Country Party conservative coalition only managed to scrape home. It received about 3 per cent less of the vote than the Opposition, but a series of small electoral anomalies provided the conservatives with 64 seats to Labor's 57.

There can be no question that a strong reason for the return of the government was the Communist scare, a scare created by the government itself; Menzies' coalition had used the Petrov crisis to political advantage. The prime minister's timing of the announcement of Petrov's defection, his subsequent press releases, and his hand-picked Royal Commission, whose much-publicized sitting climaxed the election campaign, provided the elements of a masterpiece of political contrivance. The first tangible result of the Petrov affair was an electoral victory for the conservative government; in retrospect, perhaps one might conclude that it was not Labor that had been responsible for the campaign's sordid aspects.

13 Facts, falsity and filth

Despite Menzies' initial haste in selecting the Royal Commission, and the sense of urgency conveyed by its first rapidly arranged meeting during the election campaign, it was to be fifteen months before it reported. On 11 June 1954 the Royal Commission sat for one day in Sydney, and then, a full month after the election, it reconvened in Melbourne for the first in a series of major hearings at various locations. The Sydney sitting introduced Arthur Herbert Birse, the official translator and interpreter. Aged sixty-five, a man of undisputed ability, he had been Churchill's interpreter at Teheran, Yalta and Potsdam. Francis Hamilton Stuart, chief of protocol in the Department of External Affairs, also appeared and outlined the department's communications with the Soviet embassy after Petrov's defection.

Taking of evidence would not be completed until the end of March 1955. There were several delays. The first arose from a flaw in the rushed Royal Commission Act, which meant that witnesses could not be compelled to answer questions. Then there was a shortage of courtroom accommodation. The Albert Hall had reverted to its normal round of concerts and dances. Canberra residents would not have tolerated an extended occupancy of the hall by the Petrov inquiry; its gala opening was enough. Next Petrov himself became ill and could not give evidence for more than a month, by which time the Royal Commission was ready to rise for Christmas. Eventually the Commissioners published their report in August 1955. Although there has never been any suggestion that these delays were intentional, they had the effect of keeping the crisis in the headlines for nearly a year and a half after Menzies' initial announcement in April 1954. Petrov gave evidence for the first time in Melbourne on 30 June 1954, outlining his career and the nature of his employment.

The Soviet espionage system was (and is) divided into the two areas of political and military intelligence.[1] At the time of Petrov's defection, the military branch was known as the GRU and the political branch was known as the MVD. Parts of the Soviet espionage system have been termed, at various times, the RU, GPU, OGPU, NKVD, MGB, KI and KGB, as well as GRU and MVD. There are two forms in which international espionage can take place. The first is by means of a Legal Apparatus, the Soviet term for an espionage organization operating in a foreign country under the control of a member of the Soviet embassy staff, who has an overt diplomatic post and thus enjoys the advantages and immunities of that status. Such a controller is called the Resident. Then there is the Illegal Apparatus, a Soviet espionage organization operating in a foreign country under the control of a person other than a member of the Soviet embassy staff. He consequently enjoys no diplomatic immunity. The leader of such an organization is termed the Illegal Resident. Petrov gave evidence that he was the temporary Legal Resident from late 1951 until his defection in 1954.

Through the first week of July, Chief Counsel Windeyer questioned Petrov. Windeyer had an idiosyncratic courtroom style, entirely lacking in emotion or flair. He spoke very slowly, but not deliberately, seemingly stumbling towards his submissions. (It is said that when he led the 20th Brigade to the Red Beach landing in New Guinea in 1943, he had spent the night before reading Macaulay.) Mrs Petrov gave evidence for the first time on 8 July, and caused quite a stir because of her comparatively youthful good looks[2] and her smart new clothes, apparently provided by ASIO.

Although the Petrovs' evidence on their intelligence functions was taken without much controversy, this was not the case with Petrov's disclosure, on 6 July, that he had received £5000 on the day he defected from Richards, the deputy director-general of ASIO.[3] Until this point there had been no suggestion that bribery was involved in Petrov's decision to defect; indeed, Richards had given a description of the defection day when he appeared as a witness at the pre-election Canberra session,[4] and it now seemed obvious to the Opposition that he had been instructed to avoid mentioning the matter of the £5000. A prominent Labor politician, Allan Fraser—who was later found to be mentioned in the documents—had anticipated this disclosure in a brilliant article before the election: 'The obvious truth emerges, that Petrov ... purchased his future economic security in Australia by the sale of his documents.'[5] In the light of this new information the question arose: were the Petrov papers authentic espionage documents?

The first to be examined was Document J. In Canberra, Windeyer had called it a 'farrago of facts, falsity and filth'; he said that it was in English, and was thought to be the work of an Australian.[6] Rupert Ernest Lockwood, a prominent Communist journalist with the *Tribune*, was first mentioned in this connection on 30 June.[7] Earlier that month he had published a pamphlet entitled *What is in Document J?* The Royal Commission drew attention to Lockwood's publication and forbade its further distribution, but the ban had little effect. Lockwood's counsel, the Communist barrister Ted Hill,* appeared before the Commission on 1 July, in his client's absence, and stated that Lockwood had written a document in the Soviet embassy in Canberra in May 1953, but that he did not know if this was the Document J before the Commission.[8] At this stage, neither Lockwood nor Hill had seen Document J.

After some legal delays† Lockwood appeared, upon

---

*Edward Fowler Hill, today chairman of the Australian Communist Party (Marxist-Leninist); at the time of the Royal Commission he had been secretary of the Victorian State Committee of the Communist Party since 1949 and on the Central Committee of the national organization since 1948 (see *Transcript*, pp. 2580–81). Hill and his wife were the only foreign guests of the Chinese Communist Party at the National Day celebrations in 1966; for Hill's part in the celebrations and his association with the Red Guards, see the *New York Times*, 31 October 1966.

†Lockwood had issued a £10 000 writ against Windeyer for slander. It was based on the faulty and hasty legislation of 14 April 1954, which did not

subpoena, before the Commission on 9 July. He refused to answer questions, stating: 'I feel that any answers required of me here would be used to frame criminal charges against me.'[9] When sitting was resumed after the weekend, Lockwood again refused to answer questions.[10]

Mrs Petrov now began to verify the pre-election forecasts that she might be as valuable a witness as her husband.[11] Her evidence was that a man, accompanied by the Tass representative Antonov, had typed a document for three days in the Soviet embassy in May 1953.[12] She then gave a most unsatisfactory courtroom identification of Lockwood. When cross-examined by Hill, she told the tribunal that Lockwood had been suggested as the author of the document by an ASIO officer.[13] Mrs Petrov, however, soon changed that evidence to indicate that it was she who had first mentioned Lockwood and the typing of the document, not the ASIO officer.

On Tuesday 13 July, Fergan O'Sullivan made his first appearance.* O'Sullivan had been press secretary to Dr Evatt from 1 April 1953 until the previous month, when on 4 June he was dismissed by the Labor leader, having confessed to writing Document H. This, the second Petrov document in English, consisted of three closely typed pages containing short reports on forty-five journalists, all members of the parliamentary press gallery in 1951; at that time O'Sullivan had been a member of the *Sydney Morning Herald*'s gallery contingent. Document H, like Document J, has never been

---

provide the Crown prosecutor with privilege; the amendments legislated in August of the same year were made retrospective to save Windeyer. For a discussion, see W. J. Brown, ed., *The Petrov Conspiracy Unmasked* (Sydney: Current Books, 1957), p. 265. Further delays were caused by his counsel's High Court appeal to the effect that Document J was irrelevant to the terms of reference of the Royal Commission; see *Transcript*, pp. 93–96, 169–71 and 175–84.

*Fergan O'Sullivan (b. 1927), journalist for the *Sydney Morning Herald* 1950–53; when Evatt travelled abroad in 1953 (following the famous 'visa incident' of Document J), he lent his home to O'Sullivan; see *The Petrov Story*, p. 241.

published, but according to the Royal Commission's report the details supplied were concerned with

The subject person's religion—whether it was Roman Catholic or Protestant; whether he was radical or conservative, Left-Wing Labor or Right-Wing Labor; whether he drank or was talkative; his financial position, his marital status and the number of his children; and of one it was said that he was 'promiscuous'.[14]

When O'Sullivan appeared he refused, like Lockwood before him, to answer questions about the document he was alleged to have written.[15] At the end of the day's proceedings, however, the Royal Commissioners asked to confer in private with O'Sullivan's lawyer.[16] The next day, O'Sullivan admitted his authorship of Document H.[17]

With the origin of Document H determined, the Royal Commission returned to Document J. O'Sullivan, having admitted his guilt, became a 'friendly witness' and was questioned about the document. On 15 July, Mr Justice Owen disclosed that, in addition to O'Sullivan, two members of Dr Evatt's secretariat were mentioned as 'sources' for information in Document J. The chairman said he was 'disturbed' about the references.[18]

There had been few incidents in the chamber up to this time. The *Tribune* reporter Rex Chiplin, who was later to be called as a witness, had been escorted from the chamber on 14 July—Petrov had mentioned his name, and Chiplin interrupted, crying out 'Liar! Liar!'[19] But, following Mr Justice Owen's disclosure of the implication of Evatt's staff, the real disturbance started. A telegram arrived from Evatt:

I request that you draw the attention of the members of the Royal Commission to the following communication. Yesterday the chairman of the Commission was reported as stating the document known as Document J quoted as sources for various matters, some of which were very confidential, three members of my secretariat. As a result of this statement I have made inquiries of all members of my present staff. Each one of them has unequivocally denied having given at any time any such confidential information to the alleged author of Document J or to any other person. I therefore feel it my bounden duty to protest at once at the making of the defamatory and injurious imputations reflecting on members of my staff. This statement has been given the widest circulation by press and radio. Moreover the imputations appear to have been made without any evidentiary support upon the assumption that events and sources said to be contained in Document J are truly and accurately stated by the author thereof. The course taken in naming persons by obvious reference to a small group is quite opposed to the basic procedures of justice which were outlined at certain stages of the Commission. No notice having been given, injury to individuals is immediate and may be irreparable. I therefore request that a copy of this protest be embodied in the proceedings of the Commission. Herbert Evatt, Leader of the Opposition and of the Federal Parliamentary Labor Party.[20]

Another telegram followed the next day, in which Evatt indicated that any members of his staff required to give evidence were prepared to do so voluntarily, but would prefer to appear at the sittings scheduled for Sydney the following month.[21]

There was now an opportunity to test Petrov's oral evidence. He stated, but provided no documentation, that he had been in contact with a Melbourne man, Andrew Fridenbergs. He said Fridenbergs had helped him and an MVD cadre-worker, Platkais, in EM activities. Fridenbergs, an immigrant who had been a lawyer in Latvia, denied this. However, his alibi for one meeting in June 1953 was broken by his employers; then there was the report of an ASIO tail who had observed a Platkais–Fridenbergs meeting. Petrov's oral evidence was thus proved accurate.[22]

The Royal Commission also showed great interest in one Walter Seddon Clayton, a former functionary of the Communist Party. A subpoena had been issued for him, but he could not be located. Windeyer said: 'Circumstances suggest that he does not wish to be found. ... He is, we believe, a person who may have information of vital importance to Your Honours' Inquiry.'[23] Frederick George Godfrey Rose, a Communist employed in the Commonwealth public service until March 1954, was called. He refused to answer questions, but it was obvious, from Windeyer's approach, that ASIO was asserting that in mid-1950 Clayton had been introduced, at Rose's home in Canberra, to an External Affairs employee, Miss June Barnett, and that Clayton had attempted to enlist her aid in obtaining information from the External Affairs Department.[24]

The Royal Commission completed its Melbourne sittings on 23 July. It rose because of pressure on courtroom accommodation in the Victorian capital, as well as the weaknesses in the Royal Commission Act passed hurriedly in April. By this stage, both Petrovs had given their life histories, O'Sullivan had admitted writing Document H, and the Crown seemed well on the way to declaring Lockwood the author of Document J. The suppressed information about Petrov's payment had been disclosed. Several days' evidence had been heard *in camera;* some of it has never been published, while the publication of the Petrovs' evidence on the French diplomat, Madame Rosemarie Ollier, was delayed several weeks.[25]

14 The fingerprint of a man's style

Parliament reconvened in Canberra at the beginning of August, and there was immediately bitter debate on a bill that proposed changes to the Royal Commission Act. The new legislation visited severe penalties on witnesses who refused to answer questions. Responsibility for witnesses' security from injustice and intimidation would rest entirely with the three Royal Commissioners and counsel assisting the inquiry. Labor Members firmly believed that publicity surrounding the defection and the Royal Commission had cost them the election, and were still angry at the government's failure to reveal, during the Canberra Royal Commission session before the election, that Petrov had received £5000 when he defected.

Menzies nevertheless introduced the corrective legislation with no reference to the storm the Royal Commission had created.[1] He virtually ignored two questions from Labor firebrand Eddie Ward. Finally, when Evatt circulated a press release that compared the Petrov affair to the Zinoviev letter, Menzies was stung into comment. The prime minister defended the Royal Commission and the way it was carrying out its investigation. Evatt and Ward attacked the Commission for its Canberra sitting, and intimated that they doubted the Petrovs' story.[2] Senator McKenna, in the Upper House, was similarly aggressive, being particularly critical of Menzies' selection of the Royal Commissioners.[3] The government's majority allowed the amending legislation to pass through both Houses, and the Royal Commission would now resume investigation with its full powers restored.

The politics of the Petrov affair took on a new dimension a few days after the debate in Parliament, when, without consulting his party, Evatt decided to appear as counsel for the two members of his staff named by the Commission. Allan John Dalziel, who joined Evatt's secretariat in 1940 and had been his private secretary since 1945, was one.[4] The other was Albert Grundeman, a young man who started out as a messenger boy in the public service, was co-opted to Evatt's staff in 1941, and had subsequently risen to the post of assistant secretary.[5] Dalziel and Grundeman were subpoenaed by the Royal Commission on the basis of information in Document J. On the first day of the Sydney sittings, 16 August, Evatt requested permission to inspect the document. The Royal Commissioners refused. However, they did allow him to see those sections referring to the two men in question.[6]

For the next few days Evatt's principal concern was to clarify the authenticity of Document J. He wanted to examine the typewriting, and the handwriting in the document's margins. But when he told the Royal Commissioners that he anticipated calling an expert in these matters, they made it clear that they were only interested in hearing evidence from the tribunal's specialist, Inspector J. Rogers.[7] The tribunal then adjourned for the afternoon of 17 August, at Evatt's request, while he and Inspector Rogers examined parts of the document. Evatt announced the following day that there had been a 'conspiracy' behind the manufacture of Document J.[8]

This opinion was supported by Lockwood, who was now back on the stand. This time, because of the new law, he was compelled to answer questions. Asked whether the document had been produced by him, he replied that some of it was very similar to his work and some of it was not his at all.[9] In particular, Lockwood said, the document he typed at the Soviet embassy the previous year was 170 pages long, while Document J consisted of just 37 pages. Lockwood emphasized that, although Document J covered some of the areas with which he had dealt in May 1953, it also included new material.

Windeyer, in Canberra, had already disclosed the three sections into which Document J was divided. The first dealt with Japanese interest in Australia, the second with American involvement in Australia, and the third, just one page (J-35), was headed 'Dr Evatt'.* Evatt was convinced that J-35 could not have been written by Lockwood alone, because of a particular incident related there. This concerned the difficulty it was supposed that Evatt would have in getting a visa to travel in the United States in 1953. Only O'Sullivan, Dalziel and Evatt were present at the relevant discussion, which took place in George Street, Sydney, outside radio station 2KY, before the 1953 Senate election campaign.[10] Dalziel denied giving any information to Lockwood, and the Commissioners accepted his evidence.[11] Lockwood disclaimed authorship of J-35. When asked to mark any parts of Document J that were not his work, Lockwood marked the whole of J-35 as well as many other sections.[12] Evatt was convinced that O'Sullivan had a hand in the manufacture of the crucial page.[13]

Faced with this conclusion, the Royal Commission allowed Evatt, his juniors and the Communist barrister Hill (appearing for Lockwood) to inspect Document J in its entirety from Friday 20 August.[14] That weekend Evatt pored over the document, and he returned on the Monday more convinced than ever that it was a fabrication.[15] He claimed that J-35 had at some stage been 'physically isolated' from the other pages, and that it had subsequently been 'rung in'.[16] There was physical evidence, in the form of staple marks and pin-holes, that Document J was not manufactured in the form it was presented to the Royal Commission.[17] Windeyer then pointed out that the thirty-seven pages had been stapled together after Petrov's defection. Evatt was not entirely satisfied with this explanation, and there was more to his case: he claimed that the handwritten capital letters appearing in the margins of the document, as a method of footnoting, were not Lockwood's. Lockwood said the capitals appeared to resemble his, but that this method of footnoting was

---

*At that time Windeyer did not disclose Evatt's name—this came on 16 August. He had said that J-35 referred to 'some local political matters' (*Transcript*, p. 25).

'foreign' to his work.[18] Inspector Rogers, under cross-examination, found dissimilarities between the document's capital letters and Lockwood's.[19]

Ever since 16 August, when he first appeared, Evatt had effectively taken charge of the Royal Commission proceedings. The opening session before the May election, and its suppression of the information that Petrov had received payment, emphasized the political aspects of the Royal Commission. But, until Evatt's Sydney appearances, few doubted the Petrovs' evidence. Within ten days of his appearance, however, Evatt seemed well on the way to proving that Petrov, together with others, had fabricated Document J. As the case progressed, the Royal Commissioners, particularly Ligertwood, received Evatt's submissions with increasing hostility. This was no doubt partly a reaction to the Labor leader's overbearing manner; essentially, Evatt himself was directing the investigation of Document J, even though his appearance required the Commission's permission. Mr Justice Owen commented that Evatt no longer seemed to be appearing for Dalziel and Grundeman, but rather for himself.[20] The Commissioners continually interrupted his cross-examinations of Rogers and the Petrovs, insisting that he clarify his conspiracy charges.

Finally, on Friday 27 August, after a barrage of interruptions from Mr Justice Ligertwood, Evatt spelt out his charges.[21] He claimed that Document J had been brought into existence for a 'local political purpose': the damaging of his clients, himself and, by association, the Australian Labor Party. Document J, he contended, had no Soviet intelligence value.[22] Lockwood had not written it: as well as the handwriting and methodology, 'the fingerprint of a man's style' denied his authorship of the document. Lockwood's knowledge of certain incidents, demonstrated in his published works, disagreed with Document J.[23] There was also much underlining in pen and pencil on the carbon copy that was Document J; Evatt contended that this indicated that the document had been 'hawked around' by the Petrovs before being handed over in April. This phrase was used by Evatt and then the Royal Commissioners many times from 16 August to 7 September.

On 30 August, Evatt asked the Royal Commission for permission to call an expert witness on handwriting. After daily prevarication, the request was denied four days later.* Apparently the Commission wanted no evidence conflicting with that of Inspector Rogers. But Evatt was not so easily deterred. He broadened his charges: not only was Document J a forgery, but so were the Moscow Letters (Documents A to F).[24] It was Evatt's contention that ASIO files had been used to construct many of the character sketches in these alleged espionage documents. As a result, on 31 August he asked the Royal Commission's permission to inspect the security service's dossiers under supervision.[25] He attacked Richards of ASIO for accepting Document J without testing its authenticity.[26]

On 1 September, the chairman instructed Windeyer to find an advocate for ASIO because it appeared that its officers were being attacked. Most ASIO agents were apparently employed part-time, and there had been a considerable increase in its funds in the years after 1949—beyond this, little was known about the organization, although the Royal Commission was uncovering a good deal of information. At any rate, Sir Garfield Barwick, the most successful practising lawyer in Australia at the time, was secured to defend ASIO and any of its officers who came under attack, and the next day, 2 September, he presented himself.[27]

Evatt, meanwhile, continued his examination of Document J, but the ASIO defence had provided a convenient interruption. In the five days before the Commission rose for the weekend on Friday 4 September, he had advanced his case little. That Friday afternoon, the tribunal released the evidence of a previous session held *in camera* in Melbourne.[28] On 20 June the Petrovs had given evidence, largely hearsay, that in 1951 Madame Rosemarie Ollier, second secretary of

---

*For this remarkable progression, see *Transcript*, pp. 609/9–11, 632/1077, 689/902–12, 717–18, 721/1–2.

the French embassy, had received a watch via the Tass agent Pakhomov for her services to the Russians. According to their evidence, she had been in contact with MVD agents for a number of years, her last meeting being with Petrov in March 1954. It was the MVD goal, according to the Petrovs and their papers, to obtain the French ciphers through Madame Ollier.* Madame Ollier was not at the sitting; she had been withdrawn from Australia to Noumea on 21 May.[29]

Evatt took exception to this disclosure. He publicly attacked the French government and its ambassador, the Royal Commission and the Australian government for allowing the situation to arise.[30] The Royal Commission, he said, was not a function of the French government. Moreover, the Australian government should never have published the Petrovs' evidence, which made allegations that Madame Ollier was not allowed to answer. Evatt stated his belief that she was innocent of the Petrovs' charges: 'She is being defamed as a spy, apparently on the say-so of two paid informers.' The French ambassador, Louis Roche, demanded a withdrawal from Dr Evatt.[31] He did not get it. On 6 September Evatt sent a cable to the French premier, Pierre Mendes-France, asking him to intervene and repeating his charge about the 'two paid informers'.

Public opinion reacted violently against the Labor leader, and so did the Royal Commission. Later Evatt and Madame Ollier, a former Resistance fighter, were to be vindicated when a French court cleared her of any wrongdoing and she was reinstated to the French diplomatic service.[32] Evatt had claimed that the absence of the fingerprint of Lockwood's style had convinced him that Document J was a fake; there

---

*Petrov seems to have been extraordinarily ambitious in the professed objective of his approaches to Madame Ollier. If he were truly attempting to obtain the French ciphers, rather than simply compromising the French diplomat and therefore acting as an *agent provocateur*, he was aiming at heights not achieved by the most accomplished intelligence systems; it is widely believed that at that time no major counterintelligence organization had comprehensively cracked the cipher system of another.

can be no doubt that in his instinctive, emotional rush to the defence of Madame Ollier, an innocent and defenceless stranger, there was the authentic fingerprint of Evatt's style.

On the next sitting day, Monday 7 September, the Royal Commissioners withdrew Evatt's leave to appear before them. The chairman, after one and a half hours' deliberation, stated:

You have said that your published statement was made in your capacity as a public man. This emphasizes the conflict between your two capacities, which makes it impossible for you to approach the elucidation of the facts with the impersonal detachment proper to an advocate. [33]

Protesting at this stance, Evatt argued that his two capacities were no more in conflict than the Royal Commissioners' dual functions: as judges of the Supreme Courts of their respective states, they might well have to deal with criminal proceedings against people about whom they were already hearing evidence as Royal Commissioners.[34] Evatt's speech was in vain, however, and his expulsion stood. When he withdrew from the chamber, his juniors—Gregory Sullivan and Philip Evatt —together with Hill and their solicitors, walked out of the Commission.[35]

On the same day Evatt was banned from the Commission, the Commissioners indicated their intention of issuing an interim report in the light of the controversy surrounding the documents.[36] Because of the Commissioners' action, Evatt could not cross-examine two of the most important figures in the Petrov affair. The first was Richards, the deputy director-general of ASIO, who was due to appear the very day Evatt was banned; Evatt wished to cross-examine him on the circumstances surrounding Petrov's defection and the handing over of the documents. The second was Dr Michael Bialoguski, whom Evatt had asked to be subpoenaed on 30 August. Bialoguski appeared on 9 September. He then disclosed that he was an ASIO agent (or 'helper', as Windeyer insisted on calling him), who had been in contact with Petrov since 1951.[37] Bialoguski outlined his association with Petrov. Sir Garfield Barwick appeared for Richards, but not for Bialoguski.

Sullivan and Philip Evatt returned to the Commission on 13 September because Sir Garfield wished to cross-examine Dalziel and Grundeman. An unusual position arose: they did not have to ask for permission to reappear before the Commission—it had never been withdrawn, even though they had walked out following the ban on Evatt. Evatt himself reapplied for leave to appear on 16 September.* The Royal Commissioners dismissed the application, but they did publish, at Evatt's request, a part of J-35 the following day.[38] Without their leader, Sullivan and Philip Evatt attempted to destroy Petrov's credit as a witness. They tried to get Bialoguski to confirm that Petrov was a drunkard. Bialoguski rejected the suggestion in his Royal Commission evidence, although his book and his conversations with the authors give a strong impression that Petrov was an habitual drinker.[39]

At the end of September the Royal Commissioners called for final addresses for their interim report. Philip Evatt spoke for a day and a half, but was interrupted by the Royal Commissioners more than a hundred times.† Hill followed, and then Sir Garfield Barwick spoke. Technically he represented ASIO, but in effect he put forward the official government case for the Petrovs. Windeyer himself gave no summary. The three addresses having been completed by 8 October, the Royal Commissioners stated that the conspiracy charges had not been proven.[40] They rose, nevertheless, to write their report, which as they had foreshadowed dismissed all Evatt's charges.[41]

---

*For Dr Evatt's submissions, see *Transcript*, pp. 915–20. They are, as usual, quite brilliantly presented, but there is a strange humility in them—quite different from the tone of the Labor leader's former appearances.

†At one stage the chairman even said: 'Mr Evatt, I think you ought to be ashamed of yourself' (*Transcript*, p. 1057/*640*).

W. J. V. Windeyer, Q.C., senior counsel assisting the Royal Commission on Espionage
(COURIER-MAIL)

Petrov arrives at the Royal Commission hearings
(NEWS LTD)

Escorted by ASIO officers (Richards at rear), the Petrovs leave the High Court in Melbourne after the Royal Commission ended its sitting for the day on 8 July 1954 (NEWS LTD)

Dr Herbert Vere Evatt leaves the courtroom at Darlinghurst on 16 August 1954 after the opening day of the Sydney sittings, when he made his first appearance for staff members Allan Dalziel and Albert Grundeman (NEWS LTD)

15 The Moscow Letters

The Royal Commissioners were anxious to unveil, through the hearings, a history of the MVD in Australia. Petrov had told them all he had learned as the alleged MVD Legal Resident since 1951, and also gave information on Soviet espionage activities in Australia before his arrival, which he said he had picked up as gossip. The Royal Commissioners accepted the documents he brought with him as verification of his claims in their entirety.[1]

According to the Petrovs' oral evidence, instructions from the Moscow headquarters of the MVD were conveyed to Australia in the following manner. Undeveloped 35 mm negatives were sent by diplomatic bag periodically throughout the year to the embassy in Canberra. The embassy cipher clerk, recognizing a mark on the outside of the parcel, delivered the negatives to the MVD Resident, who then developed and enlarged them (each frame was one page of a letter). Certain phrases and code names were decoded by the Resident's cipher clerk.* It was the practice of the MVD to destroy the 1950 letters in early 1952, the 1951 letters in 1953, and so on. By February 1954, the originals of the 1952 letters were due to be destroyed, according to normal procedure. Petrov gave evidence that on the twentieth of that month he led his wife to believe he had disposed of the six 1952 letters; as a result, she signed a document sent to Moscow testifying that they had been destroyed.[2] If his wife were not to defect with him, she could thus claim that she was unaware he had stolen the documents. These letters comprised Documents A to F before the Commission, known as the 'Moscow Letters'.†

---

*The Petrovs were examined and cross-examined on this technique several times. Their story was always consistent. A concise account appears in the *Report*, pp. 41–56.

†Again, the Petrovs were examined on this topic several times. Their story, which is the official one also, appears in the *Report*, pp. 34–67.

It was claimed that there were three sources for another body of documents, the G Series: some were original copies (in one Sadovnikov's handwriting) of a number of Moscow Letters from the period 1945–49; others were Petrov's copies of documents from a sealed envelope marked 'N' that Pakhomov had handed him in 1951; other documents in the G Series, all in Petrov's handwriting, were notes from the 1952 and 1953 Moscow Letters, and from one received in 1954 before his defection. From these documents, and the Petrovs' evidence, the Royal Commission reconstructed the history of the MVD in Australia since 1943.

Petrov gave evidence, apparently supported by ASIO information that has never been made public, that the first MVD Resident in Australia was one Makarov. From 1943 to 1949, Makarov held, successively, the overt embassy positions of referent, third secretary and first secretary. His chief cadre-worker was the Tass agent Nosov. Makarov's successor as Resident was Sadovnikov, who from 1949 until April 1951 was overtly second and then first secretary. Nosov's successor as Tass agent and chief MVD lieutenant was Pakhomov, who arrived in mid-1950. When Sadovnikov returned to the Soviet Union in April 1951, Pakhomov became temporary Resident. Petrov stated that Pakhomov, who was under the disadvantage of being stationed in Sydney, relinquished this role to him at the end of 1951, once Petrov had established himself in Canberra. As head of the Legal Apparatus, Petrov enjoyed the services of several embassy cadre-workers, in addition to Pakhomov, who remained in Sydney. Kislytsin, the overt second secretary and Mrs Petrov's constant companion to Darwin, who arrived in 1952, and Antonov, the Tass agent who succeeded Pakhomov in the same year, were important reinforcements mentioned in the Moscow Letters. Mrs Petrov, after feeling that she was being observed by ASIO, carried out MVD paperwork inside the embassy. Platkais, a Latvian, arrived at the beginning of 1953, overtly as an attaché, and was active in EM work. Further, Kharkovetz, a press attaché from 1951, and Kovaliev, a commercial attaché from 1952, although not regular members of the MVD, were co-opted by the Moscow Centre for work in Australia.*

The Moscow Letters and the G Series named about 120 Australians, code names being alloted to one-third of them.†. Those mentioned included Members of Parliament, journalists, businessmen, émigrés from Communist countries, and members of various peace groups and the like. The allocation of a code name, the Royal Commissioners were anxious to point out, did not necessarily imply any sinister connection between the MVD and the holder of that name; it simply meant that this individual had been under MVD observation long enough to be given the name.[3]

Just as the government's pre-election publicity had foreshadowed, several Labor politicians were mentioned in the Petrov papers. But these revelations had failed to disclose that (disregarding Documents H and J, which have never been published) several conservative politicians were also named. Altogether there were eight Labor men and five conservatives involved. They were Menzies, Casey, Fadden, McDonald and Senator McCallum, representing the Liberal and Country Parties, and Evatt, Calwell, Allan Fraser (referred to as 'Frazer'), Falstein, Russell, former Governor-General Sir William McKell, and Senators Morrow and O'Byrne for Labor.[4] Petrov emphasized that none of them had wittingly given information to the MVD, but that in some way—sometimes because of mere friendliness or perhaps talkativeness while drinking—they had aroused MVD attention. To the MVD they were active or potential 'in the dark' informants. Both Evatt and Menzies were mentioned, together with Fadden and Calwell; assuming the authenticity of the documents, the appearance of these leaders' names may well indicate the naivety of MVD work in Australia. It could indicate also that Petrov's predecessors had exaggerated the

---

*These were the findings of the Royal Commission; see *Report*, pp. 89–92. If one accepts the Petrovs' evidence, they are reasonable findings. The question, examined later, is whether or not the Petrovs embroidered their evidence.

†The names and code names, with several omissions, appear in Appendix 1 of the *Report*, pp. 304–417. (See Appendix 2 of this book.)

success of their efforts. At any rate, the Royal Commission found all the politicians innocent of any wrongdoing. Most of them had volunteered to appear before the Commission, but the Commissioners were satisfied to receive written declarations that were read into the transcript.

Unlike the politicians, journalists were subpoenaed by the Royal Commission. It must be understood that journalists, who receive much 'off the record' information from politicians, are particularly interesting subjects for espionage purposes. The examples of O'Sullivan and Lockwood have already been discussed, but in addition to the former—Lockwood is not mentioned—nine other journalists were named in Documents A to G. They were Ian Gray MacInness, Herbert Victor Birtles (referred to as 'Birtles B.'), Frederick James Maclean, Colin Simpson, Clement Byrne Christesen ('Christisen, S. B.'), Stanley Clive Perry Turnbull ('Turnbull, K.'), Rex Chiplin, and Forbes Keith Miller. An 'Olsen O.' is also mentioned as a journalist, but the Royal Commission could not identify him. (It may be of significance that, when arrested in Queensland in 1956, Petrov gave his name as 'John Olsen'.)

All but one of them, the prominent author Colin Simpson, who escaped with a declaration, were subpoenaed. Their political affiliations were examined, and they were questioned on their associations with the Tass agents Nosov, Pakhomov and Antonov. Only in the case of Rex Chiplin, whose actions had inspired the 'nest of traitors' incident and who had interrupted Petrov during the Melbourne sitting, were there any real suspicions. Chiplin knew Nosov, Pakhomov and Antonov; he had even introduced O'Sullivan to Pakhomov, who subsequently obtained Document H from the journalist.

In the sphere of commerce, the commercial attachés Krutikov, Galanin and, from 1952, Kovaliev were instructed by the MVD to establish worthwhile contacts with businessmen.[5] Seven were named in the Moscow Letters and the G Series—Solomon Kosky, John Dahl Arup (referred to as 'from the firm of Arup'), Bruce Joseph Milliss ('Bruce Milis'), Alfred White, Albert Keesing, Walter Thomas Kirk and Arkadie Yakovlevitch Wassilieff ('A. Y. Vasiliev'). They and several others were called before the Commission. Most held left-wing or Communist political views, but their contacts with the commercial attachés seem to have been innocuous. Their trips to Communist countries gave every indication of being directly related to their businesses. The Royal Commission's report found that these businessmen had not engaged in espionage activities although it concluded that Moscow may well have wished to use some of them in forming an Illegal Apparatus in the future.

Moscow Letter D-6, allegedly of 6 June 1952, set out a plan for establishing an Illegal Apparatus in Australia.[6] A Czech immigrant, Vincenc Divisek, was named by Petrov as Moscow's proposed Illegal Resident.[7] He had emigrated to Australia in 1949. Divisek's testimony was that he had worked for the MVD in Czechoslovakia during World War II, and that when he decided to emigrate the MVD had renewed contact with him, giving him instructions for contacting their Australian network. As soon as he arrived in Australia he told his story to the Commonwealth Investigation Service, but, whether by accident or design, he gave incorrect dates for his proposed meetings with the MVD. Although he never approached the MVD in Australia, by 1952, according to Petrov's documents, the Moscow Centre was again interested in contacting its former agent.[8]

Emigré work by Petrov and Platkais was also related to forming an Illegal Apparatus.[9] In addition to the Fridenbergs case, dealt with in Melbourne in July, the Royal Commissioners examined seven cases in Sydney. These seven people were mentioned in the Petrov papers.* The Royal Commission was unable to identify three of them and Petrov could not help with others, professing that he had never contacted them.[10] The conclusion drawn by Hill was that the documents were forgeries: Petrov had never received such instructions.

---

*The Royal Commission declined to name those individuals it could identify. In the documents they were referred to thus: 'Gutwach', 'Shirokhih', 'John Rosser', 'Nicolai Vassilievich Klenov', 'Vladimir Baskovsky', 'A. I. Galeznik (Antony Chalesnik)' and 'Kastalsky'.

Other solutions may be that Petrov was an incompetent who did not follow his instructions, or that he had stolen authentic MVD documents and was lying about his own position within the espionage organization.

The G Series documents in Sadovnikov's handwriting indicated that an agent known variously as 'K', 'Klod', 'Clode', 'Claude' and even 'C' had obtained documents from the External Affairs Department from about 1945 to 1948.* ASIO, which was briefing Chief Counsel Windeyer, was quite obviously convinced that the Walter Seddon Clayton mentioned in the Melbourne sittings was this agent. For months the subpoena on Clayton could not be served. Then, in March 1955, he turned up in Sydney.[11] By this time, two important pieces of information had been given in evidence: a Miss Bernie, who had worked for Evatt in 1944 and 1945 when he was external affairs minister, said she had handed copies of documents to Clayton; the Communist brother of an External Affairs officer, George Legge, had arranged a meeting between Clayton and Legge in June 1948.[12] Clayton, for his part, acknowledged meeting Miss Bernie, but claimed their meetings were simply to discuss her personal problems as a young Communist; no documents had been passed.[13] Allan Dalziel testified that Miss Bernie could not have had access to any confidential documents because her work wholly concerned Evatt's constituency duties.† In the case of the Legge meeting, Clayton admitted its occurrence, but denied that he had asked Legge to pass him any information.[14] The G documents listing 'K''s contacts were carefully examined by the Royal Commissioners. Hill attacked their authenticity, but the Commissioners remained convinced of Clayton's guilt.[15]

---

*The inclusion of the 'C' is extraordinary, for the Russian 'C'—and the G Series is in Russian—is pronounced like the English 'S'; the Russian 'Klod' is pronounced like the English 'Claude'.

†Miss Bernie worked for Evatt from 20 November 1944 to 12 April 1945; she was involved solely with constituency business and had never met her employer. See *Transcript*, pp. 1332/*240*, 1338/*578*, 1345/*867*, *870*.

Other Petrov testimony also appeared suspect. Petrov gave evidence that when he had a car accident on Christmas Eve, 1953, he was on his way to a rendezvous with Madame Ollier in Cooma. In the Senate, however, Dorothy Tangney produced documents refuting this claim.[16] The licensee of a hotel in Eden—five hours drive from Cooma—swore that Madame Ollier booked into the hotel that day and had attended all three meals. Finally, Petrov accused the French diplomat of meeting with him on 8 March 1954.[17] On this occasion she was supposedly conveying to Petrov the secret information that the vessel *Radnor* was carrying arms to the French forces in Indochina. The poverty of this 'secrecy' is exposed by the fact that a waterside workers' strike was directed at this ship—and reported on the front page of several daily newspapers—on the basis of the same information that Madame Ollier was alleged to have divulged to Petrov. This was ten days after Petrov himself had his first meeting with ASIO. He could only have been contacting Madame Ollier to cause her harm after his defection. The Royal Commissioners, despite these contradictions, found Petrov's evidence valid. As mentioned earlier, Madame Ollier was exonerated by a French court and reinstated in the diplomatic service of her country in January 1956.[18]

There was one more case where Petrov's evidence was widely perceived as unreliable. Petrov gave information that the MVD had passed US$25 000 to Lance Sharkey, general secretary of the Australian Communist Party, in 1953.[19] The Petrov papers contained no reference to this transaction, for Petrov said the instruction had been given by coded telegrams. The money had been sent by diplomatic bag to Canberra, and Petrov passed it to Antonov, who was in turn supposed to have handed it over to Sharkey. Petrov claimed that he had counted the money when it arrived, and that it was in bundles of five and twenty-five dollar notes—he seems to have been unaware that there was then no such thing, and never had been such a thing, as an American twenty-five dollar note. The date Petrov gave for the delivery of the money was, from his point of view, most unfortunate. Sharkey was at a meeting of the Central Committee of the Communist Party on the day in question, 16 October 1953, and the usual ASIO tail verified this testimony. When faced with the weight of contradictory evidence, Petrov specified a few other dates, but these were also unsatisfactory because Sharkey was not in New South Wales at the time. Eventually, 'some date in October' was decided on.[20]

Petrov was not involved in the GRU (or military intelligence) operation in Australia, and the nature of espionage is such that as a member of the MVD he would have been kept from knowledge of GRU activities. ASIO had its suspicions, however, and Petrov told the Commission all that he had heard about GRU operations. The Royal Commission concluded that such activities had been carried on in Australia by a series of Residents from the opening of diplomatic relations in 1943 to at least 1953. The report listed the suspected Residents; it also stated that the GRU was interested in secrets shared by Australia with other Western powers, and the Woomera rocket range in South Australia—one of the reasons why MI5 had pressed the Australian government to establish ASIO. No GRU documents were handed over by Petrov, but his G Series of documents named four scientists who held important government and military posts in the 1940s. Unlike the Gouzenko experience in Canada, the Australian Royal Commission found that none of these scientists had given information to the Russians.[21] They were Wilbur Norman Christiansen (referred to as 'Christinson'), Donald Stewart Francis Woodard ('Don Woods'), David John Morris ('Dave Morris') and Leonard Ulysses Hibbard ('Hibbard L. U.').

Despite the contradictions in the Petrovs' evidence, it had been proven, just as the government had predicted before the election, that 'at least the outlines of espionage' had been set by the MVD in Australia. The Royal Commission's report, published on 22 August 1955, took the Petrovs to be witnesses of truth.[22] Probably a better conclusion is that they were witnesses of partial embroidery. The Royal Commissioners recognized this in their final recommendation; despite the

availability of a solid Crimes Act, and their findings that the
Petrov papers were authentic and that Clayton was the leader
of a spy ring from 1945 to 1948, they concluded: ' ... prosecution of none of the persons whose acts we have considered
in our Report would be warranted'.[23] But many questions
remained unanswered. Was Petrov a genuine spy? Why had
his defection coincided so neatly with Menzies' electoral
purposes? And were the documents Evatt had so fiercely
criticized the genuine article?

16 The suspect spy: Beria's man

During the August 1954 sitting of Parliament, before his appearance at the Royal Commission, Dr Evatt had released a statement to the press:

I believe that when the tangled skein of this matter is finally unravelled the Petrov–Menzies letters case will rank in Australian history as an equivalent to the notorious Zinoviev Letter which was used to defeat a Labour Government in the British elections of 1924, or the burning of the Reichstag which ushered in the Hitler regime in 1933.*

The conspiracy accusation was more strongly articulated during the Royal Commission sittings and in the major parliamentary debate on the Commission's report in October 1955. Evatt was convinced that the Petrovs were not MVD agents and that their documents were forgeries. He suspected that Bialoguski had provided Petrov with ASIO information that subsequently appeared in the fabricated MVD documents. Further, Evatt felt that the timing of the separate Petrov defections was designed to have the worst possible effect on the Labor Party's electoral chances. He accused Menzies of complicity in this matter. For an assessment of these charges, perhaps some of the gravest in Australian political history, three areas of doubt must be resolved, centring on the Petrovs' credentials as active MVD agents, the timing of their defections, and the authenticity of the Petrov papers. In this examination, it will be important to scrutinize the roles played by people other than the Petrovs.

---

*Menzies read this indignantly into Hansard on 12 August 1954 (pp. 282–84).

Evatt believed that Petrov's position in Australia was simply that of third secretary in the Soviet embassy, that he was not a member of the MVD but merely a career diplomat. Most experts on Soviet intelligence disagree with the Labor leader. David J. Dallin accepts both of the Petrovs' evidence on the internal workings of the MVD: it coincides with, or supplements, all other information obtained from MVD defectors and CIA infiltrators.[1] Allen Dulles, head of the CIA at the time of defection, accepts Petrov as temporary Resident, a view also held by Rebecca West.*

Intelligence defectors are extremely important to rival security services: the defector can describe the internal organization of his former service, he can identify his former colleagues when they work in foreign countries, and he can give the names and characters of the people at his former headquarters.[2] With this in mind, it is important to realize that the Western security forces with which Australia shares intelligence information have never indicated that they doubt the Petrovs' evidence on the MVD.[3]

Rastvorov, an undisputed MVD agent who defected in Japan before the Petrovs in 1954, endorsed their claims of MVD affiliation up until 1950. In that year Rastvorov left the Moscow Centre for Japan. Although he knew nothing of the Petrovs' activities after 1950, he verified in a letter produced at the Royal Commission that 'Proletarsky', as Petrov was known in the Soviet Union, 'was a relatively well-known officer among Soviet Intelligence personnel at Moscow in the late 1940's'.† The letter told how Rastvorov had taken English classes with Mrs Petrov in Moscow from 1948 to 1950, when she was a second lieutenant and later a captain in

---

*Allen Dulles, *The Craft of Intelligence* (New York: Signet Books, 1965), pp. 112, 132, 133; for the role of Petrov's disclosures in the Burgess and Maclean case, see Rebecca West, *The New Meaning of Treason* (New York: Viking Press, 1964), pp. 233–37. For Petrov on the two British spies, see his article in *The People* (U.K.), 18 September 1955.

†Yarii Aleksandrovich Rastvorov's letter was sent to ASIO, which had requested it, by the FBI. It was dated 7 October 1954, but was not read into the transcript until 2 December 1954; see *Transcript*, p. 1652/567 and 577.

the MVD. Mrs Petrov was not a member of the Communist Party in 1948, but was a candidate and had been accepted before 1950. It was Rastvorov's recollection that Petrov had reached the rank of major or lieutenant-colonel by 1950. He said that the Petrovs were first NKGB and later MGB agents in Sweden. All this agreed with the Petrovs' Royal Commission testimony. Rastvorov knew nothing of their posting to Australia.

It would have been unusual for a man aged over forty to occupy such a low position at the embassy as that of third secretary. The Australian security forces suspected Petrov from the start, according to evidence at the Royal Commission, and set out to follow his movements.[4] Petrov himself often felt that he was being observed.[5] The ASIO files that were handed over to the Royal Commissioners at the sittings confirmed his suspicions.[6]

The Petrovs' history, as described at the Royal Commission and in their book, conformed to the usual MVD pattern. Yet it would seem, from the evidence presented, that Petrov carried out his espionage duties in Australia in amateurish fashion. The degree of sophistication and expertise that was expected or tolerated of the Petrovs, if they were MVD agents, was low. Petrov admitted that the preparation he underwent for his Australian role was very limited: he was, prior to the Canberra posting, almost exclusively trained in SK work. It may well be that he exaggerated his position in the MVD network in Australia, but it is difficult to believe that he was not an MVD agent of some kind.

Still, Australia could not be considered as important to the Soviet apparatus as the United States and Britain, or even Greece, Italy, West Germany and many other countries. The celebrated 'Illegal Resident' Colonel Rudolf Abel had a radio transmitter in his New York apartment, and so did the Kroger house in London,* but the Soviet embassy in Canberra

---

*See *The New Meaning of Treason*, pp. 265 and 282, and *Transcript*, p. 130/387–89. There is speculation that Morris and Lona Cohen, members of the Rosenberg spy ring, after fleeing New York in 1950 went to Australia and

had no such equipment. Seen in this light, one can appreciate that Petrov's posting was fairly unimportant, even if he were Resident. The sophistication displayed by Abel in his work, as opposed to the apparent naivety of Petrov in his, conforms in many ways to the normal situation in most professions, where practitioners show varying degrees of expertise and capability despite the same basis of training. Perhaps Petrov was a bad espionage agent. In his book he claims to have received the Red Star in 1938,* but this may well have been the reward of a 'party hack'. Perhaps Petrov did not wish to return to Russia because the new regime would have no place for an incompetent 'hack', particularly one who had been sponsored by the deposed and now dead Beria.

The thesis that Petrov was either a low-grade MVD Resident or simply a sloppy cadre-worker is further illustrated by the meeting places he chose for his contacts with Bialoguski and others. In Melbourne, he seems to have met Fridenbergs in inconspicuous settings—parks and railway stations—while in Sydney he seems to have chosen quite obvious venues. He met two scientists, 'X' and 'Y', in their own homes, accompanied on both occasions by a witness, Bialoguski.† He visited the Russian Social Club and Australia–Soviet House and spoke to members of these pro-Communist groups. Petrov's overt capacity as the Voks representative and consul gave him great freedom to move among these people, but if he were operating as an MVD agent, it was certainly with limited expertise.

One can only conclude, from the overwhelming weight of

New Zealand before reappearing in Austria under the name of Kroger in 1954; see *The New Meaning of Treason*, p. 281.

Empire of Fear, p. 91. The award carried with it several perquisites: a stipend, a free rail journey each year to any part of Russia, a free pass to bathhouses, and the privilege of going to the head of ticket lines. When MVD agents are posted to foreign countries they leave their awards behind, for Western security services could thus determine their MVD ranks.

†For accounts of these meetings, see *The Petrov Story*, pp. 87–89 and 150. One non-secret meeting between Petrov and Wassilieff, a Melbourne businessman, is described in the same source, p. 103.

evidence, that both Petrovs were members of the MVD. Whether Petrov was temporary Resident is debatable, but if his documents were authentic then he probably did hold that position. If the conspiracy theory has any validity, it must be seen in the light of the fact that the Petrovs did have MVD affiliation. The conspiracy must centre around the defections and the documents themselves.

17 The suspect defection: a drop at Dream Acres

'Success on chicken farms seemed to have a strong grip on Petrov's imagination,' Dr Bialoguski noted on 27 November 1953 at about the time he had finally been reinstated with ASIO. Petrov had arrived at Bialoguski's Sydney flat unexpectedly that night and seemed preoccupied with the success stories of many new settlers in Australia. By this time the proposed deal to go into a partnership in the Adria had virtually fallen through.

'If you had a choice, which of the openings that are around would you prefer?' Bialoguski asked Petrov as they relaxed over drinks in the flat.

'Chicken farm,' was the reply.

To Bialoguski, he seemed to say it 'in the manner it has been said by thousands of others, in a thousand places, when they have decided the time has come to step out of the frontline of the economic battle'.

It so happened that Leo McMaugh, Bialoguski's brother-in-law, a dentist in the outer suburbs of Sydney, owned a chicken farm that he wished to sell; within a few days Bialoguski arranged for Petrov, under the assumed name Peter Karpitch, to inspect the farm with him.[1] It was called Dream Acres. Petrov liked it and acted the part of a potential buyer convincingly, making such remarks as 'There will have to be improvements' when Bialoguski leaned against a fence and it fell over. On the way back to town, Bialoguski revealed that because he had recently sold some Ampol Exploration shares at a good profit he was prepared to buy the farm for Petrov. 'He raised mild but unconvincing protests,' Bialoguski reported.

'Talk to your wife about it,' suggested Bialoguski, 'and let me know your decision as soon as possible. What do you think yourself now?'

'I think it will be all right, I think we shall be able to take it over,' Petrov said.

'Back in the flat we had a whisky to wish the deal success.'[2]

On 1 December 1953, Colonel Spry called a special conference in Canberra on the Petrov defection.[3] ASIO was preparing the way a full five months before the event actually took place. By 16 December, Petrov had intimated that he might defect without his wife.[4] A week later, Beria was executed after being found guilty of high treason at his Moscow trial,[5] and on 29 December ASIO instructed Bialoguski to contact Petrov following his car accident on Christmas Eve.[6] As there was no police record of the accident, it must be concluded that the Russian was under surveillance by ASIO agents other than Bialoguski. This activity, in December 1953, seems to show ASIO anxiously awaiting the Petrov defection.

The accident, in which the embassy Skoda driven by Petrov was forced off the road by a lorry and burst into flames, gave yet another indication of Petrov's inefficiency and another motive for defection. He confided to Bialoguski: 'Take a look at this. The insurance on the car expired in 1952. It's my place to look after these things. I should have had the car reinsured. Now I suppose this bastard Generalov will make me pay for it. Where will I get the money?'

'Forget your troubles, this is New Year's Eve, a time to enjoy yourself,' said the sympathetic Bialoguski.

'Petrov took me at my word and we embarked on a big night which began at the Russian Club and continued with visits here and there, and ended at my flat at six the next morning. Both of us were sick and sorry when we went our respective ways on New Year's Day.'

On 7 January Petrov again arrived in Sydney, and the following day the net closed on him. ASIO henceforth had the power to force his defection or to ruin him—if it had not already gained that power. On this day Bialoguski took Petrov to clinch the deal at Dream Acres, after Richards had

Mrs Petrov arriving at court in her favourite outfit on 2 September 1954. Later in the day she broke down under cross-examination by Ted Hill. 'You are trying to put this woman on the rack,' shouted Mr Justice Owen, the Commission chairman, before he adjourned the hearing to allow her to regain her composure. (NEWS LTD)

Rupert Ernest Lockwood, the Communist journalist whom the Royal Commissioners found to be the author of Document J (NEWS LTD)

Fergan O'Sullivan (left), former press secretary to Dr Evatt, arrives at the Royal Commission with his solicitor, T. Meagher, on 13 July 1954. O'Sullivan confessed to being the author of Document H. (NEWS LTD)

Walter Seddon Clayton, a former member of the Communist Party, was directed to appear before the Royal Commission in July 1954. When he could not be located, Chief Counsel Windeyer concluded: 'Circumstances suggest that Clayton does not wish to be found.' After emerging in March 1955 and giving evidence, he was accused by the Commission of being the link man in a channel of information from the External Affairs Department to the MVD. (NEWS LTD)

equipped him with the latest in electronic bugging devices—a portable tape-recorder.

'The day of our visit to Castle Hill did not begin auspiciously,' Bialoguski wrote later. 'Early in the morning I heard Petrov walking about the flat, and it crossed my mind that he was drinking, but I fell asleep again. I awakened finally at about 10 a.m. and found that Petrov had been having a few; he was obviously boosting his morale before making the trip.'

Bialoguski told Petrov he had to see a patient, and went to meet Richards at 1.30 in the afternoon to get the tape-recorder. He recalls that it was bulky, and made a quite audible humming noise when turned on. Although the temperature was about ninety degrees, Richards, masterminding what was to be hailed as Australia's greatest feat of counterespionage, seriously suggested that he wear an overcoat to conceal the device. Eventually Bialoguski hid it in his underpants. Richards also handed him £50 to give to Petrov as a deposit on the farm.

Later that day, as Bialoguski drove Petrov past the old Sydney Stadium in Rushcutters Bay, he noticed Richards begin trailing them in another car. But they had not gone very far when Petrov insisted that they pull up at a pub in Parramatta Road for a few beers. Richards drove past with a long face. Switching the tape-recorder on by fiddling in his trouser pockets, Bialoguski recorded a toast to success at Dream Acres while they were drinking in the bar, and they set off again. On the way he handed Petrov the £50, and told him the owners would insist on a completion date for the transaction:

'April,' said Petrov.

'All right, let it be the first of April,' Bialoguski replied. 'Make it the fifth.'

Bialoguski's second wife* later wrote that Petrov was so

---

*Bialoguski's first marriage had broken up in 1949. This story by his second wife, from whom he was then separated, appeared in the *Daily Telegraph* on 5 and 8 June 1955.

drunk at the farm that the McMaughs had qualms of conscience in taking his £50. He was described as sitting sipping whisky (which Bialoguski had produced from the car while concealing the tape-recorder, with its vital conversation, in the boot) and dropping spoons and savouries on the floor around his chair.

'He is so drunk he doesn't know what he's doing,' commented Mrs McMaugh.

'Everything is quite all right. He drew the money out of the bank yesterday when he was sober,' Bialoguski reassured her.[7]

It seems incredible that ASIO, having clandestinely provided a Soviet diplomat with the deposit for a chicken farm, and having recorded a conversation in which he named the day when the deal would be concluded, did not tell the prime minister, to whom they were supposedly responsible. Yet Menzies asked Parliament and the people to believe he did not hear 'the name of Petrov' until 10 or 11 April, three months later. He may not have been informed of Petrov's identity at this stage, simply the circumstances; or he may not have been briefed at all, in which case ASIO, under Colonel Spry, had—as Dr Burton charged—taken over and was running a secret government of its own.

Dr Beckett's July approach to Petrov had shown the Russian that the specialist had some connection with ASIO. Consequently a meeting was arranged between Beckett, Bialoguski and Petrov, and took place at Beckett's house on 23 January. At this, Beckett told Petrov that he would put him in touch with some 'influential friends' should he decide to defect.[8] Back at Bialoguski's apartment, Petrov appeared upset at the thought that his wife might not accompany him, and he persuaded Bialoguski to travel to Canberra the following weekend to discuss the matter. There Bialoguski advised them not to return to Moscow. But still Mrs Petrov was not receptive to the suggestion: 'There is no use trying to talk me into staying here,' he reported her as replying.[9]

By February, ASIO was sure that Petrov would defect soon—perhaps forgetting the 5 April date mentioned by Petrov and recorded on Bialoguski's tape. On 17 February, a circular was distributed to the heads of all Australian government departments, informing them of the imminent defection of a Russian diplomat.[10] Menzies, as head of the Prime Minister's Department, should have seen this. If, as he claimed, he was unaware of ASIO's activities (thus admitting his negligence in the security sphere), he had nevertheless been given official notice of the defection a month and a half before it happened.

Petrov turned up in Sydney on 19 February. He and Bialoguski immediately contacted Dr Beckett.[11] At Beckett's fashionable home, Petrov, through Bialoguski, asked the doctor to contact his 'influential friends' because he wished to defect. Richards took the telephone call, and a meeting was arranged for the next day at Bialoguski's flat. The appointment was broken by Petrov.[12] This is where some conspiracy theorists feel that Petrov was actively tempting ASIO with his defection. In his Royal Commission evidence, Petrov claimed that when he returned to Canberra that day, 20 February, he pretended to destroy, in accordance with normal procedure, the MVD documents that later became the Moscow Letters.[13] If there were any MVD documents, this was probably the date he began to collect them, and, if the Petrov papers were forgeries, this is about the time he began to fabricate them.

Another appointment was made with Richards for 27 February.[14] Again Petrov failed to keep it. The next day, however, he arrived in Sydney.[15] Bialoguski called Richards to the flat. Petrov said to Richards, 'I will tell all I know about the work of the Soviet government in Australia.' According to Richards, Petrov 'hinted that he knew a great deal'. Advocates of the conspiracy theory agree that from this point Petrov was actively bargaining with the security service over the documents he eventually handed them on 3 April. It is important to appreciate that, when a diplomat defects from a Communist country, it is the usual practice to give him financial assistance.[16] But there is very little evidence to indicate the basis on which it was decided to pay Petrov £5000. The official story is that Bialoguski and Spry happened to mention the same amount, and this was agreed on.

By this February meeting, however, two of the four recognized stages of the bargaining process had taken place. First comes the demand for cash (this, advocates of the conspiracy theory would say, could have begun with Petrov communicating to ASIO that he needed assistance); then comes the tempting offer of a sample (this would be Petrov's intimation to Richards that he knew a great deal about Russian intelligence activities in Australia). In most cases this is followed by the demand for a larger sum and, finally, delivery of the goods.[17] No evidence exists, however, that Petrov haggled over money. If he did, one could not expect ASIO, the Petrovs or Bialoguski to admit it. Bialoguski told the authors in 1974:

I took the initiative on a lump sum offer of cash. It was my idea from start to finish. Petrov protested that cash was of no importance. But although he was protesting, I simply disregarded what he was actually saying. I thought he was protesting because he was mixed up about how he wanted to appear to me. I simply anticipated the reaction of any person in his position. I told Richards to show him some money—not necessarily to give him any. There is a chemistry of cash.

Following the February meeting, on 3 March, Richards withdrew £5000 in cash from ASIO funds. He was to carry this money around in a satchel for the next month.[18] On 19 March, Petrov again arrived in Sydney, and was told by Bialoguski that ASIO would give him £5000.[19] That night Richards brought the money to the flat and showed it to Petrov 'as a guarantee of good faith'. Bialoguski left the room while Petrov and Richards arranged a method of contacting each other. According to Richards, Petrov said on this occasion that he would 'back up what he had in his head with documents'. Again there is a suggestion of the bargaining process. A rendezvous was arranged for the next day in Fitzroy Gardens, near where the El Alamein fountain now stands in Kings Cross.

Richards met Petrov and they walked across Macleay Street to an apartment in the 'Cahors' block.[20] There,

Richards asked Petrov two questions: 'Can you tell me whether you know of any Australians who have passed on to the Soviet people in Australia information about their country which could endanger its security?' and 'Do you know the nature [of the information], or can you get reports of theirs?'. According to Richards, Petrov replied: 'All I will say now is that during the war and after there were serious situations existing for Australia in the Department of External Affairs.' Richards' interrogation of Petrov demonstrated his ignorance of a basic rule of intelligence work: if one exposes an agent, one tries to establish what that agent himself wants to find out because it is a very good indication of how much he knows. Instead, Richards directly stated to Petrov that he was interested in Australians who had espionage dealings with the Soviet Union, and in documents that proved this contact. It would not be unreasonable to suspect that Petrov may have constructed documents with this in mind.

Petrov has claimed that he did not begin assembling the documents he brought with him until after this mid-March meeting.[21] But he also gave evidence at the Royal Commission—repeated in his book—that he had caused the important destruction certificate to be falsified on 20 February.[22] Consequently he must have been gathering documents from that date.

Richards, meanwhile, stationed himself in Canberra and held regular evening meetings with Petrov up until 2 April.[23] At the Royal Commission, this information had to be coaxed from Petrov.[24] During these meetings he did hand over some clothes in preparation for the defection, but much more must have gone on than this.[25] The motive for the meetings was not mentioned in the Royal Commission's report and has never been explained.

Petrov gave evidence that he came under attack at the party meeting in the embassy on 31 March.[26] The Soviet diplomat was two hours late for his rendezvous with Richards that evening. On the same night, Petrov's consular safe was raided by Generalov and the first secretary, who found in it a document that should have been in a more secret safe—a serious offence.[27] Once again, Petrov was frightened of what the ambassador, 'that bastard Generalov', would do. April Fools' Day 1954 saw him smuggling the documents out of the embassy after the raid of the previous night. He first hid them under his mattress, and later wrapped them in a copy of *Pravda* and put this in his travelling bag.[28] That evening he left some clothes with Richards in preparation for the defection. During the night, ASIO kept watch on the embassy and diplomats' houses in case the movement against Petrov expressed at the party meeting amounted to greater suspicion than he had indicated.[29]

Petrov left home casually on the morning of 2 April, taking care not to arouse suspicion in his wife that anything was unusual that day.[30] He flew to Sydney, ostensibly to welcome an incoming group of Russian diplomats, including his successor, Kovalenok, who were arriving by ship. Richards sat right behind him on the aircraft. By 2.30 that afternoon, in the flat where they had met on 20 March, Petrov showed Richards the documents. He signed an application for political asylum and told Richards, for the first time, that he was the MVD Resident. Petrov was allowed to take the documents with him when he left the flat—an extraordinarily trusting move on Richards' part. He then contacted Bialoguski and spent the night in the doctor's apartment.

The next morning Bialoguski drove Petrov into downtown Sydney. He took a taxi to the ship, met the new Soviet diplomats and took them, again by taxi, to Mascot airport.[31] Then, without waiting for their aircraft to take off, he walked out of the passenger lounge and stepped into the back of Richards' car. Richards had been waiting outside. But, in what must have been a nervous interlude for the ASIO man, on the way back to Kings Cross Petrov indicated he still had some 'unfinished business' to conclude. He left Richards' car and took another taxi to the Kirketon Hotel, where he gave some expenses money to a Soviet diplomat about to leave for New Zealand.

Petrov then celebrated his defection. As he said in his book: 'My journey back to the rendezvous with Richards was not quite direct and took a little time. When we settled back in the car and we were on our way to the safe house, he asked anxiously, "You were longer than I expected, what happened?" I explained that, feeling thirsty, I had looked in at a bar for a quick one on the way.'

Richards drove Petrov to the ASIO house, where he was given the £5000 he had been promised. Bialoguski meanwhile called an ASIO telephone number and was informed that Petrov was safe. Petrov finally handed over his documents to Colonel Spry at eight o'clock on the night of 3 April 1954.

All evidence indicates that Mrs Petrov was unaware of her husband's intention to defect on 3 April. She had dismissed the idea whenever they discussed it, though at times she did indicate some marginal interest. Their marriage was not a particularly close one, and there is no reason to doubt the testimony that Petrov kept her ignorant of his contact with ASIO from February.[32] Because, before 20 April, she quite clearly intended returning to Russia, her role in the alleged conspiracy must be limited to her endorsement of the Petrov papers' authenticity.

Petrov himself was apparently considering defection as early as the beginning of 1953, as Bialoguski had reported, and by December of that year he was prepared to do so without his wife. Menzies should have been aware of ASIO's involvement from at least September 1953, when Bialoguski saw Yeend, and as ultimate head of the security organization he should have known much earlier than that—certainly when Beckett approached Petrov in July 1953. He has rarely been accused of negligence in his other duties, and there is little reason to believe that he broke from his usual practice in this case.

On the published record, Bialoguski is notably reticent about his role after 27 February 1954.[33] It was Evatt's belief that in this period he supplied Petrov with ASIO information that was used in the forging of the documents. The official story is incomplete. Indeed, the more facts one gathers the more likely the conspiracy theory becomes. It seems entirely possible that, in February and March 1954, Petrov was bargaining with ASIO over the conditions for his defection.

Petrov stated to the Royal Commission that he first thought of defecting in mid-1953, when his wife was in disfavour with Ambassador Lifanov. Mrs Petrov, however, was not interested in defecting because she was afraid for her family in the Soviet Union. Bialoguski for his part has always stuck to his story that he thought Petrov was a likely defector from the time of their first meeting in July 1951. At any rate, there is every reason to believe that ASIO knew Petrov was ready to defect by the beginning of 1953, when the Movement organ *News Weekly* published its article of 28 January.

The course of events leading to Petrov's defection in April 1954 had aroused Dr Evatt's suspicions. The meeting with Richards in February and the many meetings between March and the defection, when coupled with the physical condition of Document J, reinforced the view that the defection was part of a political conspiracy timed to hurt Evatt and the political prospects of the Labor Party. Evatt had accused O'Sullivan of helping to manufacture Document J sometime after May 1953; he accused Bialoguski of supplying Petrov with ASIO dossiers for the compilation of some other documents; he accused Petrov of 'hawking' Document J around so that the Russian could receive a good price for his defection. The dearth of information on these people's movements from February to April 1954 is suspicious, and the conspiracy theory remains worthy of consideration because of this silence.

In all this, the most conspiratorial—and still undocumented —element remains the series of meetings between Richards and Petrov on at least twelve occasions from 28 February to the time of the defection. It has been suggested they were manufacturing, or at least embroidering, the documents that were to prove so helpful to Menzies.

18 The suspect documents: ringing in the pages

Espionage is universal and the techniques of the craft are very much the same whatever the allegiance of the organization. To maintain that there was a conspiracy one must, besides questioning Petrov's MVD affiliations and his associations with ASIO, particularly in February and March 1954, closely examine the documents he handed over in April. Evatt contended that the Moscow Letters of 1952 were forged by Petrov in such a way that some of his public activities, especially those that had come under security observation, would appear to corroborate them. The mentioning of O'Sullivan in the Moscow Letters would lend support to Evatt's theory.[1]

Petrov's MVD responsibilities, as described at the Royal Commission, and as laid down in the Moscow Letters, conformed to the universal practices of the intelligence craft.[2] But so they should have if he were involved in a conspiracy. His activities with a dying Russian woman, as recounted at the Royal Commission by Bialoguski, who had accompanied him, compared well with Moscow Letter F-10.[3] But this was to be expected if the document were forged. The Moscow Letters contain a great deal of extraneous material; so did Colonel Abel's correspondence in New York in 1957.[4] Again, Petrov would have known that this was the usual practice. The same argument applies in the case of the negative instructions that appear in Petrov's Moscow Letters; the Moscow Centre often told its emissaries what *not* to do.[5]

But Petrov had an obligation to contact those people mentioned in the Moscow Letters: 'It must be remembered that a member of the Communist Party is obliged to act on all instructions originating from the authority in charge of the section to which he belongs.'[6] In his evidence, however, he indicated that he did not do this, giving rise to the accusation that the names appeared in the documents as part of the political conspiracy of which Evatt spoke. The argument is that people were named there simply to cause hurt, and contact was never made because genuine instructions for such action had never been given.

Among the documents in the G Series were notes, in Petrov's handwriting, on the alleged Moscow Letters received in 1952 and 1953, and on one Moscow Letter received before his defection in 1954. The conspiracy theorists argue that Petrov took notes from his own forged 1952 Moscow Letters, and that the other notes were concocted from imaginary letters of 1953 and 1954. For the Sadovnikov letters in the G Series, the Royal Commissioners relied on Mrs Petrov's evidence. She said that she had worked for Sadovnikov, although it was later revealed that the period amounted to little more than a month; yet she claimed to recognize Sadovnikov's handwriting on the basis of this short experience.[7] Windeyer compared Sadovnikov's signature in English to the Russian writing in G-1 through to G-3 and G-5 through to G-10. The chairman, however, did not accept this as corroboration of Mrs Petrov's evidence, for the English signature was in very laboured handwriting.[8] The Commissioners decided to rely on Mrs Petrov's opinion; nevertheless Evatt's handwriting expert, Dr Monticone, after comparing photostated copies of the documents with an authentic Sadovnikov sample, dismissed the similarities and declared them to be forgeries.[9]

There were numerous instances where individuals named in the G Series had been investigated by ASIO before Petrov's defection in 1954. Miss Frances Bernie and Miss June Barnett had both been interviewed by ASIO in 1953, after the 'nest of traitors' episode.[10] If Petrov and Bialoguski conspired to manufacture these documents, one of them would need to have known of these two women. ASIO had interviewed both Bernie and Barnett, and Bialoguski was its agent. Further, Bialoguski had infiltrated the many peace organizations in Australia in the late 1940s, and had been instructed by ASIO to collect biographical details of their members.[11] Many of these people, whose names also appear in Bialoguski's book, were cited in the G Series documents. For the Royal Commissioners to find that the alleged spy ring of 1948 was in fact active, they had to prove, first, that the documents handed over to the security service were in Sadovnikov's writing, and, second, that the contacts described therein did take place.

The G Series was held to have corroborated the suspicions of 1948. But although the Royal Commissioners found that in that year a spy ring had been operated by Walter Seddon Clayton—the notorious 'K', 'Klod', 'Clode', 'Claude' or 'C'—Petrov denied any knowledge of it; the only information he could provide was hearsay evidence, based on conversations with Pakhomov, who arrived in Australia in 1950, and Kislytsin, who arrived in 1952.[12] Petrov did not identify Clayton as 'K'. For Clayton to have been head of such a network, he would have needed to know people in the Department of External Affairs and at least one Soviet diplomat. Clayton's evidence—and he was questioned many times on this point—was that he knew no Soviet diplomats.[13] No evidence was offered by the representatives of Menzies' government to indicate that he had been in contact with the staff of the Russian embassy. In the External Affairs Department, Clayton knew only two people: Miss Bernie and George Legge. He knew of two others, but said he neither knew of, nor had met, several individuals named by Windeyer, including Miss June Barnett, the chief witness against Frederick George Godfrey Rose, a former public servant in the Department of Postwar Reconstruction. The Royal Commissioners attempted to establish, as mentioned earlier, that Clayton had been introduced to Miss Barnett, an External Affairs employee, at Rose's house in Canberra, and that he had tried to get her to hand over information from the department. Miss Barnett, in turn, could not identify Clayton.[14] He denied receiving any document from Miss

Bernie, although she gave evidence that she had passed documents to him in 1944–45, when she was employed by Evatt. She could not recall at the Royal Commission the nature of the documents she had allegedly handed over. Clayton admitted meeting with her, but simply as a fellow member of the Communist Party. No evidence was called by Windeyer to corroborate Miss Bernie's claims.

The question of 'K''s identity becomes more complex in the light of other information. The president of the Russian Social Club in the late 1940s and early 1950s was Mrs Klodnitsky.[15] Bialoguski had met the Klodnitskys in 1948, and afterwards saw a good deal of them. He has written that the Klodnitskys kowtowed to the Pakhomovs at the club and entertained them often in their home. Mr Klodnitsky was known by the nickname 'Claude'; the Klodnitskys' son was called Bill Claude. It seems a strange coincidence that these people, active in the pro-Communist Russian Social Club, had names so close to the code name given in the G Series documents. On the basis of a forged G Series, Petrov could well have meant ASIO to deduce that one of the Klodnitskys was the leader of an espionage network. But the Klodnitskys were not called before the Royal Commission.

One hallmark of forgery is the inclusion in a document of information that was not available at the alleged time of composition. Document G-9 contains this reference:

Falstein—aged about 40, Jew, former member of parliament, noted for his leftist speeches, very much wanted to go to the Soviet Union.[16]

It was the Royal Commission's conclusion that this was a copy of an enclosure to a letter sent to Sadovnikov by the Moscow Centre in 1949.[17] The information was allegedly drawn from their dossier on Max Falstein, a Labor Member of Parliament who lost his seat in the federal election of 10 December 1949.[18] It usually took a month for a letter to be written in Moscow and delivered to Canberra; thus, unless

Moscow was prompter (and more up-to-date) than usual, this information could not have come from a 1949 letter. Also, because of the normal disposal procedure, the very latest Sadovnikov could have made a copy of the 1949 letters and altered the information would have been the first few months of 1951; but even then Falstein was not 'about forty'. By 1954, however, the information on age and former occupation was correct. It is difficult to avoid the conclusion that the G Series was at least partly forged.

Despite these inconsistencies, the Royal Commissioners concluded that the evidence 'clearly shows the suspicion held in 1948 well-founded'.[19] As Dr Burton said in October 1955:

I recall my surprise at the revelations of the code names and the system of espionage made public as though it had come from Petrov. I had known of this general picture five years previously. It was the 1948–49 British Information rehash. It seemed to me strange that it had been presented as new. Then I was called as a witness. It was clear to me at the hearings and subsequently confirmed to me that the Commissioners at that time had not been informed of this early information. This was a thing I could not at the time understand. Bailey and Spry were both there. I knew the matter had been one of great secrecy; but it seemed to me strange that the Commissioners had not been informed. In fact, this information was vital to show that Petrov was not in fact the MVD man supposed, and that he was merely producing the information of suspicions already known to military intelligence and security.[20]

Burton remains convinced that ASIO gave Petrov access to the information and names provided by MI5 at the time of the Lapstone Hotel incident.

Of all the Petrov papers, Document J received the closest scrutiny. The Royal Commissioners concluded, despite Evatt's conspiracy claims, that Lockwood alone had typed Document J on 23, 24 and 25 May 1953.[21] Evatt contended that Lockwood was not the sole author of the document presented to the Royal Commission, though Lockwood admitted that he did type a document at the Russian embassy at that time. According to Hill's evidence, Lockwood, when he became aware of the content of Windeyer's opening address, felt that he was the author of the document described therein.[22] He had contacted fellow-Communist Hill because he anticipated being called before the Royal Commission. Lockwood then published a pamphlet, *What is in Document J?*, which the Royal Commissioners termed Exhibit 46. When the differences between Document J and Exhibit 46 were pointed out to them, they argued that Lockwood had written the pamphlet in a deliberate attempt to confuse the Royal Commission. The evidence seems to indicate that this theory was invalid.

Dr Evatt began to suspect that Lockwood might be innocent when, as previously noted, one section of Document J revealed an awareness of the American visa discussion between himself, O'Sullivan and Dalziel in 1953. During the Melbourne sittings O'Sullivan had sworn that he could not remember being in Canberra at the time when, Lockwood admitted, he was writing a document in the Soviet embassy. But, when the Sydney sittings began, O'Sullivan admitted that he had been in Canberra at the relevant time. Philip Evatt, in his summary, accused O'Sullivan of perjury in Melbourne. The Royal Commissioners did not let Evatt pursue this topic, but if it had been proven that O'Sullivan had perjured himself then all his evidence in denial of writing or helping to write Document J would have been dismissed. In Sydney, O'Sullivan admitted that he met with Lockwood one evening after Lockwood had been typing at the Russian embassy during the day. Grundeman drank with them in a hotel for about twenty minutes.[23] It was Dr Evatt's theory that this meeting had been staged by O'Sullivan, perhaps at Petrov's instigation, so that Grundeman could be used as a named source in the manufacture of Document J.

Document J was a carbon copy—the original, the Petrovs said, had been sent to the Moscow Centre.[24] Mrs Petrov stated that she herself had sent the document to Moscow,[25] but Petrov claimed that he had done so. One of them was obviously wrong. Petrov had at first indicated that Document

J was a 'most secret document' and that it was sent to Moscow as an original.[26] When an inconsistency was pointed out, however, he changed his evidence and said it was an ordinary document—according to Moscow Letter F-13, 'very secret' mail was to be sent as undeveloped negatives.[27]

Comparing Document J with Lockwood's previously published work, Mr Justice Philp conceded: 'I quite agree that there may be something in the suggestion that there is a difference in literary style.'[28] Further, Document J, according to Dr Evatt, contained factual flaws that Lockwood would never have made. Experts believe that forgeries can be exposed on the basis of internal evidence.[29] Indeed, some of the incidents incorrectly described in Document J were correct in Lockwood's Exhibit 46, which the Royal Commission had seen as early as 13 June 1954. One particular story in Document J, referring to 1950 instead of the correct date, 1949, would almost certainly not have been the work of Lockwood.[30] He had not made the mistake in Exhibit 46, and, as there was an election in 1949 and the incident described had, according to Lockwood at least, a particular effect on that election, it is difficult to imagine him letting this slip through. On page J-24, Nielsen Park was spelled correctly, yet in Lockwood's Exhibit 46 it appeared as 'Nielson Park'.[31] Inspector Rogers gave evidence that the double hyphen appearing in both Document J and Exhibit 46 was not commonly used in typing.[32] He claimed that this helped point towards Lockwood's authorship. Miss Caroline Rook, a stenographer, contradicted this evidence, adding that she had always used this method, and produced a standard typewriting manual that backed her assertion. Then she devastated the Crown by disclosing that she, and not Lockwood, had typed Exhibit 46.

In Document J, the name of the Movement-influenced Labor politician J. M. Mullens was misspelled twice as 'Mullins', the more usual English form.[33] Dr Evatt contended that much of the internal evidence of Document J pointed to foreign authorship—in this case, the incorrect use of the conventional English spelling. On page J-25, Mullens was described as a 'clerical politician', an expression not used in Australia. Evatt felt this also pointed to a foreign author.[34] Further, Mullens' electorate was given incorrectly, and Evatt believed that this error would not have been made by O'Sullivan. Thus, while he was convinced that O'Sullivan had a hand in the writing of the document, he felt that there was also a foreign contributor. This, he was sure, was Petrov.

The physical condition of Document J also aroused Evatt's suspicions. It was in a severe state of disrepair, and portions where the carbon copy was difficult to read had been typed over as originals.[35] Evatt's explanation was that it had been hawked around by Petrov while he was bargaining over a price for his defection. Extensive underlining was held to support this contention.[36] The marks were in blue, red and lead pencil as well as in ballpoint pen, the various colours perhaps indicating that several people had re-read the document at different times.

Mrs Petrov told the Royal Commission that she had seen Lockwood type most of Document J, and stated that only one typewriter was employed.[37] When the handwriting and typewriting expert, Inspector Rogers, indicated that two typewriters had been used, she withdrew her first statement. Rogers gave evidence that pages 1 to 14, from page 18 through to half of page 26, and finally page 35 of the thirty-seven page document had been done on one typewriter. Pages 15 to 17, from the lower part of page 26 to page 34, and finally pages 36 and 37 had been typed on another.[38] Dr Evatt said that page J-35 was 'physically isolated' from the other parts of Document J. This was certainly so as far as the typing was concerned.

Evatt questioned Richards about the handwritten numbers that appeared at the top of each page of Document J— J-1, J-2, etc.—with the exception of J-35.[39] Eventually Windeyer gave evidence that the numbers had been written in by one of his juniors. This would seem to indicate that J-35 was separated from the other pages after Petrov's defection, evidence of the interest its contents created.

Frederick Rose (left), a Communist employed in the Commonwealth public service, with his solicitor, Max Julius. It was alleged that Walter Seddon Clayton had been introduced to Miss June Barnett at Rose's home in 1950, and that he had tried to persuade her to hand over information from the External Affairs Department. (NEWS LTD)

June Barnett, an External Affairs officer, gave evidence that in 1950 Frederick Rose had introduced her to a man she believed to be a Communist Party official, who had walked her round the block and suggested that she provide information from the department. She could not remember his name, and stated that Clayton bore no resemblance to him. (NEWS LTD)

Evatt quits the Royal Commission on 7 September 1954 after his leave to appear had been withdrawn (SYDNEY MORNING HERALD)

On J-35, the visa incident that first aroused Evatt's suspicions had the capital letters 'BQ' handwritten in the margin next to it. This was the method by which footnotes were indicated in the document. On J-37, where such notes were listed, no 'BQ' appeared.[40] This heightened the physical detachment of J-35 from the rest of the document.

Pages J-36 and J-37, which gave the sources for the document, were the only pages in which the first person was used.[41] This might indicate that the 'sources' were compiled at a different time, or by a different person. The pinholes and staple marks suggested to Evatt that the full thirty-seven pages were not originally stapled together. He summarized his findings on Document J after being dismissed from the Royal Commission:

It is beyond dispute that Document J has been physically manipulated in such a way that one vital page was never physically attached to any other portion of the same group of documents. Moreover, that self-same page had clearly been attached to one or more separate documents which were not produced by Petrov to Security officer Richards. In other words, that vital page was 'rung in' before Security services received the document, while, at the same time, Petrov seems to have 'rung out' one or more other documents which were not produced.[42]

The evidence certainly indicates that his summary was fair.

The many questions arising from the internal evidence of the Petrov papers have never been satisfactorily answered. Dr Evatt expressed doubt about all but two of the documents. Although he was only allowed to partially investigate Document J, the evidence against its authenticity is substantial, and perhaps, if given the opportunity, Evatt could have confirmed his suspicions of Documents A to G. From the inconsistencies that have been made public, that possibility must have been great.

19 ... Couldn't put it together

If there were something wrong with the documents, and if there were something less than convincing about the timing of the defection, the Royal Commission—Ming's men—failed to reveal it. Even if one grants the validity of Petrov's information on the MVD, and its value to Western intelligence services, the facts surrounding his defection and the production of the documents still allow the possibility of a political conspiracy.

Petrov was prepared to defect nearly two years before he finally took that step, and for more than a year beforehand he had been investigating business opportunities, apparently with an eye to the future. During this time he had met with Madame Ollier, Fridenbergs, the scientists and others. He even took Bialoguski along with him to several of these meetings, as if to have a witness for his activities. Lockwood had been induced to write a document at the Soviet embassy, and Petrov had allegedly passed US$25 000 to Sharkey. Meanwhile, he had been involved in Bialoguski's negotiations on the Adria deal. In March 1954, after putting the deposit on the chicken farm, naming his defection date, and even conferring with ASIO, he held a final meeting with Madame Ollier. This telling chronology climaxes with the silence of February and March 1954. The evidence invalidating the Petrov papers must be coupled with this series of activities after his decision to defect. Thus, the accusation that Petrov was manufacturing his documents in February and March, as well as bargaining with ASIO over the defection price, cannot be quickly dismissed.

In terms of the results achieved, the case for the establishment of the Royal Commission on Espionage is suspect. In fact, one of the great ironies of the Commission's appointment lay in the transcript of evidence it produced. Although the Commission was purportedly set up to expose enemy intelligence operations, its transcript provided a most revealing dossier on ASIO methods and internal organization.

The Commission admitted hearsay evidence, generally inadmissible in a court of law. Had ASIO carried out its own private investigation, this hearsay evidence would not have been publicized, but could have been weighed for what it was worth. The Royal Commissioners requested and obtained ASIO's confidential files, but did not publish them. The Commission in effect duplicated the work of ASIO, which briefed Chief Counsel Windeyer. If the Petrov documents were forged, and had fooled just ASIO, then the local political ramifications would have been far less serious. But the appointment of a Royal Commission destroyed this possibility by advertising the Petrov information. The poverty of this very information is indicated by the fact that there were no prosecutions as a result of the long and expensive investigation. If the Petrov documents were authentic, and if government departments had been able to prove that leakages of information had taken place, then the culprits determined by the Royal Commission should have been prosecuted under the Crimes Act. We are left to conclude either that no information was passed or that the documents themselves were forgeries. Perhaps both suspicions are correct.

There was much criticism of the Royal Commission while it sat, and again once it had presented its report. Most of the objections centred around the way it was conducted and its interpretations of the admissibility of evidence. Evatt believed that the Royal Commissioners had, from the very first sitting, accepted the Petrovs as witnesses of truth.[1] He felt that once he had begun to break down this impression the Royal Commission became hostile to him.

There was just one Royal Commission that could establish some precedent for the Royal Commission on Espionage. In Victoria in 1949, Mr Justice Lowe had conducted a Royal Commission into the Communist Party. A former party member, Cecil Sharpley, had fallen out of favour with his fellows and had given information to the Victorian police.

He had accepted a monetary reward for this and had been assured that he was immune from prosecution. With this in mind, Mr Justice Lowe said of Sharpley: 'The credibility of such a witness is heavily suspect.'[2] The Petrovs had also been given money, and Colonel Spry had assured them by letter that they were immune from prosecution. Mr Justice Lowe continued: 'I have not acted on Sharpley's evidence to prove any allegations except where I find it admitted or not denied by the persons affected, or corroborated by the evidence, whether written or oral, which I accept or where I think the circumstances are much more in favour of the truth than the untruth of the story.'

In contrast to this precedent, we find Mr Justice Philp instructing Windeyer in February 1955: 'I would like to say that as Petrov is not represented here, it is your duty to put [the case] from his point of view as highly as possible. That is how I feel. It is a very awkward situation because Petrov's personal future in Australia may depend a great deal upon this matter.'[3] Windeyer replied: 'And if there be any matter which tells particularly in favour of the credibility of Petrov or Mrs Petrov, I shall put it, because the opposite point of view has been put, and put forcibly, by my learned friend [Hill].' In their report the Commissioners make the point that Windeyer was not appearing for the Petrovs.[4] They state in the transcript, however, that they had asked Windeyer to determine whether the Petrovs were under any 'duress'.[5] As a result of this request, which must have been made before the opening of the Royal Commission, Windeyer entertained the Petrovs in his home and then went to a football game with them before the first sitting. But in the report the Commissioners claim Windeyer had 'refrained ... from having any conference whatever with the Petrovs, whether upon the statements or otherwise'.*

A number of events reveal further interaction between

Report, p. 61/177. Either the Royal Commissioners were wrong here, or Windeyer, in assessing the Petrovs' duress, chose not to speak to them at his home or at the football.

those involved in the Royal Commission. In December 1954 when the Commission had investigated little more than Document J, which was questioned so strongly by Evatt and Hill, the secretary to the Royal Commission, Mr Herde, gave a Christmas party. Among the guests were the Petrovs— the people whose evidence the Royal Commissioners were supposed to be scrutinizing.* Members of ASIO also attended. At much the same time, the Royal Commission on Espionage sent out its own Christmas cards. The direct association between the Commission and ASIO can be seen in the way Bialoguski received his subpoena—Bialoguski's security contact delivered the document, not a member of the CIS.[6]

The law knows no politics, yet the Royal Commission made a point of determining people's political leanings. One former army major who was called to appear admitted to Communist sympathies, and was asked if his superiors had known of these views. Learning that they had, the Royal Commissioners demanded their names.[7] A similar approach was adopted when Dalziel appeared before the Royal Commission just before it rose in March 1955, and was asked about his relationship with the Tass representative Nosov in the 1940s. Dalziel, a militant Presbyterian, recalled that he had once taken the Communist to church to show him how he worshipped.[8] The Royal Commissioners questioned Dalziel on this as if there were something sinister in his motives.

A good deal of information that appeared in the Royal Commission's report had not been submitted in evidence at the hearings. For example, during the uproar that developed when William Harrison Bird was questioned on 6 December,† Mr Justice Ligertwood had admitted his ignorance in relation to the Communist Party:

*Owen, Philp and Windeyer were guests, in addition to the Petrovs; see *The Petrov Conspiracy Unmasked*, pp. 119–20.

†The hearing was adjourned and the courtroom cleared after the public gallery had applauded Bird for his answers to the Royal Commissioners and to Mr G. A. Pape, who was appearing with Windeyer to assist the Com-

Ligertwood (to Bird): Do you belong to a Communist Party district, or anything of that kind?

The witness: No. Do you know anything about the party?

Ligertwood: I'm afraid I do not.

The witness: Well, why don't you read something and find out? You can easily learn what its ideas are, its aims and ambitions, and you can find out what its general set-up is insofar as organization is concerned.[9]

Ligertwood must have relied on the knowledge of his two legal brothers, or done a good deal of reading before the Royal Commission's report was drafted, for it contains a large section devoted to the history of the Communist Party and its organization in Australia.[10] Similarly, the report gives a good deal of biographical detail on J. F. Hill, the brother of Lockwood's Communist advocate. Most of these details had not been elicited from Hill himself, nor had they been presented at the Royal Commission by other witnesses.

Mr Justice Ligertwood, who seems to have been the main offender in the incidents on which most of the criticisms were based, showed his legal metal in an attack on Dr Evatt when the leader of the Opposition made his reapplication to appear in September 1954:

Ligertwood: We are told to inquire into espionage; we are not here to inquire into this alleged conspiracy against the Labor Party, which, as I say, is fantastic.

Dr Evatt: Well, your honour, what is fantastic, with the greatest respect, is your honour's comment without hearing the evidence or argument.

Ligertwood: Very well, I take the full responsibility for that.[11]

Windeyer, in his opening address, indicated that there were seventy names in Document J. Only four of these were revealed at the Royal Commission. The names of Dalziel and Grundeman were given during the July sitting of the

---

mission. Bird, secretary of the Victorian branch of the Seamen's Union, told the Commission he was a Communist 'and proud of it'. He said he would not know Walter Seddon Clayton if he 'fell over him', and then told Pape to 'dry up'.

Commission, together with the names of two Catholic Actionist Labor Party dissenters. One of them, a former Labor MP, appeared before the Royal Commission but did not come under attack, unlike Dalziel and Grundeman—this was characteristic of the Commissioners' attitude to 'friendly witnesses'.

The legal principles on which the Royal Commission operated also came under fire. Again, Mr Justice Ligertwood was perhaps the worst offender. He seems to have had no respect for 'privilege' in evidence: he asked of Lockwood, 'Have you instructed your counsel not to examine those two witnesses?', and then several times he demanded of Hill, 'Tell us if Lockwood is the author.'[12]

Hearsay evidence is not generally admissible in a court of law, and there has been much discussion as to whether it should be admitted at Royal Commissions. Windeyer, in the opening session, indicated that it could be admitted by the Royal Commissioners if they thought fit, although he warned that it should be avoided. He said at the time that they were looking for the 'best evidence'.[13] The Royal Commission's report spends a page defending the practice.[14] In January 1955, when Dr F. Louat, Q.C., appeared before the Commission representing Ric Prichard Throssell, the point was cleared up.

Dr Louat: ... I've got to object to it. That is, hearsay. Is it the practice of the Commission—so that I will be quite sure—to admit hearsay from any source, from wherever Mr Petrov may have heard it?
The chairman: Not only is it the practice, it is the duty.
Dr Louat: Any sort at all?
The chairman: Yes.[15]

Commenting on the Gouzenko Royal Commission, the *Canadian Bar Review* had said: 'Against all the rules of law, the Commission admitted in evidence hearsay and what is called secondary evidence; that is, something short of producing actual proof.'[16] The Lynsky Royal Commission in England in 1948, generally regarded as a model of fairness, summarized its views on the topic: 'In coming to a conclusion as to the conduct of any individual witness, and in particular, whether any allegation made in reference to him has been justified, we have had regard only for such evidence as would properly be admitted in a case in which he was party and his conduct was in question.'[17] Hearsay evidence could not be admitted in such circumstances.

There were further variations from the courtroom norm. Mrs Petrov, for example, carried notes into the witness stand, a practice forbidden in a court of law. When it was pointed out to Mr Justice Owen that she was referring to this material, he replied, 'She did not look at it very much.'[18] Mr Justice Owen had missed the point.

Leading questions were asked of Petrov several times and he always replied accommodatingly:

The chairman: Who told you that had happened? Pakhomov?
Petrov: Yes—Pakhomov.[19]

And then there was this extraordinary exchange about meeting places:

The chairman: Is it about five miles from Queanbeyan?
Petrov: That's right.
The chairman: Sixty-eight miles from Cooma?
Petrov: That's right.
The chairman: Eighteen miles from Tharwa?
Petrov: That's right.
The chairman: Six and a half miles from Canberra?
Petrov: That's right.
The chairman: Sixty-six miles from Goulburn?
Petrov: That's right.
The chairman: Forty-four miles from Yass?
Petrov: That's right.[20]

Few Australians know their country as well as that. The only conclusion could be that Petrov was answering a leading question.

20 The geography of fear

Over the three decades since the Royal Commission, Petrov has lived in hiding under an assumed name and the protection of ASIO.

Over ten years ago, Dr Bialoguski described him to the authors as a 'pathetic figure': 'freedom is in your own mind. All Petrov did was to change the geography of his seat of fear. He defected from one gaol to another. . . . When he defected Petrov should not have concealed his identity. He should have said; "Here I am. I am Vladimir Petrov . . . this is my dog, this is my wife." '

Petrov's whereabouts have been clothed in official secrecy since the Royal Commission — with occasional brief bursts of sad notoriety. He came under police notice as a result of a brawl at Surfers Paradise in 1956, when he was found wandering trouserless in the street with a bloody nose. He gave the false name 'John Olsen'.

In September 1974, the weekly *Nation Review* published the information that the Petrovs were living in the Melbourne suburb of East Bentleigh, under the names of Sven and Maria Allyson. When a team from the ABC television show *Four Corners* visited, Mrs Petrov drove to the East Bentleigh police station and reported that she was being harassed.

The attorney-general then, Labor's Senator Lionel Murphy, later announced that he was contemplating introducing laws to protect people like Mrs Petrov against such intrusions. It would have been a supreme irony if the Petrovs' role in the history of the Labor Party had been commemorated by such legislation. Petrov had suffered severe heart attacks between his defection and 1974, and, partly paralysed, spent much of that year in Montclair Hospital at Brighton, Melbourne. He was visited constantly by his wife.

In 1984, on the eve of the release of the papers, Melbourne *Truth* newspaper defied a D notice prohibiting publication of details concerning the Petrovs with a front page photograph showing a tragic old man in a wheelchair in another Victorian nursing home. Mrs Petrov who had been visiting him regularly was also traced. Coincidentally, Labor was once more in power, and the Attorney-general, Senator Gareth Evans, became involved in moves to protect the Petrovs' privacy.

In October 1984, Dr Halley Beckett, the eye specialist recruited to talk to Petrov, was living, now aged seventy-five, on the Gold Coast. He said that he had seen Petrov once after the defection, when he was very ill.

Menzies' former private secretary Geoffrey Yeend, now Sir Geoffrey, was in 1984 permanent head of the Australian Prime Minister's Department.

Michael Bialoguski died in England two months before the release of the Petrov papers in 1984. Until his death, Bialoguski considered that he personally was made a scapegoat. He found it difficult to resume his medical practice after the interruptions of the affair, and later went to England, where he became a general practitioner.

One intriguing development of the Petrov saga concerns the British agent, Roger Hollis, who had discussions with Burton in 1948, and helped establish ASIO and select its original agents. He became director-general of MI5, from 1956 to 1965, and was later knighted.

In 1984, Chapman Pincher asserted, in a book titled *Too Secret, Too Long*, that Sir Roger was the spy of the century, and the 'fifth man' in the network of Soviet 'moles' including Burgess, Maclean, Philby and Blunt. A former MI5 'mole hunter', Peter Wright, now living in retirement in Tasmania has publicly made a similar claim.

Rupert Lockwood, the author of at least parts of Document J, now living in retirement in Sydney, theorized at the time of the release of the Petrov documents that 'Petrov was a decoy to divert attention from Kim Philby, Anthony Blunt, Hollis and other Soviet agents who had penetrated MI5.'

Brigadier Sir Charles Spry, an active seventy-four-year-old, in November 1984 told Anthony McAdam of the *Bulletin*; 'I've heard all the evidence against him and I would have to hear considerably more detailed evidence, not supposition, before I accepted that Hollis was a Soviet spy.'

Dr John Burton left the public service and politics for an academic career, which he continued in London and the USA.

Rex Chiplin was later managing director of Rupert Murdoch's Cumberland Press in Sydney. In 1974 he revealed to us that Mrs A's name was Mercia Masson. He had seen her at North Sydney railway station that year.

In 1974, Evan Whitton of the *National Times* found Walter Seddon Clayton — the man the Royal Commission judges said was the centre of a Soviet spy ring — a pensioner living in a New South Wales coast resort.[1] Clayton claimed that, in 1957, ASIO had offered to let him name his own price to work for them. He declined. He told Whitton that he had never done anything of a subversive nature and had never met a Soviet citizen in his life. Clayton believed he had been singled out for attack by the Commission because he had been in charge of the Communist Party's printing presses and other underground operations when the party was declared an illegal organization between 1940 and 1942. 'If the present government suddenly declared the Liberal Party an illegal organization, members would consider it their duty to carry on underground. It's part of democracy,' he said.

'We scoffed his baked snapper, got down to what he calls a "noggin" or two of his rough red. For an alleged superspy, he struck me as being a pretty good cook,' Whitton concluded.

Fergan O'Sullivan, the author of Document H describing the political and other tendencies of the Canberra press gallery, went to work for a country newspaper in New South Wales, and then became, oddly, press secretary to a minister in the then Labor government of that state. Later, before retiring to the country, he was more appropriately placed as press secretary to a conservative minister in the subsequent coalition government.

Albert Grundeman left Canberra and any connection with politics. He went to Queensland and died there in 1957.

Allan Dalziel remained with Evatt until the end of the Labor leader's political career. Later, after falling out with the new leadership of the party, he wrote for the rebel Labor journal *Century*, and completed a biography of Evatt before his own death in 1973.

One of the consequences of the Royal Commission was that the Menzies government wished, in its usual way, to reward the chairman, Mr Justice Owen, with a knighthood. But it would have been odious to make the senior puisne judge of the New South Wales Supreme Court a knight, when the chief justice himself, appointed by the Labor government of the state, had not been thus honoured. Accordingly the federal government prepared the way by giving Chief Justice Street a KCMG in the Birthday Honours in 1956, and then awarded Owen the lower grade, a KBE, in the New Year's Honours in 1957.[2] Ligertwood was made a knight bachelor in 1956 by the conservative South Australian government, and Philp received a KBE in 1958, when the Queensland government passed into conservative hands. Colonel Spry was given a CBE in 1956 and Richards an OBE the following year. Spry was knighted in January 1964. Chief Counsel Windeyer was appointed to the High Court of Australia in 1958, and received his *ex officio* KBE the following month.

Menzies should have emerged from the affair with a tarnished record, but the effect on his public image was the opposite. Despite his denials to the contrary, it seems likely that he knew of the impending defection as early as September 1953, and the probability is great that, as ultimate head of ASIO, he was aware of the Petrov operation before then. The prime minister's actions after the defection typify the complete political animal, for he took every advantage of the opportunity to score a victory over Evatt. He delayed the defection announcement until the last possible moment before Parliament was due to rise for the election, and failed to warn Evatt, with the result that he was absent from the chamber. The coalition's election campaign of April-May was riddled with anti-Communist rhetoric. Menzies secured his own Royal Commissioners for that arbitrary method of investigation, and then had them hold a sensational sitting just before the election. Alongside the exhaustive press releases and the blood-curdling 'leaks' by Fadden, the omission at the Canberra sitting of any mention of the £5000 paid to Petrov appears glaring. When Evatt became involved in the Commission hearings, Menzies sat back to watch his political destruction. In Parliament, during the two heated debates on the Royal Commission, the prime minister showed his disdain by scorning to come to grips with Evatt's grave charges.

The accusations of conspiracy made by Evatt are most convincing when viewed in the logic of the printed transcript. But logic was the very method he did not employ in publicizing his charges. The allegations were made sensationally, and became more and more shrill as the investigation progressed. Evatt's overbearing manner, and his patent intolerance of Mr Justice Ligertwood's slower mind, did not endear him to the Royal Commissioners. These characteristics also alienated the public. Evatt's lack of communication with his fellow lawyers extended into a lack of understanding of the electorate. Once he was convinced of a Petrov conspiracy, he even went so far as to write to Molotov, the Soviet foreign minister, who naturally denied the Petrovs' story.* Evatt, following his appearances at the Royal Commission, had to face a leadership challenge by Calwell in October 1954. On 5 October he had released a press statement bitterly attacking Movement influence in the Labor Party, particularly in the Victorian branch, and indicating his intention of taking remedial action. This, coupled with his appearance at the Royal Commission against caucus wishes and the implication of his staff, was too much for the dissident Labor element in Victoria. They split with the ALP at the March 1955 federal conference in Hobart, and formed the Australian Labor Party (Anti-Communist), later to become the Democratic Labor Party. Thus, before half his term of office was over, Menzies called a federal election for 10 December. Exploiting the disastrous Labor split, the conservatives won a large majority at the election; they were to govern the country, virtually by default, until 1972.

---

* This was disclosed during Evatt's dramatic speech in the debate on the Royal Commission's report; see Hansard, H. of R., 19 October 1955, pp. 1694-1718.

21 Those who forget the past

Politics is theatre: it tends to reflect life, but also to exaggerate some of its genuine emotions, as well as its superficialities, for dramatic effect and advantage. In this way it is sometimes able to reveal great and essential truths. But the reverse proposition need not hold: the theatrical performance or the public political stance that is instantly most popular, and that involves a conscious distortion for dramatic effect, is not always the one that proves to have lasting merit for its audience.

The second coming of Menzies, in December 1949, was heralded as a new era for Australia. According to the rhetoric of the 1950s, free enterprise was to flourish untrammelled by doctrinaire socialism, and the welling spring of communism was to be staunched in the nation's breast. A dispassionate view, twenty years later, shows much of the private sector to have prospered not from free enterprise, but from ever-increasing subsidies and protection, with new business undertakings thwarted by restrictive practices and obstacles to entry that were conveniently ignored by those in power. The struggle against communism was equally bogus.

For at least six years, to the December 1955 election when Labor was so humiliatingly defeated, a great McCarthyite drama was played out in Australia. Sometimes in concert and sometimes, it appears, independently of one another, ASIO, the CIS and the Liberal–Country Party government persecuted political nonconformists and others, Communists and fellow travellers. The audience, everyday Australians, had no difficulty in deciding which side to support; authority, professing to act under the patriotic impulse, will almost always defeat the individual. The victims were rarely prosecuted, for they rarely committed crimes; but they were silenced and dishonoured. Indeed, as Bruce McFarlane recently pointed out, in academia 'the Class of '54 ... have been traumatized into silence'.[1] Others had to quit the country.

'Kicking the Communist can' became an everyday phenomenon, promoted by the era's most sensational public events, the Petrov defections in 1954 and the Royal Commission of 1954–55. Most of those who lived through the Petrov affair can recall the excitement, and most of those who didn't have heard of it. The extraordinary thing is not that Australia had its very own McCarthy era, with a McCarthy-like inquisition, but that so few people are aware that this is what it was. As Santayana said: 'Those who cannot remember the past are condemned to repeat it.'

The Petrov affair focused attention on the role of the Australian security services, and of ASIO in particular. In a democratic and tolerant society, what should their function be? Clearly we need an organization composed of a small number of specialists trained and active in counter-espionage; *ad hoc* forces would in all probability be difficult to organize quickly and would, of course, lack training. Equally clearly, such an organization needs to be kept under the closest scrutiny; it must not be an agent of an incumbent government, acting against its local political opponents, nor should it be allowed to become a secret force in its own right. ASIO has been both. Its 1971 report on Dr Jim Cairns, then in Opposition and leading public demonstrations against Australia's involvement in the Vietnam War, was clearly inappropriate; so was the philosophy Burton attributed to Spry of second-guessing and actively opposing the foreign policy of an elected government.

The 'tangled skein' of the Petrov affair may never be unravelled. From what is known, however, there are some important conclusions. The affair was basically relevant to domestic politics, for despite the Petrovs' espionage information the crisis they created (or became part of) had little to do with their MVD roles. The question remains: was the Australian security service, in this instance, a local political instrument of the conservative government? The result, as noted above, was a modified Australian version of the McCarthy era. The Royal Commission criticized political nonconformity, sought out and publicized Communists, and, equating communism with disloyalty to Australia, destroyed their reputations. In a larger sense the crisis, stage managed by Menzies, provided a catalyst for the split in the Labor Party that kept it in Opposition until 1972. And at the root there remains the definite possibility that a local conspiracy lay behind the Petrov defection and the Petrov papers. One may conclude that there was, indeed, a nest of traitors operating in Australia when Casey used the phrase with such telling effect in 1952; one may also conclude that the people to whom Casey was referring were not the real traitors.

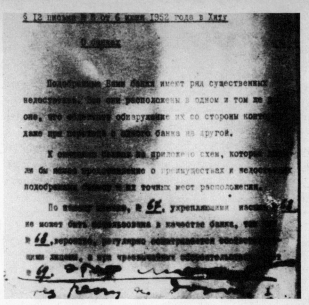

The Royal Commission released this photograph of Document D-23, found to be a letter to Petrov from the Moscow Centre dated 6 June 1952 (NEWS LTD)

The Commission's literal translation of Document D-23 (see over for decoded version) (NEWS LTD)

Paragraph 12 of Letter No.3 of 6 June, 1952,
to HITA.

Concerning Banks

The banks selected by you have a number of defects. They are all located in one and the same area, which facilitates their detection by the office, even if you move from one bank to another.

The description of the banks was not accompanied by sketches which would give a clear idea of the advantages and defects of the selected banks, and of their exact location.

In our opinion, No.67, supporting the No.68 embankment, cannot be used as a bank, because No.68 is probably regularly inspected by the appropriate persons, and in exceptional circumstances might No.69.

(x^1)

Footnote relating to insertion handwritten on the original document.

(x^1) — "this bridge not across the river, but across the road".

Paragraph 12 of Letter No. 1 of 6 June, 1952,
to CANBERRA.

Concerning Secret Hiding Places
for Documents.

The secret hiding places for documents selected
by you have a number of defects. They are all
located in one and the same area, which facilitates
their detection by the counter-intelligence, even if you move
from one secret hiding place to another.

The description of the secret hiding places
for documents was not accompanied by sketches
which would give a clear idea of the advantages
and defects of the selected places, and of their
exact location.

In our opinion, a crack between the boards,
supporting the railway bridge embankment, cannot
be used as a secret hiding place for documents,
because the railway bridge is probably regularly
inspected by the appropriate persons, and in
exceptional circumstances might be guarded.

($*^{1}$)

Footnote relating to insertion handwritten on
the original document.

($*^{1}$) - "this bridge not across the river,
but across the road".

Document D-23 deciphered (NEWS LTD)

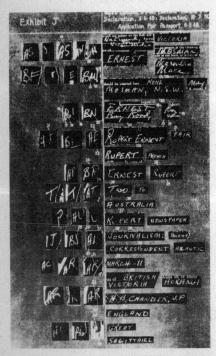

Using various public documents
and a receipt, the Royal
Commission set out to identify
the handwritten notations on
Document J as Lockwood's. This
photograph released by the
Commission compares the
reference system used in
Document J (left) with
Lockwood's own writing.
(NEWS LTD)

Appendix 1:
Submission by Dr J. W. Burton
to the Royal Commission
on Espionage

Version compiled by Dr Burton using notes
from which the original was dictated and
typed under security conditions

SUBMISSION 1

That the activities of the Soviet representatives in Australia were,
in many respects, not out of line with the current practices of
other missions, and that any specific evidence of Soviet espionage
or counter-espionage should be examined in the light of a detected attempt by Australian intelligence authorities to plant an
agent in the Australian Embassy at Moscow.

The present is the first time there has come to the attention of the
Australian people knowledge of some of the activities which
accompany diplomatic life. It has come to public attention through
the defection of an agent—a Soviet agent. Understandably, in the
public mind the impression has been created that Soviet diplomatic
activity in Australia was exceptional, being activity designed to
threaten the security of Australia and her friends, and having
nothing to do with the legitimate protection of any Soviet interests.
Mr Windeyer has suggested that Soviet 'behaviour is an abuse of the
hospitality which the nation accords diplomatic representatives'
(p. 29).

The second term of reference of the Royal Commission requires
Your Honours to inquire 'whether espionage has been conducted
or attempted in Australia by representatives or agents of the
Union of Soviet Socialist Republics'. The popular acceptance of
the existence of espionage, due to announcements and statements
made, should not prevent a careful examination of the question.

On any absolute standard of behaviour, any diplomatic activity
which is dishonest and an abuse of diplomatic privilege must be
condemned, and the motives carefully examined. On any moral

basis, there can be no excuse for espionage, attempts to obtain information illegally, or any irregular acts by the Soviet or by any other power. Nevertheless, the fact is that extra-diplomatic activity, under protection of diplomatic privilege, is common practice. It is therefore necessary to examine the practices of other foreign powers, and of Australia too, before a judgment can be made as to what activities, if any, of the Soviet representatives fall into the category of 'espionage'.

For example, revelations at this Commission of Soviet practices in Australia are paralleled by the recruitment of Australians to visit overseas capitals from where they return educated in and propagating a particular policy which may or may not be in the best interests of Australia, by the use of attaches in Australia who report on the political activities and beliefs of Australians who are critical of the policies of other countries, by Embassy or Consular contacts with Australians willing to report on other Australians, by the use of foreign business houses in Australia for these and other purposes. Monies said to have been offered or given by Soviet agents are small in comparison with subsidies received from other foreign representatives and agents by private organisations and by persons for propaganda purposes, to influence trade union development, and even for electoral purposes. Presents said to have been offered by Soviet agents for services rendered are mean as compared with the generous Xmas and other presents and entertainments which are given selected press, business and official representatives in Australia. Concentration on junior officers who are easily flattered by such attention is a common characteristic of this diplomatic practice. If Soviet agents have made presents to Australians they have not acted any differently from almost every other foreign mission. From this point of view it is perhaps not justified to single out Moscow in words such as were used by Mr Windeyer: 'In other words, Moscow sought not merely to gain political intelligence by legitimate contacts whether official or unofficial or social, but to seduce public servants from their allegiance by blandishments or suborn them by bribes' (p. 29). Furthermore, the description of Soviet methods, 'conversion, compromise, and corruption' (p. 12), equally applies to the techniques of other powers, if it is desired to put the worst interpretation on all these diplomatic practices.

While in principle the giving and the accepting of gifts from foreign representatives is wrong and should be discouraged, knowledge of the acceptance of a gift should never imply, in the absence of other evidence, that any Australian has acted against the interests of his country, nor should it ever be implied, in the absence of other evidence, that there was any attempt to make him do so. In this connection I would like to state that while the gift practice is widespread, and while entertainment is concentrated on key people, there are few if any capitals in the world where there is less response, less corruption, than in Canberra.

Turning to espionage, as distinct from conventionalised methods of obtaining information and promoting points of view, here again Soviet activity is paralleled by the activity of other powers, particularly the 'great powers'. It is condoned even by Australian practices. The Japanese Embassy was wired before the last war. External Affairs officers in one friendly country successfully conducted espionage, by means of bribing key communications officers and having access to official messages, because an emergency situation affected Australia. Both acts could be justified by the circumstances of the time, at least in the view of Australia. Where is the line to be drawn between 'espionage' of this nature, undertaken to protect a national interest in the foreign country concerned, and 'espionage', which must be regarded as a deliberate attempt to threaten the foreign country without in any way being associated with the protection of a national interest? Where is the line to be drawn between justifiable and unjustifiable 'espionage'? Whatever line is drawn should be the demarcation line for ourselves as well as for other powers.

In making a judgment or drawing the line between justifiable and unjustifiable Soviet espionage in Australia, there is one Australian attempt at espionage in Russia which should be noted. Counsel has drawn attention to the fact that an important part of Soviet espionage in Australia seemed to be related to counter-espionage. There were attempts, it is stated, to ascertain who were espionage agents on our United Nations Delegations, and at our missions overseas. Interest was shown in persons who might be Security agents in the press and other sections of the community, presumably in case any were one day sent to Russia, the United Nations or any point important to Russia. There seemed to be a belief in Moscow that a Russian interest was being protected by ascertaining the names of Australian intelligence officers. Why? An explanation might be found in the following episode, the details of which—name, dates and so on—are omitted here but are on the relevant file in External Affairs. Some time ago the Australian staff at Moscow was in difficulties because of the lack of an officer who knew the Russian language well. Day-by-day living in Moscow, as well as the work of the Embassy, required the services of a good linguist. No one being readily available in the Department, a search was made outside. A recommendation was in due course made to the Department from an Australian intelligence organisation, through the defence liaison officer of the Department. The person recommended, an Englishman, was duly appointed, and to save delay was sent immediately to London even before receipt of a Soviet visa. Official visas were not normally delayed, but this one never arrived. The officer was held in London for a time, where he resigned without asking to be returned to Australia. It was some time later that it was learned by the Department that the person in question was an experienced intelligence officer who had operated against the Russians in the Middle East, and was apparently known to them. Only passing reference was made to the matter by Soviet officials in Canberra, but from that time onwards it was quite impossible for the Department to make any useful contacts with the Soviet Ambassador or his First Secretary. Social entertainments of senior officers, which had been regular though not frequent, were terminated. Attempts which I had previously made to discuss regularly proposals before the United Nations, and policies Australia was promoting, had to be discontinued. Informal explanations that an error was made and that External Affairs would not knowingly take part in attempted espionage were not believed or accepted. The records will show, also, that the work of the Embassy at Moscow from that time became more difficult and less useful, until, in fact, I as Secretary of the Department had no option but to recommend a severe curtailment of the mission, if not its withdrawal.

Some recommendations are made at the conclusion regarding diplomatic activity in the light of this experience.

It is submitted that the activities of the Soviet representatives in Australia were, in many respects, not out of line with the current practices of other missions, and that any specific evidence of Soviet espionage or counter-espionage should be examined in the light of a detected attempt by Australian intelligence authorities to plant an agent in the Australian Embassy at Moscow.

[Submissions 2 and 3 have been deleted by the publisher on legal advice.]

SUBMISSION 4

That Petrov would not be a reliable source of important information.

Attempts have been made to build up the importance of Petrov as a means of building up the importance of his defection, and to justify the dramatic moves which followed it. His salary, the highlights of his career, have been misrepresented to show his high standing in the M.V.D. Your Honours on more than one occasion have expressed surprise at evidence which shows his high standing, and by reason of the way the evidence has been presented have come to the conclusion that a 'big fish' was caught, whereas it was thought something relatively small was being hooked.

I am aware of the testimony sent from a former Russian spy through American agencies regarding the status of Petrov. I submit that the source of this 'evidence', and the channel through which it was communicated, both demand that it be treated as of no value. The only evidence which can have any weight is the evidence taken before the Commission, and as that depends upon the word of Petrov it must be treated with reserve.

The evidence before the Commission reveals Petrov as a person who would not normally be a source of important information or have much understanding of M.V.D. procedures. Petrov's whole experience has been communications work (pp. 67–69), except for a period when he claims he was given responsibilities in respect of the security of seamen (p. 79). His claims in this respect seem most unlikely, having in mind the administrative arrangements which would be required to run a cipher office and also carry out the executive work required to watch and to transfer seamen. He has had no M.V.D. or any other intelligence training (p. 99), nor has Mrs Petrov. He came to Australia with no diplomatic rank, to take the place of an officer who was a communications officer, and who had no rank (p. 89). He was subsequently appointed a Third Secretary to give him status for Consular duties—the lowest of all diplomatic ranks (p. 89). (Several times, for example p. 9, it is wrongly stated or implied that Petrov came to Australia with the rank of Third Secretary.) When Petrov arrived in Australia the M.V.D. representative at the Embassy was a First Secretary, which is a high diplomatic rank in a service as large as that of the Soviet. He was assisted by another high-ranking officer (pp. 9–10). The suggestion is that Petrov took over the duties of this First Secretary after the latter had returned to Russia, and also directed the second M.V.D. officer (p. 10). A far more likely explanation of the facts is that Petrov was no more than a cipher officer at any stage, and as such received and sent messages to and from the M.V.D. officer or Tass representative as required. From time to time he was required to carry out certain duties under clearly stated instructions—the kind of instruction which would be sent to an inexperienced officer in the absence in Canberra of any responsible intelligence officer. Petrov's lack of real knowledge about notes brought over by him, his personal behaviour, which called for several reprimands from his seniors, and many other pieces of evidence reveal him as a communications officer who, by reason of the communications he handled, might have had some knowledge of espionage and M.V.D. affairs, just as the officer handling Australian Security Organisation messages would have some knowledge of Australian Security affairs. Petrov's salary, the size of which surprised Your Honours (p. 145), indicates no more than that he was a communications officer with some consular responsibilities.

The question of Petrov's salary needs to be dealt with in some detail because of the way in which the facts have been presented to Your Honours, and because of the importance which Your Honours seemed to attach to wrongly presented conclusions. Counsel said, 'The point about this is that the high salary which this man was paid is some indication of the importance, in the eyes of Moscow, of the work on which he was engaged. This was not an ordinary salary: this was an M.V.D. salary—not the salary of an ordinary Embassy official' (p. 145). Your Honour the Chairman was impressed with the amount stated as salary and said, 'I must say that to me those figures are quite surprising' (p. 145). Even more surprise was shown at the salary of Mrs Petrov, and the comment was made by Counsel, 'Mrs Petrov, Your Honours, was obviously a highly paid and important person' (p. 157). Your Honour the Chairman said, 'They would not send people to Australia at these rates unless they were likely to be of some use to them' (p. 157). In the context, this observation implies that the Petrovs must have been of more use than their stated diplomatic and clerical duties implied.

The facts in the evidence are:

In 1954 Petrov received R4,000 per month.

R3,000 per month were paid into an account in Moscow.

R1,000 per month, stated as £101, was paid in Australia.

Of the amount paid in Moscow, that is R36,000, some 10,000 to 20,000 was taken out in the form of compulsory loans.

A suit cost R1,200 which at A£ = R9 is worth £133.

A pair of shoes cost R400 which is worth £44.

On the assumptions that the minimum loan was paid, and that cost of living adjustment requires the rate of exchange to be increased by four (which is an undervaluation in terms of External Affairs calculations for their officers), Petrov would receive £101 in Australia per month, and £700 in Moscow per year. His total income would be, therefore, about £1912 per year.

On the assumption that the whole of the sum paid in Moscow is available to him, that is R36,000 or £A4,000, or adjusted for exchange, £A1,000, Petrov would still have a total salary of only £A2,212.

It is necessary to examine this salary in relation to the salaries of Australians and others in the same diplomatic or consular rank. The official estimates do not give a total of Australian allowances, because of a system of accounting which does not make this possible. But the estimates presented to Parliament show that four officers received £5,056 in salary and £19,000 in allowances. On any reasonable guess this leaves a Third Secretary with at least £3,000. A United Kingdom Third Secretary in Moscow receives £4,807 (stg) and in Paris £5,300 (stg).

These are facts which Your Honours could reasonably have expected to be given during the evidence on Petrov's salary, and if given Your Honours, and the public, would not have been misled as has been the case. These facts are all so well known to the Department of External Affairs, the Public Service Board, to the Government itself which at one stage took certain decisions regarding the Moscow Embassy on a careful analysis of costs, exchange rates and salaries, that it is a matter of very great surprise and concern that Your Honours have been misled.

Every foreign and cipher service has its Petrovs—men who reach middle age, who have not been promoted to carry out responsible duties, who have some knowledge of secret matters which some of their seniors do not possess, because of documents and messages they handle, who have become disgruntled believing that they should be given greater responsibilities, and who stop at nothing in their attempt to compensate and build up their prestige. Several examples could be given in our own Administration. These officers are an administrative problem, and frequently, according to their temperament and integrity, are a danger in many ways to the Administration. It is from officers such as this, harbouring a deep grievance, that disloyalties arise. Petrov was one such man.

It is submitted that Petrov would not be a reliable source of important information.

SUBMISSION 5

That the disclosures of Petrov add nothing fundamental to knowledge the Commonwealth Government and Security had obtained from British sources more than five years ago, and that this fact should be published.

The reason for taking my evidence in Private Sitting was that it dealt with, amongst other things, information which had been regarded as of the utmost secrecy during the term of my office as Secretary of the Department of External Affairs.

During the hearings of November 2nd I realised that Your Honours were not then in possession of certain background information which I had assumed would have been made known to you either by the Director-General of Security, or by the Solicitor-General, if not by the Prime Minister when he invited you to undertake the investigation. I refer in particular to the fact that, even before Security had been established, certain detailed evidence indicating the possible existence of Soviet espionage in Australia, and some knowledge of the Australians thought to be involved, including descriptions and Russian code names, had been brought to the notice of the Australian Government by British authorities. It was, in fact, this information which led to the establishment of a Security Service under the Chifley Administration in 1948–49.

Apparently it was not thought necessary or desirable by those advising and instructing Counsel to make known all the details and circumstances of this British information. Yet this information, in all its details, is fundamental to the investigation by Your Honours, for it shows that the general purport and a great deal of the details of the information which have come before the public as a result of the present Royal Commission were known to the present Government when it took office in 1949. While new names have been published, and new documents have been produced, there are no facts so far published which add in any fundamental way to the knowledge which was at that time in the possession of the Government and of Security. Indeed, nothing so far published indicates a seriousness or urgency which was not present five years ago, and which then was not considered sufficient to justify any dramatic action. On the contrary, in so far as Petrov's evidence seemed 'to draw some threads together' (p. 4), it has shown that some of the early disclosures based on British information were alarmist and not based on any real evidence. This applies in particular to the allegations regarding a 'spy ring'.

The fact that the Government and Security had obtained from British sources many years ago the basic knowledge attributed to Petrov should be made public without delay. The public was told by the Prime Minister immediately after the defection of Petrov that 'As far as we've gone there are very few if any surprises to the Australian Security Service among the names revealed.' Counsel confirmed this during his opening before Your Honours. The real reason was not given—indeed the suggestion was made that the information given by Petrov demonstrated the efficiency of Security, which had already been watching most of the Australians concerned.

It is not known to me whether the original reasons for secrecy regarding British sources still apply. This is a matter on which the evidence of British authorities should be taken first hand. (Indeed, the views of the British authorities on the procedure of a public inquiry, and examination of communications passing between Australian and British Security authorities and between the Governments of the two countries on the matter, are of great importance in ascertaining all the relevant facts regarding Soviet espionage in Australia.) It is most unlikely that after all this time the secrecy of the British source would now be important. Moreover, one may suppose that the present inquiry has already destroyed this source, if in fact it was still in existence before the Petrov incident.

Even though the British authorities still wished the Australian Government to refrain from indicating the early source of its information, some means should be found of making public the essential facts. Matters of far greater importance to Australia than the protection of an exploited source of intelligence are involved. One day, without doubt, the fact that the Government already had the basic knowledge will become public property by one means or another. To avoid widespread disillusionment in Australian governmental practices and in judicial inquiries, it is better that the information become available in some way as a result of the present investigations.

It would be most useful to Your Honours if a detailed statement were produced showing what information was obtained from the British source originally, what had been obtained by Security as a result of investigations based on the British information, the dates on which it was obtained, and what additional knowledge Petrov added.

It is submitted that the disclosures of Petrov add nothing fundamental to knowledge the Commonwealth Government and Security had obtained from British sources more than five years ago, and that this fact should be published.

SUBMISSION 6

That Petrov's defection was at a time of great political moment and that there was no security reason for an investigation at that time.

The secret British information already referred to was communicated in 1948 under strict conditions in order to safeguard its source, which was at that time being tapped continually and constantly, and indeed day by day. No use could be made of this information which would in any way reveal that the Government was in possession of it. Consequently, if the source was still secret in 1954—which seems most unlikely—the defection of Petrov, while adding nothing of vital concern to the knowledge possessed by the Government and by Security, could have created a new situation. Security could have been enabled through Petrov's defection to make use of some of the information which previously it could not use for fear of revealing a secret source of information. More open investigations by Security of persons known to be concerned in the alleged espionage could have become possible. In other words, it could have been that advantage was taken of Petrov's defection to build on information previously available to Security, including the probable existence of some Soviet espionage and some particulars of it, but which for special reasons could not before be used in the normal way.

From a Security point of view it would have been a proper procedure to take advantage in this way of Petrov's defection. The procedure would call for no comment if it were not for the fact that the time chosen for making use of this information, that is the time of Petrov's formal request for political asylum, happened to be a time of great political moment. It is presumed that the information, having been kept secret for some five years without apparent danger to the country, could have been kept secret for a few more weeks or months without prejudice to Australian security. The evidence which has been added by Petrov's defection does not justify an 'urgent' inquiry. Furthermore, the methods of investigation decided upon on the one hand were not without political significance, while on the other, they endangered personal reputations, the work of Security itself, and Australian-Soviet relations at a time when the greatest possible caution and discretion were demanded.

In spite of the fact that there was no new urgency created by Petrov's defection, and that ordinary Security investigation would have been the appropriate method of inquiry, the Prime Minister stated on April 13 that he would like to have deferred appointment of the Royal Commission until the new Parliament met, but there 'should be no avoidable delay'.

Your Honours are not required to examine the political circumstances associated with the establishment of the Commission.

Your Honours are asked to inquire into Soviet espionage—whether or not that inquiry was prompted by political considerations. But a true evaluation of Soviet espionage cannot be made without consideration of the way in which this espionage has been brought to public attention. The question arises, for example, would not equally or even more startling revelations have been made, had attention been drawn, for local political purposes, to the non-diplomatic activities of other foreign missions? So far as the published evidence goes, there has not been revealed any facts or circumstances which in any way justify the Prime Minister's remarks, or the establishment as a matter of urgency of the present Royal Commission.

It is submitted that Petrov's defection was at a time of great political moment and that there was no security reason for an investigation at that time.

SUBMISSION 7

That the Security Organisation which has been developed could be a dangerous political instrument, and that its activities are relevant to the present inquiry.

The fact that Security had years previously the basic information and much of the detailed information revealed during the present inquiry, the fact that this information was finally used in a political situation, and the fact that the Prime Minister misled the Parliament and the public as to the urgency of the inquiry, reveal a deliberate use of the Security Organisation for political purposes, and imply a criticism of or an allegation against the Security Organisation itself.

It should be emphasised that any such criticism is a criticism of a system, of an organisation, of an institution: the persons conducting the organisation cannot be held responsible for conducting it in a way desired by the Government.

The history of the establishment of the Security organisation is of both interest and relevance. During the visit of the British Intelligence Officers in 1948, a large Russian Delegation came to a conference held at the Lapstone Hotel. After consultation with one of these officers, I made the suggestion to the Prime Minister that in view of the allegations of an espionage network in Australia it would be useful to employ existing facilities to screen the Russian delegation, and to ascertain their contacts in Australia. I argued further, to the Prime Minister, that even though there were no outcome of such an investigation, it would be useful to demonstrate to the British authorities that the Australian Government was able to safeguard the security of the country without a special security organisation with wide executive powers, thus introducing for a first time in Australia the European secret police institution. Mr Chifley was most reluctant to give approval for the extraordinary measures—or so it seemed then—which were to be taken, including phone-tapping, the wiring of hotel rooms, reporting by drivers and External Affairs officers attached to delegations, and so on. He finally agreed, placed one of the British officers in charge of the operation, and State police and Commonwealth officers, including Spry, were called in.

The experiment had no results which were helpful in counter-espionage: the Russians appeared to make no attempt to contact Australians, and Australians no attempt to contact them. It nevertheless demonstrated the extent to which a permanent organisation engaged in counter-espionage and using these techniques would quickly spread distrust and suspicion throughout the community, and which indeed could create the conditions such an organisation is designed to avoid. G.P.O. technicians were amazed at their instructions, and in fact questioned them. Car drivers and departmental officers and many others, who for the first time saw in operation phone-tapping, reporting on guests of the Government and other such measures, realised that Australia was capable of the same techniques as totalitarian states. It was an unpleasant experience from this point of view, and while such procedures might be advisable in a particular situation, under the specific direction of the Prime Minister as was so in this case, their continuation on a permanent basis, by persons with a long-term interest in finding evidence of espionage, and without any possibility of detailed control, appeared to be introducing the devices of the enemy as a means of combatting him. I wrote a report on this experiment which I sent to the Solicitor-General, in which I strongly urged the greatest possible caution in the establishment of any new organisation.

In the light of information given by British officers, and as a result of strong appeals at a high level from the British Government in relation to information to be obtained from the United States, a Security Organisation was established by Mr Chifley, Dr Evatt, and Senator McKenna (who was acting Attorney-General for some of the time), and being aware of the dangers, the organisation was placed under a member of the judiciary. Its executive powers were meant to be limited, and it was intended that it should be kept strictly within the bounds of essential counter-espionage. Every step was taken to ensure against the development of a situation in which there would be throughout the community 'spies, pimps and informers'.

The fears which Mr Chifley had then, and which led him to place the organisation under a member of the judiciary, have proved to be well-founded. Under the new government the control was handed over to a professional service intelligence officer, and this placed civilian security on the same footing as the service intelligence organisations, to which reference is made below. Furthermore, this appointment created a link between Security and the Defence Departments and associated organisations whose stranglehold on foreign policy acquired during the war was under the Chifley administration gradually being broken.

The organisation developed step by step away from the British model on which it was based, toward the American type which is so strongly criticised by many British officers. The evidence before the Commission, the way it was obtained, and the type of person employed by Security to obtain it, make this abundantly clear. The presence or the widespread belief in the presence of Security officers, paid and voluntary, in many organisations including universities, Church-sponsored organisations, public utilities, the press and so on, and the existence or the widespread belief in the existence of phone-tapping and mail opening, place Australia in the category of countries which have failed to maintain their free institutions.

I cannot emphasise too much that in these remarks no reflection is made against the senior officers concerned. It is necessary to distinguish between persons and the system in which they work. My remarks are directed solely at the system which has been introduced and developed in recent years, for which only the responsible Ministers of the Crown can be held responsible. Indeed, anyone who undertook the responsibilities of Security in its present form, with its wide executive powers, and with opportunities for confidential contact, through agents, with the press and leading citizens, would feel it a duty to employ the same techniques, the same type of people, and to direct the whole organisation to ensure that no person with ideas which he personally regarded as dangerous should at any time be able to win public respect or public confidence. Indeed, he would feel it his duty to employ the whole organisation to keep or place in power governments whose foreign and defence policies he personally considered would best protect the security of the country. The fact that better informed persons held different views would not hinder him in protecting the country against them. That would be his duty, and is, I suggest, the duty of Security as presently constituted. In this sense the Security Organisation is a dangerous imitation of the kind of system it is created to prevent, the system against which Australia maintains it must be defended.

It is not for me to argue whether Petrov was produced at a given time because it was thought helpful by Security to ensure a continuation of present defence and foreign policies. There is at least some evidence that Petrov was in close touch with Security, and indeed assisting it, many months before his formal defection This evidence requires careful collation, and because of the way in which Counsel assisting the Commission has been briefed and instructed this work should be done by Counsel briefed for the purpose, with a right of suggesting to Your Honours the calling of new witnesses and the recalling of past witnesses. Nor is it for me to argue whether Petrov, if he really came over at the time stated, was exploited for a political purpose. Even assuming there had been such political manoeuvres, Security would have only been doing its duty under its present charter if in the view of its senior officers the government should not be changed.

Something of this nature happened before the Japanese war when Naval Intelligence became worried at the attitude and contacts of many members of the then Government—that is the same Government as to-day. Undoubtedly the service intelligence organisations had a great deal to do with the sudden change in press comment and the subsequent change of government. There was no inquiry— nor should there have been—by the incoming Government, even though it had this evidence of close contact with the Japanese on the eve of war. This example is given to stress the fact that in certain circumstances we tend to employ methods and organisations of the enemy in order to combat him. The Security Organisation has introduced, as a permanent feature of Australian government, procedures which once were tolerated only in an emergency situation.

Still without making personal criticisms—for everyone should be entitled to his own views on these matters—it is right and fair to state that many service personnel, including Spry, have held and probably still hold a view which would lead them to assume certain political responsibilities. It was because I opposed the assumption by intelligence and defence organisations of policy and political power that I, as Secretary of External Affairs, was led into conflict with the Defence Department and with Spry personally. At that time Spry was taking part in an intelligence organisation with which other countries were associated. A small group of people were 'initiated' by a special oath of secrecy over and above the normal, and adequate, oath taken by public servants. Certain matters of direct concern to foreign and defence policy were to be known to these persons and these only. I refused to co-operate in this, and took no special oath, on two grounds. Firstly, I was expected to have knowledge which I could not share with the government and those responsible for policy decisions, and secondly, I was expected to mix the work of intelligence with the work of maintaining good relations with foreign countries—an impossible position. I reported my attitude to the Prime Minister, and appointed an officer who was to attend meetings of this group only when matters of foreign policy were to be discussed, and with instructions to report to me any matter which was relevant to the work of the Department.

I have no doubt intelligence officers consider that they should take policy and political responsibilities when in their view the political representatives concerned are not deemed to be reliable or capable of keeping information secret. But I strongly urge that this argument if held valid would undermine the whole fabric of parliamentary government. It is prevalent in the service organisations and in the Defence Department, and now also, I believe, in Security. Again, this is not a criticism of the persons concerned, but it is a criticism of the systems which have been continued and developed since the war, and of the governments which have given positions of power and responsibility in civilian matters to service officers who hold this view. It is a criticism of a system which in practice places foreign and defence policy, and now internal security, in the hands, not of the Parliament or the Executive, but of intelligence organisations.

These matters are very relevant to the inquiry which Your Honours are conducting, because the facts of Soviet espionage and Australian treason can so easily be coloured, misinterpreted, suppressed or even manufactured, if those responsible consider some greater purpose is to be served. These are matters on which Your Honours could properly comment and recommend.

It is submitted that the Security Organisation which has been developed could be a dangerous political instrument, and that its activities are relevant to the present inquiry.

SUBMISSION 8

That there are many observations and recommendations which the Commission could make which would help to offset some of the damage done, and which would make a positive contribution to Australian security.

Freedom for External Affairs to pursue its objectives

It is of the utmost importance to the long-term security of Australia that External Affairs should be free to pursue friendly relations with all countries without fear of reprisals at a later stage by another government or by the Defence Department or by Security. For External Affairs, contacts with unfriendly countries, the sending of Diplomatic Missions to unfriendly countries, concentration on the policies of unfriendly countries, is far more important than activities in relation to known allies. One year Australia is at war with Japan and Germany. Another Australia regards these countries as allies. The same about front has been true of Russia and China. At present there are fears and inhibitions preventing the Department making the kind of recommendations which it has a duty to make. Defence and Security dominate foreign policy, either directly through Ministers, or indirectly through intelligence organisations. It is characteristic that the foreign policy of Australia hinges on two military defence pacts. The main contacts of the Department are allies in these pacts. The Australian foreign office has no real contacts with or knowledge of countries which the Government regards as unfriendly, and no officer can afford to show too much interest in studying these countries. The officer who works for improved relations with Russia and China and the countries of Asia, on which Australian security in the future ultimately depends, is suspect: he wins the favour of the Government, and promotion, if he joins in the continuous planning and plotting and the drafting of false and misleading statements which are calculated to keep our relations with those countries on the least friendly level. During the hearings of the Royal Commission there has been a reflection cast on the Department, not the officers at present in favour of conducting a virtual defence policy, but upon officers who conceive the duties and responsibilities of the Department in different terms. It should be made clear that the Department should at all times be free to promote the most satisfactory relations, without any fear whatsoever of political disfavour or demotion as has happened during the last few years, and more especially as a result of Security activities. Unless some pointed comments are made in this respect, the present position will continue: the poorer type of officer, the more timid, the least independent in thinking, the compromising, will continue to exercise their influence on the younger members and set the same pattern for the future.

An examination of diplomatic practice

Recommendations might usefully be made by Your Honours regarding diplomatic practice. There can be no complaint about the behaviour of other countries if we are not prepared to observe the same principles which we lay down for them. It is suggested that the Government be advised to examine the position with a view to a formal statement of its own position, and an international convention to regularise certain practices, and to ban others.

Relations with Russia

As a result of the Petrov disclosures and the way in which his defection was handled, diplomatic relations were broken off between Russia and Australia. The disclosures do not contain anything which justifies the statements made against the Russians by members of the Government and by Counsel, particularly having in mind Australian attempted espionage. It is suggested that a recommendation should be made that, on the basis of an agreement regarding diplomatic, including trading and consular activities, representatives should again be exchanged.

Academic freedom

In the atmosphere of mistrust and suspicion which has been created as a result of the action of the Government in establishing the Commission, academic freedom has been threatened to an important degree. Cases could be quoted of persons not receiving appointments because of political affiliations or past statements. Others have been refused permission to leave the country to pursue studies. The exaggerations which have characterised the hearings of this Commission have had widespread effects throughout the community in unexpected ways, and only Your Honours can offset these effects.

Nest of traitors

The Security Organisation

It is submitted that there be a recommendation to the government that the organisation be reviewed so as to eliminate some of the dangers to which reference has been made.

Loyalty of Australians

A final conclusion of anyone reading the transcript is that the evidence speaks well for the loyalty and good sense of Australians. There are in Australia all shades of opinion, but with few exceptions Australians cannot be persuaded to act in any way which can reasonably and honestly be regarded as against an Australian interest. Those who might act falsely are not confined to the 'left', and are more likely to be found amongst those who support an extreme 'right' political view-point. In any event they are extremists, few in number, and rarely in positions of responsibility.

Appendix 2:
The Moscow Letters
and the G Series
of documents

Originally published as Appendix 1
to the *Report of the Royal Commission
on Espionage*, pp. 304–417

1. In this Appendix we set out our interpretations of the Moscow Letters and of the G Series of documents.

2. The text here published of these interpretations is the result of a constant process of examination and checking to which we have subjected the documents. We have continued that process not only throughout our sittings, but up to the present time. In consequence, the text here published will be found to differ occasionally in minor respects from the text of some passages read during our sittings and recorded in the Transcript.

3. We have been able to identify all the persons referred to by code names, except in the very few instances to which we have adverted in our Report.

4. The Moscow Letters in literal translation, when referring to a person to whom a code name had been allotted before 1952, always refer to that person by that code name only. For instance, in the literal translations Mrs Petrov and Anderson are never referred to by their real names, but are always referred to as 'Tamara' and 'Yeger' respectively. In our interpretations published in this Appendix, we have in such cases replaced the code name by the real name.

5. Our interpretations here published retain code names only in phrases which indicate the initial allotment of those code names; for instance, in B.10 we have retained the phrase 'F. J. McLean, further referred to as Lot', but thereafter we have interpreted 'Lot' as 'McLean'.

6. Throughout both the Letters and the G Series of documents, we have interpreted code names of places and all other code words and code phrases, so that, for instance, 'Arkadia', 'Azimut', 'luggage', and 'planner' here become respectively 'Brisbane', 'Perth', 'mail' and 'cadre worker'. We have interpreted 'Sparta' simply as 'the

Soviet' or 'Russia', though this popular usage is perhaps not as accurate in some contexts as would be 'the U.S.S.R.'.

7. Some of the original documents here interpreted bear handwritten annotations, all of which appear to be in Petrov's hand. We have indicated the existence of these annotations in footnotes.

B.3

CANBERRA

TO PETROV

LETTER No. 1

of 2 January 1952

B.4

Paragraph 1 of Letter No. 1 of 2 January 1952 to Canberra

CONCERNING KOVALIEV

(°1)

Nicolai Grigorievich Kovaliev has departed for No. 1 (°2) to you to work in the capacity of commercial attaché, recruited before departure to our work under the code name Grigoriev.

Kovaliev has a higher education, knows the English language. He has had experience of work abroad, in 1949–51 he worked as senior economist in the Soviet Ministry of Foreign Trade in Denmark, and is described favourably.

He entered into collaboration with us willingly, declaring that he would be very glad and satisfied if he could render us assistance.

Kovaliev was thoroughly instructed as regards studying foreigners and acquisition of information of interest to the Soviet intelligence, as regards the observance of secrecy in work, and also as regards the conduct of Soviet citizens abroad.

For establishing contact with him the following pattern has been agreed:

Our worker turns to him: 'Regards to you from Moscow from Vladimir Pavlovich.'

Kovaliev's reply: 'What progress in studies?'

Our worker replies: 'Good', and names his code name.

(°1) The following is handwritten on the original: 'contacted him 4/11-52 personally M'. 'M' refers to Petrov's code name 'Milhail'.

(°2) The meaning of 'No. 1' was not reproduced in the deciphered list of insertions, and is not definitely known, but probably is 'Australia' or 'Canberra'.

B.5

We instruct you to establish contact with Kovaliev, to acquaint him with the situation and to direct his efforts towards the obtaining of useful contacts in political and industrial circles and in institutions of the government.

In view of the fact that Kovaliev has no experience of intelligence work, it is essential that you should hold discussions with him for the purpose of teaching him ways and means of conducting intelligence work and that you should render him timely assistance in the purposeful study of the acquired contacts.

After you have established contact with Kovaliev, direct him to arrange official contact with Kosky with the object of studying the latter. For the time being Kovaliev should not be informed that Kosky is our agent. We warn you that you may establish an agent connection with Kosky only with the permission of the M.V.D. Headquarters, Moscow.

In three months time after the arrival of Kovaliev in the country, we request you to send us information as to how he is engaging in our work.

B.6

Paragraph 2 of Letter No. 1 of 2 January 1952 to Canberra

CONCERNING MME OLLIER

A secret contact with Mme Ollier has already been maintained by us

B.7

for a period of more than two years; however, we do not have any positive results from work with this prospective agent.

Analysis of information concerning meetings with Mme Ollier shows that the cadre workers maintaining contact with her carried out their work in an insufficiently expert way, in consequence of which she has not so far become an agent of full value. The basic mistake lay in the fact that, having received Mme Ollier's consent to give us assistance, Sadovnikov in the first instance and now also Pakhomov failed to obtain a regular yield from her of important information to which she has access, and they did not teach her the ways and means of agent work.

During meetings with Mme Ollier, Pakhomov discusses mainly international events and questions with her, which Mme Ollier herself raises, but questions of our work are not deeply broached. Pakhomov sets her almost no task and does not succeed in seeing that she executes fully and punctually the tasks which have been set her.

In order that we should be able to make a maximum use of Mme Ollier's agent capacities, Pakhomov must in the first place ascertain what type of work she carries out at the Embassy, her daily work routine: when she starts work, when is the lunch-hour break, where she lunches, when she finishes work, etc. It is particularly necessary to elucidate all the details connected with the fulfilment of her duties as cipher clerk, namely: in what room she is engaged on cipher work, where the ciphered documents are kept,

B.8

does she have access to the safe where the cipher books are kept, and does she carry on her person the keys to this safe, etc.

It is also absolutely essential to elucidate, at first orally, the actual technique of the enciphering and deciphering of cables. The elucidation of all these details is necessary to enable us to determine what would be the best way, least liable to exposure, of effecting the acquisition of deposits of ciphers of her Embassy.

It is desirable that the meetings, at which Pakhomov will be elucidating the questions mentioned above, should be carried out at places which would allow discussions in quiet surroundings. For this purpose it appears to us that places might be suitable, located at a distance of 40 to 70 miles from Canberra. In such a place Pakhomov could at first have a discussion in a cafe or restaurant and then discuss with Mme Ollier the most important questions for our work during a walk in the park or along quiet streets.

It is also necessary to prevail upon Mme Ollier that she should, at first orally and later in written form, give information about the contents of all incoming and outgoing cables.

Draw Pakhomov's attention to the necessity of a more secret way of conducting meetings with Mme Ollier, and not to allow that he should select places for establishing contact with her in localities where she could meet her fellow workers or acquaintances.

B.9

(From Pakhomov's information of 1/xii/51 it is apparent that he met her and put her in the car near the place where the building of her Embassy is.)

In the event of Mme Ollier being granted permission to go to her native country on leave, of which she would wish to take advantage, she must be advised not to insist on a posting to some other country, but to return to Australia. However, taking into account the possibility of her transfer to another country, it is essential that before she departs on leave to France some arrangement should be arrived at with her concerning the conditions of contact (°1) in Paris, on such a basis that the first meeting should be appointed for a month and a half after her arrival in her native country, having also made provision for control meetings once a month.

In the next mail inform us concerning the existing conditions with regard to contact with Mme Ollier.

We request you to pay special attention to work with Mme Ollier and to give Pakhomov assistance in making a thorough preparation for conducting meetings with her.

We ask you to inform us about meetings with Mme Ollier and about your proposals for improving work with her.

---

(1) In the original, literally translated, the passage reads 'conditions of agreement', and the Russian word for 'contact' is handwritten above the Russian word for agreement .

B.10

Paragraph 3 of Letter No. 1 of 2 January 1952 to Canberra
(°1)

CONCERNING ANDERSON

With reference to paragraph No. 6 of Letter No. 6 of 1/xii/1951

Pakhomov must not cease his work with Anderson. On the contrary he should make this work more active, but on a more secret basis, as we have already indicated to him.

Pakhomov should strive insistently to carry out our instructions regarding work with Anderson, as set out in paragraph 3 of Letter No. 5 of 15/x/51.

We are especially interested in getting Anderson to elucidate the information indicated in the 2nd clause of the mentioned paragraph.

We request you to take the control of Anderson under your personal control and to assist Pakhomov to carry it out effectively.

Paragraph 4 of Letter No. 1 of 2 January 1952 to Canberra
(°2)

CONCERNING MCLEAN

In the Political Intelligence department of the Department of External Affairs of Australia there works, with the rank of First Secretary, F. J. McLean, further referred to as Lot.

According to Sadovnikov's description, McLean has access to secret

---

(1) The following is the interpretation of a note handwritten on the original:
'To Comrade Pakhomov
Prepare a reply together with your proposals 5/11 Petrov.'
(2) The following is the interpretation of a note handwritten on the original:
'To Comrade Pakhomov
Prepare a reply (?) 5/11 Petrov.

B.11

documents, knows well many workers in the Department of External Affairs, attends diplomatic receptions and consorts with members of the diplomatic corps.

He treated our representatives in Canberra with respect, willingly accepted invitations, and attended receptions arranged by our diplomats in private apartments.

During discussions he expressed his dissatisfaction with the Menzies government, with internal conditions in the Department of External Affairs, with the Minister for External Affairs, Spender, the chief of his department. He once related that the Public Relations department, in which he formerly worked, is engaged on the processing of all reports of a political character, which are received from Australian representatives abroad, and prepares comments and proposals concerning them. Furthermore, he is more talkative and frank when he is at a small gathering at private receptions.

According to unconfirmed data, McLean was formerly a member of the Australian Communist Party, which he left at his own wish.

One of our trustworthy agents describes McLean favourably and considers that he could supply valuable information, but for this purpose he should be skilfully and tactfully handled and be convinced that nothing that he will say will come to the knowledge of any Australians or will reflect on his service career. It should also be taken into account that McLean has a large family and is badly off materially.

Bearing in mind that McLean is of interest to us, you must study and cultivate him as a prospective agent.

B.12

We request you to keep us informed regularly about progress in the study of McLean.

Paragraph 5 of Letter No. 1 of 2 January 1952 to Canberra (°1)

CONCERNING THE STUDY OF THE DEPARTMENT OF EXTERNAL AFFAIRS

One of the most important aspects of the work of the foreign political intelligence consists of the study and survey of the Department of External Affairs of the foreign country.

Up to the present moment the Australian section of the M.V.D. has not been conducting such survey, and in consequence M.V.D. Headquarters has in effect no information concerning the Australian Department of External Affairs.

Taking note of the importance of this question, we request you to set about the study and survey of the Department of External Affairs.

For a start, compile and send to M.V.D. Headquarters a report in maximum detail concerning the Department, including official and agent information.

Beside other information, this report should refer to the following questions; brief historical data concerning the organization of the Department, its structure, its location, from whom is the personnel recruited, information about the leadership, about educational institutions where diplomatic cadres are trained, which departments actually deal

---

(°1) The following is the interpretation of a note handwritten on the original:
'To Pakhomov
Perhaps Mme Ollier can give something on this question.
Petrov.'

B.13

with matters affecting the Soviet, America, England, and as detailed information as possible concerning the heads and personnel of these departments. Do the employees of the Department of External

Affairs join together in any trade unions organizations or clubs, what do these organizations represent in themselves, what are their addresses.

Further, it is desirable to obtain information regarding procedure for the safeguarding and use of secret documents which exist in the Department, is the association of employees with the people around them controlled and in what manner, in what places is a non-official contact possible with them.

Mobilize all workers of the Australian section of the M.V.D. and recruited persons to participate in the preparation of this report, allocating among them the collection of material on separate concrete questions.

Paragraph 6 of Letter No. 1 of 2 January 1952 to Canberra (°1)

CONCERNING BRESLAND AND NORMAN HERBERT RUSSELL

Among the members of the Australian delegation which visited Russia in October 1951 were Charles Bresland (°2) (further referred to as Cook) and Norman Herbert Russell.

Bresland was born in 1926 in Perth. After completing 7 classes of school he worked as a book salesman in one of the publishing firms in Perth

---

(°1) The following is the interpretation of a note handwritten on the original:
'To Pakhomov
    Petrov.'
(°2) As explained in Chapter 7 of our Report, the name 'Brennd' here appears in the deciphered list of insertions, in mistake for 'Bresland'.

B.14

and later in the publishing firm of the Communist Party in the same place. In 1944 he joined the Communist Party of Australia. At the present time Bresland is a committee member of the Communist Party in the State of New South Wales, the secretary of the executive committee of the Eureka Youth League, progressive organization of the Australian youth in the same State, and a member of the national executive committee of that League. Bresland's wife is a member of the Eureka Youth League.

Bresland understands the Russian language well, but speaks it with difficulty. In all, he creates a favourable impression. He likes Russian music, knows many Russian youth songs and shows a great interest in Russian literature. He at all times spoke sincerely and well of everything he saw in Russia, and he assisted other members of the delegation to understand correctly the realities of life in Russia.

Bresland agreed to an exchange, not through the post, of information and literature between the Youth organizations of Russia and Australia, and he gave several addresses at which a contact could be established with him. Here are the addresses: Chas. Bresland, 59

Peel Street, Belmore, and Eureka Youth League, 40 Market Street, Sydney.

We request you to commission Pakhomov to establish cautiously an official contact with Bresland for the purpose of using him for receiving inquiries in student circles of the universities in Sydney and Canberra.

Norman Herbert Russell was born in 1922 in Sydney; he is non-Party, of middle school education—he completed an accountancy course. At the present

B.15

time he works as a clerk in the Sydney port. He is a member of the clerks' trade union. He is financially secure, lives in his own house and has his own motor car.

Russell's general outlook is that of a petit-bourgeois. Whilst refraining from taking any active part in the fight for peace he does not, it is true, decline to carry out individual assignments to that end.

Although during his sojourn in the Soviet Russell conducted himself well and promised that after his arrival in Australia he would speak nothing but the truth about the Soviet, nevertheless his behaviour arouses suspicion. While in Stalingrad, Russell met, as though accidentally, two attaches of the British Embassy, and conversed with them for some minutes. While he was in Moscow, Russell, together with N. Isaksen, another member of the delegation, secretly and without telling anyone visited the British Embassy, where he spent several hours. The following day they explained their absence by saying that, having gone out for a walk, they allegedly met a young Russian man who spoke English, who invited them to a restaurant where they sat for several hours. Such behaviour on the part of Russell suggests that there may be a contact between him and the British intelligence.

We are sending the information about Russell for your orientation.

B.16

Paragraph No. 7 of Letter No. 1 of 2 January 1952 to Canberra

CONCERNING DAGHIAN
With reference paragraph No. 10 of Letter No. 6 of 1/xii/51

In view of the fact that Daghian has not closed his laboratory and continues to work in it, meetings should be continued with him with the same aims about which we informed you in paragraph No. 4 of Letter No. 5 of 15/x/51.

We explain that, in those cases where as a result of a changed situation there arises a need to alter the aims of the study, the local section of the M.V.D. should itself come forward with its proposals, and not merely limit itself to a request for directions from M.V.D. Headquarters, as was done by Pakhomov in this case.

Paragraph No. 8 of Letter No. 1 of 2 January 1952 to Canberra

CONCERNING MORROW AND O'BYRNE

Morrow and O'Byrne are of unquestionable interest to us, and therefore it is necessary for Pakhomov to establish and maintain an official contact with them. An association with Morrow and O'Byrne should be exploited for the purpose of studying them and of obtaining the necessary 'in the dark' information from them.

B.17

Paragraph No. 9 of Letter No. 1 of 2 January 1952 to Canberra

CONCERNING SLAVIANIN (°1)

It is clear from material received that Slavianin is attempting too obtrusively to establish close relations with Pakhomov.

Taking heed of this, warn Pakhomov that he must be cautious in conversations with him, as it is not to be excluded that he might be an agent of the counter-intelligence.

Paragraph No. 10 of Letter No. 1 of 2 January 1952 to Canberra

CONCERNING SEVERIANIN (°1)

Taking into consideration the fact that Severianin is a prominent member of the Communist Party, he cannot be used in our work. Discontinue the study of him.

Paragraph No. 11 of Letter No. 1 of 2 January 1952 to Canberra

In response to paragraph No. 3 of Letter No. 6 of 1/xii/51

In case of operational necessity, Pakhomov must of course come to Canberra, but this should be done in such a way that the Tass agency work will not suffer harm.

---

(1) This is apparently a code name, and we are unable to identify the person to whom it refers.

B.18

We authorize that part of the expenses for such trips should be paid out of the operation budget of the Australian section of the M.V.D.

We agree that Pakhomov should prolong in the Department of Immigration for a further year the term of his sojourn in the country.

Paragraph No. 12 of Letter No. 1 of 2 January 1952 to Canberra

CONCERNING THE FULFILMENT OF OUR TASKS

In our paragraphs 2 and 8 of Letter No. 4 of 17 August of this year Pakhomov and Mrs Petrov were set definite tasks regarding the selection of secret hiding places for documents and places for meetings with agents which were to be used in further operational work, and also regarding the compilation of a series of reports concerning public and political leaders of the country.

So far we have no news concerning progress in the execution of these tasks.

We request you to participate in this work and to take steps to ensure that the above mentioned tasks should be executed in the near future.

Paragraph No. 13 of Letter No. 1 of 2 January 1952 to Canberra

ORGANIZATIONAL QUESTIONS

(1) The operational letters for 1950 received and kept by you in the Australian section of the M.V.D. must be destroyed in accordance with the act.

B.19

(2) We request you to communicate to us in the next mail a brief description of the motor car which has been acquired, under what cover story it has been purchased, what is the cover story for its presence in the garage of the Embassy, and what are your proposals concerning its further use.

Point out to Pakhomov that he failed to observe our directions concerning maintenance of the motor car.

We authorize Pakhomov to use the car for operational purposes only in Canberra. He must not travel in this car to Sydney.

Paragraph 14 of Letter No. 1 of 2 January 1952 to Canberra

CONCERNING MAKING AN INVENTORY OF PROPERTY

In order to establish the actual presence of property which is to be found in your M.V.D. section, you and Mrs Petrov must carry out a complete stock-taking of property and an inventory as at 1st January 1952, namely:

(1) To carry out stock-taking of the valuable property which is actually present, in accordance with form no. 1;

(2) You must estimate the approximate value, at local market prices, of such property in the M.V.D. section as has not yet been valued at the time of the taking of the inventory.

B.20

(3) To declare property which has become useless, in accordance with form no. 2.

(4) To report any changes that may have occurred in the course of the year with regard to the available property, in accordance with form no. 3.

We request you to forward to us the results of the stock-taking of the property (the deeds)—

Enclosures: forms nos. 1, 2, 3.

Pavlov.

C.2

CANBERRA

TO PETROV

LETTER No. 2

POLITICAL

of 12 March 1952

C.3

Paragraph 1 of Letter No. 2 of 12 March 1952 to Canberra

CONCERNING KHARKOVETZ

Bearing in mind the pressing need for the development of intelligence work in the country of your sojourn, we consider it possible to utilize the services of Kharkovetz for this purpose. In your last communication concerning him, Kharkovetz was positively appraised. He has been in the country long enough, he has familiarized himself with the local conditions and situation, he knows the local language. In his official capacity he has opportunities for the establishing of contacts in circles of interest to us, and, given skilful exploitation, he will be able to bring about a definite profit.

Kharkovetz's introduction into intelligence work should begin with a brief explanation being given him concerning the aims and tasks of the Soviet intelligence in its work against (°1) capitalist countries. You should hold several conversations with him in order to teach him methods of conducting intelligence work and the observance of elementary rules of secrecy. Simultaneously, his efforts should be directed to the acquisition of contacts among correspondents (°2), employees of institutions of the government and diplomatic corps (°3), with the aim of studying and selecting persons suitable for attraction to our work.

The following are handwritten on the original at the places indicated:
(°1) 'against'
(°2) 'of correspondents'
(°3) 'dip. Corps'

C.4

We request you to transmit, in the next mail, your proposals concerning the utilization of Kharkovetz. We also request you to report how he fulfils your assignment with regard to the collection of material about the organizations of the counter-intelligence.

C.5

Paragraph 2 of Letter No. 2 of 12 March 1952 to Canberra

CONCERNING NICOLAI KIRILLOVICH NOVIKOFF

As is known to you, our agent Kliment (Nicolai Kirillovich Novikoff) lived in 1949 in Sydney at the address Cricket House, 254

George Street. Instruct Pakhomov to locate him and to collect a personality report about him, in a cautious manner.

Living with N. K. Novikoff was his son Nicolai Nicolaevich Novikoff, born in 1919, who in 1949 had a photo studio. We are now interested in this son of N. K. Novikoff; therefore try also to collect information as to his whereabouts, to ascertain his ideological views, his financial situation, his circle of friends, etc.

An acquaintance between Pakhomov and Nicolai Nicolaevich Novikoff could be established on a business basis, for instance through a visit to his photo studio under the pretext of negotiations for an order of a portrait of himself or his wife.

We request you to communicate in the next mail such information as has been collected, as well as your proposals concerning the study of Nicolai Nicolaevich Novikoff.

C.6

Paragraph 3 of Letter No. 2 of 12 March 1952 to Canberra

CONCERNING POLITICAL PARTIES

In the matter of exposing the foreign political plans of capitalist states by means of agent penetration into the institutions of governments and the leading circles of these governments, one of the most important priorities is the study of political parties.

The study of political parties has not so far been carried out by the Australian section of the M.V.D. For the purpose of studying the problem and determining definite ways and means for the effecting of the study of political parties, we request you to commence collecting material and preparing short reports about each of the political parties existing in Australia, and in the first place those participating in the coalition of the government.

In reports concerning political parties it is desirable to portray the history of their origin and development, what classes of the population they bring together, the conditions of membership of political parties, their political tendencies, information regarding their leadership, their influence on the political life of the country and the activities of the government, about foreign influence exerted on any of these political parties, the activities of their clubs and printing organs, information about members of political parties who may be of some interest to us, and also your proposals concerning ways of studying them.

Employ all the personnel of the M.V.D. section and of recruited persons on the execution of this work.

C.7

Paragraph 4 of Letter No. 2 of 12 March 1952 to Canberra

We are seeking the traitor to our native land: Efim Feoktistovich Shirokhih, born in 1914 in Zalojnee, in the Mostov area of the Kurgan district.

According to information in our possession, Shirokhih is at present living with his wife in Sydney, Australia, at the postal address La Perouse.

We request you to take measures to locate Shirokhih and to inform us by mail whether he really does reside in Australia.

Paragraph 5 of Letter No. 2 of 12 March 1952 to Canberra

CONCERNING REPORTS

The reports sent by you concerning meetings with agents and with persons who are of interest to us are basically deficient in their formulation. The reports are compiled negligently, they are badly related to the code book, and are not photographed.

All this is an infringement of the elementary rules of secrecy.

We request you to take note of these observations, and, in future, to send reports in negatives together with the letter, as enclosures to the corresponding paragraphs.

C.8

Paragraph 6 of Letter No. 2 of 12 March 1952 to Canberra

For your information we notify you that the information sent by you in mail No. 6 of 1/xii/51, containing an account of the Australian Minister for External Affairs in the parliament concerning trips to the countries of South East Asia and the Far East, is not of operational interest. The information contains merely general dissertations concerning trips to these countries and conditions there, but does not reveal the true aims of this trip.

Pavlov.

D.5

CANBERRA

TO PETROV

LETTER No. 3

POLITICAL

of 6 June 1952

D.6

Paragraph 1 of Letter No. 3 of 6 June 1952 to Canberra

CONCERNING THE PLAN OF WORK

Intelligence work in Australia in 1951–52 was actually at a standstill and has not produced any discernible results. This is explained by the fact that the Australian section of the M.V.D. was not fully staffed, and you and Pakhomov were not working to a definite aim. The absence of a plan of work on the part of the M.V.D. section also had an adverse effect on the state of affairs.

The aggravation of the international situation and the pressing necessity for the timely exposure and prevention of cunning designs of the enemy, call imperatively for a radical reorganization of all our intelligence work and the urgent creation of an illegal apparatus in Australia, which could function uninterruptedly and effectively under any conditions.

In this connection the workers of the Australian section of the M.V.D. should devote special attention to the taking of measures for the preparation of conditions for illegal work (in future referred to as Novators).

The putting into effect of measures relating to illegal work is at the present moment one of the top-priority tasks, on the fulfilment of which should be engaged all the workers of the Australian M.V.D. section, including persons who have been drawn in.

Workers of the M.V.D. section must take into account that the success of the operations in preparation will in large measure depend on the timely collection of data concerning the situation pertaining to agents, the acquisition of various documents and the preparation of conditions for the entry and settling of illegal workers.

D.7

The M.V.D. section must therefore instantly begin collecting the necessary data and compiling reports, without observing any fixed time limits, and send them in instalments to M.V.D. Headquarters. For this work you may at your discretion use any cadre worker, recruited collaborator, and also the most reliable agents. For the collection of some of the data you may also exploit official possibilities open to you (lawyers of your acquaintance, members of the Australia-Russia Society, etc., without disclosing our intentions to them).

We draw your attention to the necessity of developing work with regard to the counter-intelligence, this being a new but exceptionally important line for us.

In connection with this it is essential:

(1) To take measures for the recruitment of valuable agents who have access to enemy intelligence and counter-intelligence organizations and who have possibilities of supplying us with information concerning plans about subversive activities of the British-American bloc against the Soviet and the Peoples' Democracies.

(2) To put into effect active agent manoeuvres for the exposure of the channels of transmission of enemy agents, and also for the substitution of trusted agents to the Australian and British intelligence in order to intercept and to unmask enemy agents who are being, or have already been, sent to the Soviet and the Peoples' Democracies.

The Australian M.V.D. section must here and now take practical measures for the training of agents for work in extraordinary circumstances.

D.8

In the event of extraordinary circumstances each agent should have concrete tasks allotted in advance and firm conditions should be worked out for contact with our illegal or group leader. However, the cadre workers of the M.V.D. section should carry out this work gradually and in such a manner that, when these or other questions are discussed with agents, no panic should spread among them, and so that they should not interpret our preparations as a sign of inevitable war in the near future.

Side by side with the fulfilment of new tasks, more attention should be devoted to the improvement of the direction of the work of all active agents so as to secure the most effective exploitation of their capabilities and opportunities. For this purpose it is necessary to study deeply the personal qualities of agents and to prepare thoroughly for the carrying out of meetings with them. Work must go on continuously on the improvement of ways and means of contact with agents. You should strive especially to attain a reduction in personal meetings with an agent in the street.

For these purposes it is necessary to utilize not only secret hiding places for documents but also reception and transmission points, the organization of which is a pressing task for the M.V.D. section.

Taking into account the fact that the agents available to you cannot, according to their qualities and opportunities, execute the important tasks facing the M.V.D. section, you must now (at last) begin recruitment work. In the first place it is essential to avoid the recruitment of persons whose progressive activity is known to the counter-intelligence, and to concentrate attention on the study and recruitment of persons engaged on secret work of the government and occupying leading posts in political parties and organizations, capable of

D.9

supplying us with valuable information. The work of recruitment should be carried out boldly, with forethought and inventiveness.

The work of carrying into effect the tasks that have been set should be conducted with active, aggressive methods. All cadre workers should be imbued with a sense of responsibility for the work entrusted to them, and should manifest a maximum of creative inventiveness, perseverance and also boldness and decision in carrying out tasks which face the M.V.D. section. You must render timely assistance to cadre workers and at the same time you must resolutely combat any signs of a negligent attitude towards the work, of indecision, or of cowardice.

We understand that in the conditions now obtaining, when the whole burden of the work has fallen on you alone, it has been very difficult for you to conduct active intelligence work. Having taken this into consideration, we have arranged to direct to your M.V.D.

office two new cadre workers, one of whom, Antonov, is going out to you in the month of June to replace Pakhomov.

As Enclosure No. 3 (1) we send you the plan task for Antonov.

We hope that, by the efforts of all the workers of the M.V.D. section under your correct guidance, you will fulfil the tasks set before the M.V.D. section.

As Enclosure No. 1 (2) we send you the approved plan of work of the M.V.D. section for the period July 1952 to July 1953, which has been compiled with due regard for your proposals. When putting the plan into effect it is essential to direct workers of the M.V.D. section

---

(1) Enclosure No. 3 was given by Petrov to Antonov, and accordingly was not among the documents brought over by Petrov.

(2) Enclosure No. 1 was not brought over by Petrov, because it had to be kept with the ciphers (see Exhibit D.10): Transcript, 149 (342).

D.10

to acquire agents capable of performing our most important tasks.

For the purpose of effecting a daily and thorough control over the fulfilment of the plan, we authorize its retention in the M.V.D. section on the same terms as the ciphers.

Paragraph 2 of Letter No. 3 of 6 June 1952 to Canberra

CONCERNING MRS PETROV

In connection with the fact that Mrs Petrov is engaged on the ciphering, we agree with your proposal that we should limit ourselves to entrusting her with solely technical work in the M.V.D. section, and also with the fulfilment of separate tasks which have no connection with the entering into external contacts.

Mrs Petrov should not insist on an exchange of lessons with the wife of Body, since such persistence might alert the Body couple and might frighten them off from the continuation of your acquaintanceship with them.

According to information in our possession, Mrs Petrov occasionally shows a lack of tact in her relations with the employees of the Embassy, including the Ambassador, which cannot fail to have an adverse effect on her work. In this connection, we request you to administer an appropriate reprimand to her.

D.11

Paragraph 3 of Letter No. 3 of 6 June 1952 to Canberra

CONCERNING KOVALIEV

The information you have communicated concerning the behaviour of Kovaliev shows him in an unfavourable light. Warn Kovaliev once again about the inadmissibility of repeating such actions. It is evident from your report that you regard Kovaliev, basically, as an agent for S.K. work, which is completely wrong. You must draw him actively into the work of fulfilling the intelligence tasks. Compel him to draw up detailed reports concerning his contact along official lines and constantly assist him to study and select people who might be of interest to us.

Press for the establishment of an official contact between Kovaliev and Kosky for the purpose of studying the latter. After several meetings with Kosky we shall examine the question of establishing an agent relationship with him.

D.12

Paragraph 4 of Letter No. 3 of 6 June 1952 to Canberra

CONCERNING KHARKOVETZ

It is essential that Kharkovetz should be drawn more boldly into intelligence work. Entrust to him 2 or 3 concrete studies in accordance with the plan of work of the M.V.D. section, and teach him practical work, starting with the elementary principles of the conduct of intelligence work. At the same time continue to have talks with him in order to educate him as an intelligence worker. Advise him how best to rearrange his work so that he would be able to occupy himself with the acquisition of external contacts, without which the success of our work is inconceivable.

Keep us regularly informed concerning progress in the introduction of Kharkovetz into intelligence work.

Paragraph 5 of Letter No. 3 of 6 June 1952 to Canberra

As you yourself have now become convinced, Pakhomov conducted his work with Mme Ollier incorrectly: he did not set her intelligence tasks, and did not attain their fulfilment, in consequence of which he was not able to obtain from her secret information to

D.13

which she has access. His discussions with her were conducted in a purposeless manner and their meetings brought us no profit. Pakhomov stubbornly refused to carry out our instructions to obtain from her clarification concerning the ciphers. Also, he failed to come to an arrangement with her concerning permanent conditions of contact.

In entrusting you with work with Mme Ollier, we request you to bear in mind the errors committed by Pakhomov in work with her, and to direct your main attention and efforts to the receipt from Mme Ollier of information about the ciphers on which she works, and also of other secret information which passes through her hands.

In order to establish contact with her, exploit any suitable opportunity to become acquainted with her by making use of Pakhomov's name, and to come to an arrangement concerning a meeting in secret conditions.

At the first meeting explain to Mme Ollier that in connection with Pakhomov's departure from the country, you would like to continue to maintain a contact with her, and express the hope that she will go on helping us as before, and that we need this help. Tell her that, in so far as she has access to secret documents, she can render a considerable service to the cause of peace by giving us information concerning the machinations, behind the scenes, of the ruling circles of Britain, America, France, and Australia, directed against the Soviet and the Peoples' Democracies.

Come to an arrangement concerning subsequent meetings, which we recommend to be conducted not oftener than once in three or four weeks.

D.14

From the very first meeting with her, endeavour to establish good relations with her; since much will depend upon this in your further work with her. Prepare yourself well for the meeting.

We agree with your proposal to pay her a certain sum of money. We authorise you, at the opportune moment, to hand to Mme Ollier ₤75-0-0, using the justification that Pakhomov had told you about her financial difficulties and that you, having taken into account her good attitude towards us and the services she has rendered, decided to assist her financially. Give her to understand that, if she collaborates with us actively, she can always count on our help. At your first meeting with Mme Ollier explain to her that we are interested in the development of her contacts in the diplomatic corps, and in particular ask her to deepen her acquaintanceship with (°1).

We request you to display maximum caution in your work with Mme Ollier.

You should select, in advance, the places most suitable for conducting meetings, and thoroughly check when proceeding to the meetings and after meetings.

We request you to inform us briefly by cipher concerning the establishment of contact with her and concerning the results of the first meeting, and to send us a detailed report by mail.

Send us your proposals about work with Mme Ollier in every mail.

(°1) Here follow the names of four persons on the staffs of Diplomatic Missions of other countries which, for reasons of comity, we think it proper not to publish here. There is no suggestion in the Moscow Letter or elsewhere that any of them was in any way connected with espionage. Their names are set out in the Annexure to this Report.

D.15

(°1)

Paragraph 6 of Letter No. 3 of 6 June 1952 to Canberra

CONCERNING DAGHIAN

Notwithstanding the fact that Daghian is of great operational interest to us in the matter of obtaining auxiliary agents, study and cultivation of him has been conducted in a very weak manner. You should not limit yourself to simply having talks, as Pakhomov did in his meetings with Daghian. He must be gradually led up to the execution of separate assignments. For instance, he should be asked for information about conditions in the port, what is required for the opening of some small commercial enterprise, etc.

Detailed reports must be compiled concerning meetings with Daghian, in which should be included, alongside all the questions discussed at the meeting, an account of his behaviour, his reactions to the questions discussed, and also your conclusion concerning the meeting which has been transacted. The meetings should be carried out in accordance with the prepared plan, in which a term should be set for the completion of the study. The study of Daghian should be entrusted to a new cadre worker, who is to arrive soon in your M.V.D. section.

(°1) The following is the interpretation of a note handwritten on the original:
    'To Comrade Antonov. I am acquainted with the history of the matter and I will introduce you to him at the first opportunity.
3/7 Petrov'

D.16

(°1)

Paragraph 7 of Letter No. 3 of 6 June 1952 to Canberra

CONCERNING ANDERSON

We cannot agree with your opinion that the study and cultivation of Anderson should be terminated merely because he was not elected in the trade union and was left without work. Anderson is of undoubted interest, as he has friends among workers in institutions of the government. In our opinion, the study of Anderson should be continued, instead of merely observing and recording the changes in his situation, as you propose. This study will likewise be entrusted to a new cadre worker of the Australian M.V.D. section.

We request you to collect through the facilities at your disposal, and to transmit to us, information concerning the changes which have occurred in the leadership of the trade union in which Anderson worked.

Paragraph 8 of Letter No. 3 of 6 June 1952 to Canberra

CONCERNING HERBERT STANLEY NORTH (°2) (BORN IN 1920)

In 1947–1951 Herbert Stanley North (born in 1920), a native of Australia, worked in the Australian Embassy in Moscow in the capacity of cipher clerk and administrative clerk.

(°1) The following is the interpretation of a note handwritten on the original:
    'To Comrade Antonov
3/7 Petrov'
(°2) The following is handwritten on the original:
    'Nort Herbert Stanley'

D.17

From September 1939 until November 1945 North served in the Australian navy as a wireless operator. After demobilization he worked in the Taxation Department in the city of Perth.

According to agent information dated 1947–1948, North was described as ill-disposed to the Soviet.

North was on terms of friendship with a technician of the British Embassy, Gilmore, with clerks of the American Embassy, Powers and Crawford, in whose company he regularly visited restaurants and imbibed large quantities of alcoholic liquor.

After his marriage in 1949 to an employee of the New Zealand Consulate, Healy Ketlin, he ceased to visit restaurants, began to display an interest in Russian literature and art. According to the words of North's wife, his anti-Soviet utterances were the result of the negative influence exerted on him by the employees of the American Embassy, and after terminating his friendship with them he began to interest himself in Russian culture, and to study the Russian language.

In July 1951, North left Russia with his wife for Australia.

D.18

Bearing in mind that, during the latter part of North's stay in Russia he began to change his attitude towards the Soviet, and also that he worked in an institution of interest to us, we request you to try, through the means at your disposal, to locate him, to ascertain his employment and financial situation, and whether he comes out in public with his impressions concerning the Soviet, what is his present attitude to the Soviet, and also how to approach him.

Communicate to us any information that you may collect in relation to North as well as your proposals concerning the feasibility of studying and cultivating him.

Paragraph 9 of Letter No. 3 of 6 June 1952 to Canberra

There live in Australia a series of displaced persons and traitors of our native land, who conduct suspicious correspondence with their relatives and friends in the Soviet.

In their letters they show an interest in the fate of their relatives, and in the material situation of Russian people and their partici-pation in the political life of the country; they check the correctness of their relatives' addresses, express hope of a swift meeting with them, and ask that correspondence should be maintained in secret.

D.19

Such a correspondence is conducted by a certain John Rosser from Benova, Queensland; by Nicolai Vassilievich Klenov, born in 1918, residing in the town of Albany, who signed a letter under the name

Volovik; Vladimir Baskovsky, residing at the address Newport Hostel, Victoria (using this name is Vladimir Andreevich Krasilnikov, born in 1928, who deserted from the Russian Army, and fled to the British zone of occupation in Germany).

We presume that this correspondence is being conducted not without the knowledge of intelligence organizations. It is also possible that these people are being specially prepared for transmission to Russia.

We request you to collect information about these persons through means at your disposal, and in the event of receiving data concerning the departure of any of them from Australia, please notify us by cable.

Paragraph 10 of Letter No. 3 of 6 June 1952 to Canberra

At the present time there resides in the town of Brisbane at the address Ragner Rd., Hemmant, a certain A. I. Galeznik (Antony Chalesnik), who in April 1952 wrote a letter which he addressed to our government. In this letter Galeznik expressed a wish to hand himself over to the Soviet legal institutions as a criminal of the second world war. At the same time there is nothing said in the letter about the crimes committed or about the motives which prompted him to take this decision.

Galeznik is not in our books.

D.20 (°1)

(̇ 1) This document is a duplicate of D.19.

D.21

Please inform the Ambassador about this and send an official letter, as from the Embassy, to the stated address, in which letter you advise Galeznik to approach the Embassy direct in the matter which is of interest to him. If he agrees to visit the Embassy, then receive him in the capacity of an employee of the consular department and ascertain the basic facts of the case. In conversation try to ascertain information as to his whereabouts and also the reasons which have caused him to refer to Russia, by-passing the Soviet Embassy in Australia. At the same time it is necessary to observe caution and not to resort to any measures which might expose you as an intelligence worker.

Inform us by mail concerning the outcome.

Paragraph 11 of Letter No. 3 of 6 June 1952 to Canberra

In connection with the necessity of stirring up the work of compiling dossiers on governments and public and political persons of capitalist countries, you should systematically collect and dispatch to M.V.D. Headquarters both agent and official information on the following persons:(°)

(°) It is clear from internal evidence that the remaining pages of Exhibit D should be read in the order: D.23, D.24, D.22, D.26, D.25, D.27; and that Exhibit D is not complete (see footnotes to pages D.25 and D.27). As explained earlier, the documents brought by Petrov were photographed and numbered in the order in which they were received from him.

D.23

Menzies—Prime Minister—Leader of the Liberal Party.
Casey—Minister for External Affairs.
McDonald—Minister for Defence.
Francis—Minister for the Army and the Navy.
Fadden—Minister for Finance, leader of the National Party.
McKell—Governor General.
Williams—High Commissioner of Britain in Australia.
Evatt—Leader of the Labour Party.

Paragraph 12 of Letter No. 3 of 6 June 1952 to Canberra

CONCERNING SECRET HIDING PLACES FOR DOCUMENTS

The secret hiding places for documents selected by you have a number of defects. They are all located in one and the same area, which facilitates their detection by the counter-intelligence, even if you move from one secret hiding place to another.

The description of the secret hiding places for documents was not accompanied by sketches which would give a clear idea of the advantages and defects of the selected places, and of their exact location.

In our opinion, a crack between the boards, supporting the railway bridge embankment, cannot be used as a secret hiding place for documents, because the railway bridge is probably regularly inspected by the appropriate persons, and in exceptional circumstances might be guarded.

(°1)

(°1) The following is handwritten on the original:
'this bridge not across the river, but across the road.'

D.24

Insofar as the first two hiding places are situated close to one another, after having tested them in practice by inserting some articles into them (newspaper cuttings, cigarette packets, etc.), it should be determined which one of them is the more dependable and retain that one for possible use, having worked out an appropriate signalling for it. The other, less suitable, hiding place should be discarded.

As enclosure No. 2 we send you information which may assist you in the work of selecting and using secret hiding places for documents. After studying the document burn it in accordance with an act, and dispatch the act to M.V.D. Headquarters.

Paragraph 13 of Letter No. 3 of 6 June 1952 to Canberra

CONCERNING MOTOR CAR

In order to settle the question of the sale of the motor car which is in your possession, and of the acquisition of another more suitable one in its place, we request you to inform us what sum you require for the additional payment for a new motor car.

D.22

Paragraph 14 of Letter No. 3 of 6 June 1952 to Canberra

We request you to acquire and dispatch to us by the next mail two copies of official books of reference concerning Australian diplomats abroad and foreign representatives in Australia.

Vadim.

D.26

Enclosure No. 2 to Letter No. 3 of 6.6.52

CONCERNING THE USE OF SECRET HIDING PLACES FOR DOCUMENTS

For the purpose of rendering help to the cadre workers of the Australian M.V.D. section in the working out of more perfect conditions for impersonal contacts with agents through secret hiding places for documents, we consider it necessary to draw your attention to the more important questions of effecting impersonal communication with agents and at the same time ensuring the necessary secrecy.

In this connection it is necessary to refer to the advantages and weaknesses of secret hiding places for documents, their kinds and their purposes, the basic requirements which they must possess, the basic conditions for their use, and signalling in the utilization of them.

The advantages of secret hiding places for documents:
(1) A considerable secrecy is ensured in the organization of contacts: the number of personal meetings is reduced, which diminishes the possibilities of the contact being discovered by the counter-intelligence of the adversary, and consequently also the danger of exposure.

D.25

(2) It is possible to use a trusted person of the intelligence for extraction or insertion of information in the hiding place.
(3) It is also possible to use the hiding places for the creation of reserves of material resources for the conduct of intelligence work (money, operational techniques, etc.).

Defects:

(1) It decreases the opportunities for a personal study of the agent by the intelligence worker and for effecting the work of educating the agent.
(2) One cannot exclude the possibility of a chance discovery of the information by third parties, and also by the counter-intelligence. The latter might identify both the intelligence worker and the agent, and might also exploit the situation in order to mislead them.
(3) There is the possible danger that the information might be damaged or lost, as a result of natural calamities (fire, flood) or of its destruction by animals (rodents, etc.). (°)

(°) At least one page is missing between D.25 and D.27.

D.27

(2) For the transmission of negatives.
(3) For the transmission of bulky documents.
(4) For the long term storage of information (days, months).
(5) For the short term storage of information (a few hours).

Basic requirements which secret hiding places for documents must possess

(1) Each hiding place must in the first place fulfil its functional purpose, i.e. it should be of such a size that the necessary mail could be transmitted through it. Of course, one and the same hiding place can sometimes be used for different purposes. Nevertheless, the M.V.D. section must have the necessary number of hiding places for various purposes.
(2) When selecting hiding places it is necessary to pay heed to the special features of the situation in the area where it is installed. Hiding places should not be arranged in the vicinity of specially guarded objects, prohibited zones, observation posts of the counter-intelligence, military guardposts, etc. (°)

(°) At least one page is missing after D.27.

E.4

CANBERRA

TO PETROV

LETTER No. 4

POLITICAL

of 24 July 1952

E.5

Paragraph 1 of Letter No. 4 of 24 July 1952 to Canberra

(°1)

For the purposes of creating better conditions for combating the activities of foreign counter-intelligence organizations, which are aimed at impeding the work of Soviet intelligence workers, and also for the purposes of timely prevention of provocation and other active measures of the adversary to this end, you should:

(a) Establish personal contact with the military intelligence officer, Comrade A. A. Gordeev, inform him of the gist of information received concerning forthcoming changes in the situation, which might prove useful for his practical work, and also concerning the concrete measures adopted by the adversary in relation to him and his agents; jointly work out and adopt general counter-measures to safeguard advantages gained, and in cases of necessity to render each other assistance over the matter in question.

(b) To take measures to elucidate the activities of the counter-intelligence organizations of the adversary in Australia, using for this purpose all the available agent resources and potentialities.

(c) When effecting contact, it is strictly forbidden for you to disclose the identities of the personnel of your M.V.D. section, of your agents, of the plans of work and the plan-tasks set by M.V.D. Headquarters.

(°1) 'Destroy' is handwritten on the original.

E.6

(°1)

In the operational reports of the M.V.D. section reference should be made to any effecting of contact with the military intelligence officer.

Corresponding instructions are being sent to Comrade Gordeev through his channels.(°2)

Paragraph 2 of Letter No. 4 of 24 July 1952 to Canberra

On the 17th October this year, in New York, the 7th Session of the General Assembly of the United Nations opens. For the purposes of successfully carrying out the preparatory work for the organizing of operational cover of the Session, and for uncovering the plans of the American-British bloc relating to the conduct of it, M.V.D. Headquarters is interested in the collection and timely acquisition of authentic information concerning the following questions:

(1) Concerning the attitude of the governments concerned on the questions of the provisional agenda of the Session and concerning the intention of the governments to table any particular questions for discussion by the Session.

(2) Detailed biographical particulars concerning the members of the delegation, the employees on the technical staff and correspondents who are sent to attend the Session.

---

(1) 'Destroy' is handwritten on the original.
(2) The following typewritten sentence has been struck out of the original document:
'These directions should be destroyed after you have become familiar with them. Report concerning their destruction, in accordance with the act, to M.V.D. Headquarters.'

E.7

(3) Helpful particulars concerning all persons on the staff of the delegation and of the technical staff establishment who are of operational interest to us.
(4) Concerning correspondence of members of the delegations to the Session with the appropriate departments of external affairs, and concerning instructions to the members during the course of the Session for the whole duration of the sittings of the General Assembly.
(5) Concerning the reactions of the ruling circles of the country where you sojourn to the speeches and proposals of the Soviet delegation.

It is desirable that you should take all measures in your power and endeavour to acquire information of interest to us. For this purpose we advise you to make appropriate use of the potentialities of Mme Ollier, O'Sullivan, and Chiplin, and also to attempt the exploitation of Body 'in the dark'.

Paragraph 3 of Letter No. 4 of 24 July 1952 to Canberra

Your letter no. 3 of 7th July of this year is very short and laconic. In it you give no information about the work being conducted by you and do not touch upon a single substantial question of the work of your M.V.D. section. In particular, you

E.8

do not write anything about the measures taken by you to establish contact with Mme Ollier, about work with Kovaliev, Kharkovetz, and others, you do not notify any particulars concerning Kastalsky, which were promised in your cable, and you do not write to say how Antonov has settled down, etc.

We request you to give us detailed information in your letters concerning the operational work of the Australian M.V.D. section and to put up concrete proposals aimed at the improvement of the intelligence work in the fulfilment of the tasks facing your M.V.D. section.

Paragraph 4 of Letter No. 4 of 24 July 1952 to Canberra

CONCERNING O'SULLIVAN

In reply to your paragraph 3 of Letter No. 3 of 7.7.52

We regard the study and cultivation of O'Sullivan as very full of promise, and therefore, with the object of enforcing it, we request you to include Antonov in this work as soon as possible. It is essential to verify the data supplied by O'Sullivan about himself and about his father. In so far as this is feasible, try to do this through Chiplin. A verification is being carried out by us in England; we shall inform you of the outcome.

E.9

In order not to draw the attention of the counter-intelligence to him, we advise that O'Sullivan should not be invited any more to the Embassy and that meetings with him should be transferred to the city, all the more so as he has already secretly met Pakhomov.

We consider that, by continuing to study and verify O'Sullivan, you can already draw him gradually into our work by way of putting before him concrete tasks which he is in a position to fulfil.

It is desirable that, when a suitable opportunity offers, you should ask him to compile for us a survey concerning the economic, political, and military penetration of Australia by America, with the inclusion of unofficial data. Warn O'Sullivan that his survey will not be published in the press and that it is required by you for your personal use. Promise him that the time spent by him on the preparation of this survey will be compensated by you.

Ascertain also whether O'Sullivan has contacts with circles pertaining to the government, the parliament, and business, and also in Liberal Party, Country Party, and Labour Party circles.

We request you to inform us in detail in every letter concerning progress in the study and cultivation of O'Sullivan.

E.10

Paragraph 5 of Letter No. 4 of 24 July 1952 to Canberra

As Enclosure No. 1(°1) we send you particulars concerning two members of the Australian delegation which was in Russia for the First of May festivities—Flood and Lewis. Both of them, in our opinion, could be used for the fulfilment of tasks which are provided for in the plan of work of the Australian M.V.D. section.

Instruct Antonov to make the acquaintance of Flood and Lewis for the purpose of studying them and (°2) using them along our lines.

Inform us concerning the results.(°3)

Paragraph 6 of Letter No. 4 of 24 July 1952 to Canberra

On suspicion of contact with the American counter-intelligence, M.V.D. Headquarters had under surveillance an immigrant Galina Mikhailovna Popova (formerly Egupova), a woman born in 1911 in the town of Tomsk, and residing until the year 1949 in Japan.

At the end of 1945 Popova became the pretended wife of a white emigre, Alexandr Vasilievich Grey (real name Serapinin). He arrived in Japan in 1945 among the personnel of the British-American Armies, with the rank of Captain of the Australian Army. In 1947 he was demobilized from the Australian Army, and he transferred to service in the American counter-intelligence in Japan.

(°1) Enclosure No. 1 was given by Petrov to Antonov, and accordingly was not among the documents brought over by Petrov.

(°2) In the original the word 'and' is struck out and the word 'for' is written above it.

(°3) The following is the interpretation of a note handwritten on the original: 'enclosure in Antonov's package'.

E.11

Despite the fact that Grey has a wife and grown-up son in Australia, he cohabited for a long time with Popova and proposed to her to transfer to Australia, whither Popova travelled at the end of 1949.

The address of Popova in Australia is not known. It is possible that she is staying at the house of Grey, who was living at Sydney at the address: In Endeavour Street, West Road.

We request that, if it should prove possible, you should establish the whereabouts of Popova in Australia and inform us of the results of your inquiries by mail.

Vadim.

A.6

(°1)

Paragraph 1 of Letter No. 5 of 27 September 1952 to Canberra

CONCERNING KISLYTSIN

The sending to you of cadre worker Kislytsin gives you an opportunity of considerably stirring up and extending the activity of the Australian section of the M.V.D.

Kislytsin is a cadre worker of the M.V.D., he is familiar with work in conditions abroad, has a command of the English language, and is fully trained for carrying out intelligence work. As Enclosure No. 1 to this Letter we send you a task plan for Kislytsin (°2). Your immediate task is to assist Kislytsin to study the situation as quickly as possible and to direct his efforts to obtaining useful contacts. In the first instance Kislytsin must be instructed to engage in the selection and study of persons who could assist the entry and settling of our illegal workers in the country, and also the study and cultivation of persons who might be of use to the M.V.D. connected with the diplomatic corps and parliament whose names have been received from Pakhomov and are listed in the attached task plan.

Upon Kislytsin's arrival acquaint him once again with the task plan and with the plan of work of the Australian section of the M.V.D., tell him in detail about the situation in the country, and give him the necessary advice and directions for the execution of the tasks which have been set before him.

---

(1) The following is handwritten on the original:
'The first page of Letter No. 5 was not printed.'
This apparently refers to the title page of the Letter, in form similar to Exhibits B.3, C.2, D.5, and E.4.
(2) Enclosure No. 1 was given by Petrov to Kislytsin, and accordingly was not among the documents brought over by Petrov.

A.7

If any additional proposals occur to you regarding Kislytsin's task plan, we ask you to inform us about them in the next mail.

Paragraph 2 of Letter No. 5 of 27 September 1952 to Canberra

CONCERNING ANTONOV

Antonov acted correctly in sending information about his first acquaintances and in notifying us about the difficulties encountered. Both we and you must deal attentively and tactfully with his first independent steps in practical intelligence work, since upon the correct beginning of this work depends its further success. Antonov is going through a difficult time now, and our task and yours consists in helping him to assess correctly his first acquaintances, among whom there may prove to be not a few local counter-intelligence agents and importunate 'friends' of the type of Stanley.

About Stanley (in future referred to as Stepan): it is known that he is a drunkard and that he has contacts in the counter-intelligence. In the past he associated with Nosov, but he avoided association with Pakhomov. Consequently the appearance of Stanley in Antonov's quarters as from the first days of his stay in the country, and also Stanley's obtrusiveness, cause suspicion and compel us to treat him with special caution.

A.8

We share your and Antonov's opinion that Stanley is apparently engaged in the study of Antonov. Warn Antonov once again that he should be cautious with Stanley, but that he should not avoid such association as is necessary within the compass of his official position.

With reference to other persons among Antonov's first acquaintances, with the exception of M. Kent Hughes, it is not yet possible to say anything definite in the absence of adequate information about them. M. Kent Hughes behaved in friendly fashion towards Pakhomov, and she is appraised favourably by him. It seems to us that she might be useful for acquiring 'in the dark' acquaintances and necessary (1) information. Conversations with her on subjects of interest to us should not be held in Antonov's quarters.

Advise Antonov to continue to extend his contacts, in the first instance among the political correspondents and among members of the parliament, ignoring any embarrassment through temporary difficulties in the spoken language.

With the object of the successful execution of this task we recommend that Antonov should take measures to establish contact with— (2), with O'Sullivan,—(2) and—(2), whose personality reports, with the exception of O'Sullivan who is known to you, we send in Enclosure No. 2.

We request you to tell Antonov that he should henceforth report to us in detail concerning his study of the situation in the country and concerning the contacts obtained by him, and that he should put forward concrete proposals regarding the study and cultivation of prospective contacts with the object of recruitment.

---

(1) 'in the dark' is handwritten on the original.
(2) The three names here omitted are included in the 'Enclosure No. 2' referred to in this paragraph. For reasons which we have stated elsewhere, we do not publish that Enclosure here.

A.9

Paragraph 3 of Letter No. 5 of 27 September 1952 to Canberra

CONCERNING KOVALIEV

The personality reports submitted by Kovaliev concerning persons with whom he has established contact testify that he is beginning to engage in our work. However, apparently as a result of the absence of positive guidance on your part, Kovaliev has dealt perfunctorily with the production of the personality reports, since he has omitted essential data which were known to him about those persons. In particular, he did not mention the bankruptcy of the firm of Arup and the legal case connected with it, and also the connection of White and Keesing with the Communist Party.

You should instruct Kovaliev in detail how he is to conduct the study of contacts and to extend contacts. In our opinion, among his contacts R. Kirk represents the greatest interest. Help Kovaliev to study the potentialities of R. Kirk for work along our lines, and his personal qualities, with the aim of determining the expediency of his recruitment.

Kovaliev's contacts, about which you notified us in Enclosure to Letter No. 4, do go through our books.

It would be desirable to obtain copies of the next issues of the periodical 'Technical Review'.

Please keep us informed about the work and conduct of Kovaliev.

A.10

At the same time we request you to let us know what measures you have taken to establish official contact of Kovaliev with Kosky.

Paragraph 4 of Letter No. 5 of 27 September 1952 to Canberra

CONCERNING KHARKOVETZ

It is clear from your reports that Kharkovetz is manifestly evading the execution of our task. It would appear that you are not able to put yourself in such a position that he should see in you a representative of the M.V.D. It is essential that you should achieve such a position that Kharkovetz would adopt a fully responsible attitude towards his obligation to assist us. Be more insistent in drawing Kharkovetz into our work, initially entrusting him with small tasks which he would be able to execute.

Paragraph 5 of Letter No. 5 of 27 September 1952 to Canberra

In order to expose and suppress the subversive activities of the American intelligence and counter-intelligence organizations against the Soviet, we request you to begin the systematic collection of information in accordance with the following specimen questionnaire:

A.11

(1)

1. Location and names of the intelligence or counter-intelligence organizations of the American intelligence and schools, their functions, structure, personnel, and practical activities.
2. Form and methods of work of the intelligence organization (agent cadres, methods of recruitment and training of agents, equipment, cover stories (2), tasks, documentation of cover stories (3), places and means of transferring (4) of agents, channels of penetration into the Soviet and the Peoples' Democracies, (5) methods of contacts with agents, etc.).
3. Co-ordination of activities of the intelligence and counter-intelligence organizations, names and functions of the co-ordinating organization, and its personnel.
4. Training of cadre intelligence workers (schools, their names, addresses, procedure for enrolment, training programme).
5. Training of agent cadres in America and in other capitalist countries, the availability of schools for training saboteurs and terrorists, (6) methods of transferring (4) agents into the Soviet and the Peoples' Democracies (5).
6. Data about the use made by the American intelligence of 'displaced persons', emigre organizations, former cadres of German and Japanese intelligence services, Trotskyists, and Titoites, (7) in intelligence work against the Soviet and the Peoples' Democracies.

The following words and phrases are handwritten on the original in the places indicated:

(1) 'Paragraph 5 of Letter No. 5 of 27/ix/52'
(2) 'cover stories'
(3) 'of cover stories'
(4) 'transferring'
(5) 'countries of the peoples' democracies'
(6) 'saboteurs and terrorists'
(7) 'Trotskyists'

A.12

7. Data concerning official (°1) collaborators and technical workers of intelligence and counter-intelligence organizations and schools (the position occupied, the nature of the work carried out, nationality, citizenship, family status, financial standing, home address, way of life, personal qualities and inclinations, traits of character, political views, connections, distinguishing marks, etc.).

8. Locations of intelligence organizations and schools (exact address and description of location), lay-out of rooms, entrances, windows, tables, safes and other depositories of secret documents in buildings occupied by an intelligence organization. (It is desirable for a plan to be drawn.)

9. The security system of the buildings of the intelligence organization (plan of disposition of guard posts), means of communication of the intelligence organization (numbers and disposition of telephones, presence of special signalling apparatus, radio stations, etc.), types and numbers of motor cars used by intelligence workers.

10. Data concerning secret meeting houses (addresses, description of location, internal lay-out) and their proprietors.

11. Data concerning drivers, boilermen, office cleaners, waiters, and other staff serving the intelligence organization and its employees.(°2)

(°1) 'official' is handwritten on the original.
(°2) It is clear from internal evidence that page 12 to 15 inclusive of Exhibit A should be read in the order: A.12, A.14, A.13, A.15.

A.14

12. Data concerning the principal foreign centres and secret sections of intelligence organizations of America, names and personality details of their chiefs, staff and personnel of these intelligence centres.

13. Data concerning the organization of contacts with intelligence sections and agents (mail, storage, use of agent ciphers, methods of protection, personal and impersonal contact, secret hiding places for documents, etc.).

14. Data concerning tasks set by American intelligence organizations to their secret sections and agents abroad as regards the acquisition of information concerning the Soviet and the Peoples' Democracies.

15. Data concerning the co-ordination of the activities of the American intelligence with the intelligence organizations of other countries.
    Notify us about the information acquired by you.

A.13

Paragraph 6 of Letter No. 5 of 27 September 1952 to Canberra

According to agent information in our possession, the Canadian counter-intelligence has worked out and sent to the counter-intelligence of the participating countries of the so-called 'special information committee' (S.I.C.) a plan of control over the purchases of strategic materials by trade representatives of the Soviet and the Peoples' Democracies, for the exploitation of these representatives and for undertaking economic sabotage against the Soviet and the Peoples' Democracies.

A.15

The plan provides for recruitment of the directors of trading companies or the creation of fictitious trading companies from among the employees of the counter-intelligence. These companies will have the task of gaining the confidence of the representatives of the Soviet and the Peoples' Democracies, and of becoming intermediaries in trade transactions so as to be informed regarding all purchases of strategic materials.

The Canadian counter-intelligence considers that the creation of this type of intelligence agent will enable it not only to discover the methods of work of the trade representatives of the Soviet and the Peoples' Democracies, but also to improve the exploitation of these representatives, and to be informed of the attitude of their employees, bearing in mind their recruitment, the possibility of compromising them, or any tendency on their part not to return home.

It would appear that the Canadian counter-intelligence has already begun to put its plan into effect in relation to Poland.

For the purpose of co-ordinating these sorts of activities of the counter-intelligence of the countries participating in the S.I.C., the Canadian counter-intelligence suggests the organization of a special Bureau. Nothing is yet known about the attitude of other countries towards this project.

We request you to take this information into account in the course of your work, and to take possible measures for its verification. Please inform us if you should receive data confirming the information given above.

A.16

Paragraph 7 of Letter No. 5 of 27 September 1952 to Canberra

The information set out in para. 7 of your Letter No. 4 of 28.8.52, should have been notified to us by you by cable. Please take this into consideration and in future inform us immediately about similar happenings.

We agree that Antonov should not go any more to the editorial office of the 'Tribune'.(1). In so far as materials supplied by the Information Bureau and Photo Chronicle(°2) through Tass, intended for the Australian press, are official(°3) and are examined by censorship(°4) upon receipt, it appears expedient to us that Antonov should come to an arrangement with the editorial office of the 'Tribune'(5) that a technical worker should be sent to him for such material when necessary.

Paragraph 8 of Letter No. 5 of 27 September 1952 to Canberra

CONCERNING ANDERSON

(Reply to para. 2 of your Letter No. 4 of 28/8/52)

The bringing about of an acquaintanceship between Antonov and Anderson should not be postponed.

You must take measures to ensure that this acquaintanceship comes into being in the immediate future and that Antonov actively engages himself in the study of Anderson.

The following words and phrases are handwritten on the original at the places indicated:

(1) 'edit. of the Tribune'
(2) 'inform. bureau and photo chr.'
(3) 'offic.'
(4) 'censorship'
(5) 'editorial office Tr.'

A.17

Paragraph 9 of Letter No. 5 of 27 September 1952 to Canberra

CONCERNING BODY
(IN FUTURE GOST)

Taking into consideration the guarded attitude of Body and the conditions which have arisen in the Department of External Affairs, we consider that you should not now for the time being insist on unofficial meetings with him. However, with the opening of the fishing season, try to invite Body again for a fishing trip with the object of promoting a closer contact with him. In conversation with Body you should elucidate in a cautious manner questions of interest to us concerning conditions in the Department of External Affairs, personality reports about Australian delegates in international organizations and at conferences, etc.

Keep us informed about the development of your contact with Body. Please also send us information about meetings with him.

Paragraph 10 of Letter No. 5 of 27 September 1952 to Canberra

(°1)

---

(1) This paragraph relates to a member of the staff of a foreign Diplomatic Mission to whom we have referred in Chapters 10 and 11 of our Report. We set the paragraph out, and report on it, in the Annexure hereto.

A.18

Paragraph 11 of Letter No. 5 of 27 September 1952 to Canberra

CONCERNING INFORMATION ABOUT PERSONS WHO MIGHT BE OF USE
TO THE M.V.D.

As Enclosure No. 2 to this Letter we are sending you information about persons who might be of use to the M.V.D. taken from Pakhomov's report.

Please acquaint Antonov and Kislytsin with them. We consider that the basic work in the study of parliamentary correspondents and members of the parliament, indicated in the Enclosure, should be conducted by Antonov.

We recommend that you should personally undertake the study of Doctor Max Stephens. You yourself may become acquainted with him by approaching him for a medical consultation.

A.19

Paragraph 12 of Letter No. 5 of 27 September 1952 to Canberra

(°1)

(°1)—This paragraph relates to a member of the staff of a foreign Diplomatic Mission to whom we have referred in Chapter 11 of our Report. We set the paragraph out, and report on it, in the Annexure hereto.

A.20

Paragraph 13 of Letter No. 5 of 27 September 1952 to Canberra

H. Shaker lives in Australia at the address: Footscray, Melbourne. According to data in our possession, Shaker, a member of the Communist Party, whilst living in Egypt, conducted Communist Party propaganda among the workers, and at one time he was manager of the 'Sabahi' factory. In 1948, as a result of persecution by the Egyptian authorities, he left on a false passport for Australia, where he is working in a factory in the town of Melbourne. At the present time there has arisen the necessity to locate him.

Without revealing Shaker's Communist Party membership, please ask Jean Ferguson, by making use of available possibilities in Melbourne, to locate Shaker on the first suitable occasion, and to collect personality data about him and, if possible, about his relatives resident in Egypt.

If this scheme proves unsuitable, think of some other way of acquiring information of interest to us concerning Shaker. However, our cadre workers should not travel to Melbourne specially for the execution of this task.

Notify the results of the search by mail.

Paragraph 14 of Letter No. 5 of 27 September 1952 to Canberra

In answer to your request we inform you that Ratnavel does not appear in our books.

A.21

Paragraph 15 of Letter No. 5 of 27 September 1952 to Canberra

CONCERNING THE MOTOR CAR

In the interest of our work we consider it more expedient to place the motor car of the Australian section of the M.V.D. at the disposal of Antonov. He should obtain a driving licence in the near future, and should use the car for operational purposes.

You, as you informed us, have an opportunity of using the motor car of the Embassy. Therefore if you come to an agreement with the Ambassador by which you secure for your use one of the Embassy cars, then the question of transport for the M.V.D. section can be considered settled.

In view of the fact that you do not hold a driving licence, we advise you not to use the motor car of the M.V.D. section, in order to avoid possible provocation.

Vadim.

A.22. A.23. A.24

Enclosure No. 3 to Letter No. 5 of 27 September 1952 to Canberra

(°1)

(°1) This Enclosure relates to the member of the staff of the foreign Diplomatic Mission referred to in paragraph 12 (Exhibit A.19) of this Letter, and accordingly we do not publish it here. We set out the Enclosure, and report on it, in the Annexure hereto.

A.25–A.29

Enclosure No. 2 to Letter No. 5 of 27 September 1952

(°1)

(°1) This Enclosure comprises pages 25 to 32 inclusive of Exhibit A. In A.25 to A.30 inclusive there are set out personality reports, based on Exhibit H, on named journalists. For reasons stated in our Report we do not publish those pages here, but we include them in the Annexure. A.31 includes a reference to a member of the staff of a Diplomatic Mission which, for reasons of comity, we do not publish here but include in the Annexure. The remaining portions of the Enclosure are set out on the three following pages of this Appendix, and are dealt with in our Report.

A.30

Russell is a member of the Parliament, a labour supporter. In conversations with Pakhomov he displayed an interest in the life of Russia and expressed

A.31

a desire to visit the Soviet. He once listened attentively to Root, who expressed himself favourably about the changes in Russia, in the upbringing of the new generation and in the building projects. He is critical of the internal and foreign policy of the Australian Government.

Russell is of interest for further study.

Max Stephens is a doctor of medicine, a Polish Jew, Australian citizen. He lives in Sydney, has a surgery in an outer suburb of the city. He is easy going, especially when intoxicated. He asked Pakhomov to approach him for help if Pakhomov should need any assistance. Evidently this was caused by Stephens's fears that Pakhomov knew that Stephens had issued a fictitious medical certificate to Nosov in return for a bribe. As a doctor he enjoys a good reputation. He is of operational interest to us. It is expedient that study should be conducted with a view to recruitment in the capacity of owner of a secret meeting house.

His address is 54 Lions Road, Drummoyne.

A.32

Senator McCallum is a member of the parliamentary Foreign Affairs Committee. He is a member of the Liberal Party, a reactionary. He is sociable, but at the same time haughty. As a result of discussions with him, Pakhomov formed the opinion that Senator McCallum has a poor knowledge of international policy, despite the fact that he is an adviser on international policy. He knows practically nothing about the Soviet and about the Peoples' Democracies.

In conversation with Pakhomov, Senator McCallum asked many questions about the Soviet, the state structure, constitution, the legal system, elections, etc., which demonstrates his desire to know more about the Soviet.

In reply to Pakhomov's questions he sometimes gave answers which threw light on the position of the Australian government in international affairs.

It would be expedient to establish a contact with him with a view to obtaining from him 'in the dark' information on questions of foreign policy.

F.3

CANBERRA

TO Comrade PETROV

LETTER No. 6/0

25 November 1952

Paragraph 1 of Letter No. 6/0 of 25 November 1952 to Canberra

We acknowledge receipt of your Letter No. 5 of 29 October with all the Enclosures.

Paragraph 2 of Letter No. 6/0 of 25 November 1952 to Canberra

As Enclosure No. 1 we send you instructions concerning the procedure of correspondence of the Australian section of the M.V.D. with M.V.D. Headquarters and of formulation, registration and the transmission of operational mail.

The present instruction should be in the personal charge of the chief of the Australian section of the M.V.D.

F.4

Paragraph 3 of Letter No. 6/0 of 25 November 1952 to Canberra

CONCERNING YOUR REPORT ABOUT THE SITUATION

In the first place we draw your attention to the fact that the report was drawn up sketchily and superficially, and does not contain the detailed information about the situation in Australia which is really indispensable to us.

The individual questions were not separated in the report. The fundamental questions, to which you devoted attention, questions concerning citizenship and procedure concerning entry, were set out unsystematically.

We draw your attention to the fact that it is impossible to state the situation in any country on six pages. When compiling a report you should be guided by the list of subjects which you have in your M.V.D. section.

We cannot accept the report sent by you as the execution by your M.V.D. section of the task set by M.V.D. Headquarters for making such a report, the time limit for which expired in October of this year.

We request you to commence the systematic collection of material concerning the situation, and to send us a report in instalments, as and when the separate sections are ready.

F.5

Paragraph 4 of Letter No. 6/0 of 25 November 1952 to Canberra

CONCERNING KHARKOVETZ

As you know, Kharkovetz has quite wide contacts in diplomatic and press circles of Canberra. However, these contacts of his have not been studied or gone into more deeply merely because they did not interest him personally, and because you did not draw his attention to this at the proper time.

You should daily render him practical assistance and draw him more actively into operational work.

We request you to instruct Kharkovetz to compile for us a full list of his contacts, indicating all the data which are known to him about them.

In further work recommend to him that he should deepen cultivation of contacts, especially in the American and British Embassies, and should begin a more thorough study of Yuill.

We request you to let us know your proposals for increasing the activities of Kharkovetz.

Paragraph 5 of Letter No. 6/0 of 25 November 1952 to Canberra

CONCERNING INTRODUCTION OF CURRENCY RE-VALUATION FOR POUND STERLING

We have learned that in Australian government circles it is expected that currency re-valuation for pound sterling will be introduced in 1952, in which connection Australia intends to change the rate of exchange of her currency.

F.6

The question of re-valuation was being discussed at a consultation of Commonwealth experts who during the course of September-October of this year were preparing recommendations for the forthcoming conference of Commonwealth Prime Ministers.

At this consultation the representatives of Canada and Australia insisted on re-valuation at the end of 1952. However, because of the opposition of the British it was decided at the consultation to recommend that the question of re-valuation should be considered at the coming conference of Commonwealth Prime Ministers in the middle of 1953.

In communicating the above material for your information, we request you to ensure that the information relating to this question is obtained.

Paragraph 6 of Letter No. 6/0 of 25 November 1952 to Canberra

CONCERNING NICOLAI KIRILLOVICH NOVIKOFF AND NICOLAI NICOLAEVICH NOVIKOFF

In February 1951 and March 1952 you were given assignments to collect personality reports on Nicolai Kirillovich Novikoff and Nicolai Nicolaevich Novikoff.

During the intervening time we have received from you only one brief report concerning N. N. Novikoff, compiled by Pakhomov. From Pakhomov's account it is evident that you know N. K. Novikoff and N. N. Novikoff, and that you had meetings comparatively often with N. K. Novikoff.

Pakhomov informed you about the statement of I. A. Smirnoff concerning the fact that he saw N. K. Novikoff in the Central Building of the Criminal Investigation Department.

F.7

Up till now you have not sent one single report about meetings with N. K. Novikoff, and it is not clear to us what you are doing in relation to him and N. N. Novikoff, and particularly what you have undertaken for re-checking information concerning the contact of N. K. Novikoff with the Criminal Investigation Department.

We request you to hasten the fulfilment of the instructions of Letter No. 2 of 12 March of this year concerning the collection of full personality reports about N. K. Novikoff and N. N. Novikoff. In the first place, ascertain the existence and nature of N. K. Novikoff's contact with the Criminal Investigation Department, and also the circle of N. N. Novikoff's acquaintances, and his past.

We ask you to communicate by the next mail the information collected and your concrete proposals concerning work with them.

Paragraph 7 of Letter No. 6/0 of 25 November 1952 to Canberra

CONCERNING REX CHIPLIN

In connection with the measures which you know to have been taken by the counter-intelligence against Rex Chiplin, we request you to exercise maximum caution in further work with him.

We consider that, apart from Antonov, none of our cadre workers should have meetings with Chiplin.

Antonov should reduce to a minimum his meetings with Chiplin in the press gallery and other places, and should only accept information from him in fully advantageous conditions.

F.8

When receiving information you should ascertain and inform us about the source from whom Chiplin receives information, and not merely its contents, as you did when dealing with the question of exchange of enciphered material between the governments of Australia and America.

Paragraph 8 of Letter No. 6/0 of 25 November 1952 to Canberra

CONCERNING F. J. MCLEAN

In the last post you informed us about the taking of measures with regard to increasing the activities of F. J. McLean. At the same time you sent us a list of responsible employees of the Department of External Affairs, on which McLean's name did not appear, despite the fact that for a period of several years he did figure on the list.

In this connection we request you to clarify, in a cautious manner, whether McLean is working in the Department of External Affairs at the present time, in what capacity, and what is the reason for his exclusion from the list. If he does not work there, then endeavour to ascertain his new place of work, the reason for his transfer, and other questions of interest to us concerning him, and especially whether this is connected with measures taken in the Department of External Affairs after the article which Chiplin published.

Inform us by the next mail concerning the results and also your proposals for increasing the activities of McLean. We request you to report also whether he attended the last big Reception in our Embassy.

F.9

Paragraph 9 of Letter No. 6/0 of 25 November 1952 to Canberra

CONCERNING A. Y. VASILIEV (further referred to as KUSTAR)

As is known to you, Vasiliev repeatedly told a number of Soviet official representatives about the possession of the secret of producing hard-wearing aviation bearings.

According to his statement the limit of the wear of aviation bearings produced at his factory was three to four times greater than that of the English and American ones. He allegedly declined to hand this secret on to the British and the Americans, despite repeated proposals, and he expressed a desire to pass it on to Russia.

It is difficult for us at the present time to decide whether the technology of manufacture of these aviation bearings is of interest to us. In order to be able to come to a final decision on this matter, we request you to obtain from Vasiliev and dispatch to us the technology of manufacture, and one or two samples, of the bearings.

In order to carry out the above measures and to determine the expediency of further work with Vasiliev, we request that it should be ascertained from him in a cautious manner whether he is the subject of the data, relating to the activities of a certain A. Y. Vasiliev in fascist organizations in Manchuria, about which you were informed in the E. M. line of work.

We ask you to bear in mind that, as a result of his frequent association with the Russians, Vasiliev is evidently under the surveillance of the counter-intelligence. This can be particularly judged by the fact that the meeting of Pakhomov and Vasiliev in Melbourne in June of this year

F.10

was for a period of two days under the uninterrupted observation of Holden motor cars S. F. 527 and S. F. 529.

Paragraph 10 of Letter No. 6/0 of 25 November 1952 to Canberra
(ᵒ 1)

CONCERNING KAZANOVA

We request you to report to us by the next mail all the information known to you concerning Kazanova, who figures in the consular files in connection with her last will and testament, and about her relatives in Russia.

As is known to you, she devised her house in favour of the Soviet, having lost all hope of making a trip to her children and grand-children in Russia.

According to her statements, her repeated pleas to her relatives to send one of her grandchildren from Russia to look after her until her death and to receive her small inheritance met with a refusal on the part of her relatives.

Depending on the availability of full particulars concerning Kazanova (1) and her relatives in Russia, we shall weigh the question of sending to Australia one of our cadre workers as an illegal worker, under the guise of a relative of Kazanova.

In connection with this we request you to visit Kazanova (`1) under a plausible pretext (`2) and to elucidate questions which are of interest to us,

---

(°1) 'Kazanova' is handwritten on the original.
(°2) 'Visit under a plausible pretext' is handwritten on the original.

F.11

especially, which of her relatives (1) resides (`2) in Russia and where, with whom does she correspond (3), does she possess any photo-graphs of her relatives, does she know them so as to recognize them by sight (°4), when did she receive the last mail, etc.

Together with Kislytsin consider measures that can be taken in this matter, and let us know your proposals.

Paragraph 11 of Letter No. 6/0 of 25 November 1952 to Canberra

We request you to hasten the fulfilment of paragraph 4 of Letter No. 2 of 12 March 1952. (`5)

Paragraph 12 of Letter No. 6/0 of 25 November 1952 to Canberra

CONCERNING THE MOTOR CAR

Both you and Antonov knew the cover story for the purchase of the motor car. In accordance with this cover story all the employees of the Embassy, Pakhomov's acquaintances, and the counter-intelligence have every reason for considering the car to be the property of the Tass agency. The authorization for the purchase of the motor car was given in an unciphered communication in the name of the directorate of the Tass agency. Therefore,

---

The following words are written on the original at the places indicated:
(°1) 'relatives'
(2) 'resides'
(°3) 'corresp'
(4) 'by face'
(5) '(search for Shirokhikh)'

F.12

Antonov's statement to the Ambassador that he knows nothing about the motor car, that no one told him anything about it in the

Tass agency, and that the motor car belonged personally to Pakhomov (which you likewise confirmed to the Ambassador),—we consider to be an infringement of the rules of secrecy, which occurred because of an oversight on your part. Your and Antonov's statement to the Ambassador caused the exposure of Pakhomov as our cadre worker.

In the situation which has now arisen, the motor car should be left in Canberra and it should be used for operational purposes after you or Kislytsin have obtained a driving licence.

Taking into consideration Antonov's statement that he refuses to take the car because he is afraid to drive a motor car in Sydney, we recommend to Antonov that, pending a final decision, he should take a course of driving lessons and that for this purpose he should use £15 out of the resources of your M.V.D. section.

Paragraph 13 of Letter No. 6/0 of 25 November 1952 to Canberra

In Enclosure No. 2 we send you 50 metres of undeveloped films.

Vadim.

F.13

Enclosure No. 1 to Letter No. 6/0 of 25 November 1952 to Canberra

No. 1

CONCERNING THE PROCEDURE OF CORRESPONDENCE OF THE AUSTRALIAN SECTION OF THE M.V.D. WITH M.V.D. HEADQUARTERS, AND THE FORMULATION, REGISTRATION, AND TRANSMISSION OF OPERATIONAL MAIL

The present instruction lays down the following procedure of correspondence, formulation, registration, and transmission of operational mail.

I. *Kinds of operational mail*

All operational correspondence is divided into very secret mail and less secret mail.

(1) Very secret mail (classification 'O' and 'V'). By very secret mail are sent operational letters and enclosures to them in undeveloped negatives, and also other very secret material.

(2) Less secret mail (classification 'A' and 'VA'). By less secret mail is sent less secret material.

F.14

II. *Kinds of operational letters*

The following kinds of operational letters are laid down:

(1) Letters concerning operational questions, as for instance concerning the preparation or the effecting of recruitment, the agent study of persons, groups and organizations, concerning questions of organizing intelligence work and other operational questions.

(2) Letters concerning organizational questions; concerning personnel, the recruitment of cadres, wages, questions of household administration and other questions.

(3) Letters concerning financial questions.

(4) Particular letters on special questions.

III. *Procedure for the formulation of operational letters*

(1) The following sole procedure for the formulation of letters is laid down:

For every line of work a separate letter is sent, to which is allotted a corresponding index (°1): intelligence = 'O', counter-intelligence = 'K', scientific and technical = 'H', Illegal = 'NL', Immigration = 'EM', Soviet Colony = 'SK', seamen = 'M', Delegations = 'D'.

(2) At the beginning of the year a consecutive serial number is allotted to each letter along a corresponding line and the index (°1) is put in the form of a fraction: for instance, Letter No. 1/O—intelligence; Letter No. 5/SK—Soviet Colony.

(°1) We are unable to ascertain the significance of the word 'index' in this context.

F.15

(3) In the local M.V.D. section the letter is prepared in an encoded way, the separate most important places in the text are expressed in ciphers, typing in the first copy, is photographed on combustible negatives, and is sent to M.V.D. Headquarters in undeveloped negatives. The cipher is sent by the same mail in a separate packet to the address of the cipher section.

The drafts of the letter and of the enclosure are destroyed, in accordance with the regulation, which is confirmed by the chief of the local M.V.D. section.

(4) Enclosed objects (money, samples, photographs, etc.) are sent in separate packets, as enclosures to the letter.

IV. *Packing of the operational mail*

(1) The operational mail is packed by the operator into envelopes or parcels (first packet) in the following order:

(a) The negatives are packed in light-proof paper on which is marked the stamp 'very secret', 'K' series, the name of the town, the code name of the addressee and the number of the letter. The packing up of the negatives in paper should be done in such a manner that in the event of necessity it would be possible to expose them to the light swiftly.

(b) Reports and material enclosures are inserted in envelopes, gummed down and sealed with five plain wax seals.

F.16

On the top right-hand corner should be written the stamp 'very secret' and Series 'K'. In the centre—the name of the town and the code name of the addressee. Below— the number of the letter.

(c) The ciphers are transmitted in the order set out in the Special Instruction.

(d) Packets with money transfers are sealed with five plain wax seals. On the top right-hand corner of the packet is written Series 'K'; in the centre—the name of the town and the code name of the addressee; below—'Enclosure No.— to Letter No.—'.

(e) Operational parcels (Radio stations equipment etc.) are sent by very secret mail, as enclosures to an operational letter, correspondingly packed and sealed with a plain wax seal. On the top right-hand corner of the parcel is placed the stamp 'very secret' and Series 'K'; in the centre the name of the town and the code name of the addressee; below—'Enclosure No.— to letter No.—'.

(f) Less secret enclosures in packets, parcels, bales (heavy mail) are not sealed. The weight of the parcel or bale should not exceed 16 Kilograms. Enclosures, the contents of which cannot be divided into two or several bales or parcels, constitute exceptions.

In the top left-hand corner is written the name of the town; in the top right-hand corner is placed classification 'N' or 'V.A.'; in the centre—Enclosure to No.—.

F.17

(g) Personal letters are sent in a separate envelope and are sealed with one plain wax seal. On the envelope is written the name of the town and the code name of the addressee; in the centre 'personal letters'.

V. *Procedure for the dispatch and receipt of mail in the local M.V.D. section*

(1) A list of documents, in accordance with lines of work, should be compiled in the local M.V.D. section in respect of all material and documents intended for dispatch to M.V.D. Headquarters.

The list should be drawn up in the following form: serial number, title of the material, from whom received, the number of pages of the main document, enclosures: a note concerning the importance of material 'V.V.' (Very Important); the list is signed by the chief of the M.V.D. section or by his deputy.

The list for each outgoing post is made up in two copies. The first copy stays in the M.V.D. section.

(2) When packing, the sender sorts out the material according

to the addressees, and subsequently packs it up in three packets.

All the first packets (envelopes) are packed in accordance with paragraph '4' (the packing of the operational mail) of the present instruction.

The second and third packets are packed in the following order:

F.18

(a) When negatives are packed, there is written on the top right-hand corner of the second (inside) packet 'Very secret' and classification 'S'. In the centre by pre-arrangement (°1) address of M.V.D. Headquarters. Below—the numbers of all the enclosed negatives without showing index (°2).

The packet is sealed with a plain wax seal, the imprint of which is known to M.V.D. Headquarters.

On the top right-hand corner of the third packet is written 'Very secret', classification 'O'; in the centre the address—'Soviet Ministry of Foreign Affairs'; on the left bottom corner—the numbers of all the negatives enclosed, without showing index (°2). Under the number —by pre-arrangement (°1) address of M.V.D. Head-quarters.

(b) When packing very secret enclosures containing documents and objects, there should be written on the top right-hand corner of the second envelope or parcel 'Very secret' or 'Secret' (depending on the nature of the enclosure), classification 'V' and 'Personal only'. In the centre—by pre-arrangement (°1) address of M.V.D. Headquarters. Below—the numbers of all the material and enclosures contained in the envelope (parcel) without showing index (°2). The envelope or parcel is sealed with a plain wax seal, the imprint of which is known to M.V.D. Headquarters.

On the top right-hand corner of the third (outside) packet is written 'Very secret' or 'Secret' and classification 'V'. In the centre the address 'Soviet Ministry of Foreign Affairs'. Below—the numbers of all the material enclosed and of the enclosures without showing index (°2). Under the number—by pre-arrangement (°1) address of M.V.D. Headquarters.

(°1) *Sic.* Quaere, the pre-arranged code address?
(°2) See footnote (°1) on F.14.

F.19

For the whole of the outgoing mail there is compiled a general list in which is shown the code name of the receiver, the numbers and the quantity of the packets. The list is inserted in the second (inside) packet, sent under classification 'O' or 'V'.

All the packets are handed over to the chief of the cipher section against a receipt and are sealed with the seals of the Embassy (Consulate).

(3) Incoming mail in the local M.V.D. section is received from the cipher section of the Embassy (Consulate), the packing is checked with seals, and is checked against the list of the mail, which is found in the first (external) packet.

(4) When mail is opened in the local M.V.D. section, the quantity of the documents and material is checked against the list forwarded by M.V.D. Headquarters.

VI. *Safekeeping of materials of the mail*

(1) The original material of dispatched mail is kept in local M.V.D. sections until M.V.D. Headquarters has confirmed its receipt, after which the material is destroyed in accordance with the act, and in the event of operational necessity it is photographed on inflammable negatives and is stored until the necessity has passed.

Incoming letters (negatives and photographic plates) are kept for not more than two weeks.

F.20

In case of necessity, notes are taken from the letters and enclosures in one copy on thin (cigarette) paper, and are kept in the safe of the M.V.D. section until the necessity has passed.

Samples, addresses, names, and other data indispensable on a long term basis for the purposes of operational work, are photographed on inflammable negatives and are kept in the safe of the M.V.D. section until the necessity has passed.

The destruction of operational documents is carried out in accordance with the act, and is confirmed by the chief of the M.V.D. section. The act is photographed and is forwarded to M.V.D. Headquarters on undeveloped negatives with the next mail. The original of the act is destroyed by the M.V.D. section upon acknowledgement from the M.V.D. Headquarters of receipt of the photographic copy of the act.

The present instruction is a guide for the cadre workers of the M.V.D. section who are connected with the dispatch and receipt of operational letters.

G.1 (°1)

(1) 'Denis'—Dalziel
(2) 'Stepan'—Stanley
(3) 'Tikhon'—Tennekuist
(4) 'Raphael'—F
(5) 'Sestra'—Bernie Francisca, Department of External Affairs.

(°1) This document is in Sadovnikov's handwriting.

G.2 (°1)

CONTACTS K

(1) 'Master'
(2) 'Tourist'
(3) 'Sestra'—Franciska Bernie
(4) 'Podruga'
(5) 'Ben'—Hughes
(6) Joe—Department of External Affairs (Archives)
(7)   —Member of the Communist Party, girl, having finished the school of the Department of External Affairs, and will go over to work in the Department of External Affairs.
(8)   —Sister of the wife of B.
(9) Don Woods—Secretary of the adviser of Doctor E. on atomic energy.
(10) 'Moryak'—Macnamara George.
(11) B.—Dep. Director of the Department of External Affairs.

(°1) This document is in Sadovnikov's handwriting.

G.3 (°1)

(1) Wilbur Christinson—'Master'. (husband of the sister of Tourist)
(2) Hebert William Tattersell—Artist.

(°1) This document is in Sadovnikov's handwriting.

G.4 (°1)

Mr C. R. Tennant 'K'
   50 Bundarra Road, Bellview
      Hill, Sydney.
         Tel. FW.1267

Christisen, S. B. 'Crab'
Rogers 'Lovky'
Christisen, N. M. 'Eva'
Ferguson—Raphael
Kosky—Priyatel
Turnbull, K.—'Teodor'
George McNamara—Moryak

(°1) This document is in Petrov's handwriting. The last seven lines were copied by him from one document, the remainder from another.

G.5 (°1)

Letter No. 2 of 14/6/48

Communicate the additional materials and the well-founded conclusions in relation to the following persons:

(1) *Bruce Milis*—progressive labour supporter, secretly assisted the Communist Party. Enjoyed the confidence of Chifley. Resided and had a trading company in the town of Katoomba.

(2) *Geoffrey Powell* (*Geoffry Powell*), photographer, under-cover member of the Communist Party. Proposed that he should transfer to work in the security service. Did he accept the invitation and where does he work now?

(3) (°2)

(4) *Dave Morris*—born 1910, major, bachelor of science, under-cover member of the Communist Party.
After finishing the University studied in England. During the second world war he worked as a technical expert attached to the General Staff in Melbourne. Studied tank matters in England.
In 1946 was sent to England to work in the sphere of military research.

(5) (°2)

(°1) This document and G.6 together form one document. Both are in Sadovnikov's handwriting.

(°2) For reasons stated in Chapter 15 of our Report, we do not publish this entry here, but we set it out in the Annexure.

G.6 (°1)

(6) *Don WOODS* (*Don WOODS*)—former secretary of the adviser of Dr E. on atomic energy of BRIGGS.

G.7 (1)

Encl. to Letter No. 2 of 10/11/49

X (1) *Joe*—born 1921, works in the archives of the Department of External Affairs. Lives in Canberra.

(K) (2) *Taylor*—judge and representative of the Arbitration Commission, labour supporter, up to 1943 was at the head of the security service in Sydney; at that time handed to the Communist Party a document which made possible the exposure of an agent provocateur in one of the regions of the Communist Party. President of the Industrial Commission of N.S.W. 'K' describes him favourably.

(K) (3) *Legge, Jack*—Chemistry scientist. Member of the Communist Party since 1936. In 1939 worked in a Troskyist Group on an assignment of the Communist Party. When the Communist Party was in an illegal situation, 'K' used the house of Legge J. for the publication of the newspaper 'Tribune'. He carried out missions of the Communist Party when he visited Scandinavia. L's wife is now engaged on scientific work in Melbourne. 'K' considers that N5 (L) inspires confidence. A relative of L works in the political intelligence department of the Ministry of Foreign Affairs.

(K) (4) *Hook, Jack*—President of the Sydney Trade Union of the Labour Council, labour supporter, one of the leading members of the Labour Party. Collaborates with the Communist Party. Holds progressive views. 'K' considers H to be a man who deserves to be trusted.

([°]1) Pages 7 to 10 inclusive of Exhibit G together form one document. All are in Sadovnikov's handwriting.

G.8

(S) (5) *Borras*—doctor of Economics, an official fellow worker of the security service, and expert on languages, a Greek. Is engaged on the instruction of Italians, Greeks, and others. Among the members of the security service he is regarded as a leftist. Lives in Canberra.

X (6) *Bernie Franciska*—born 1923, Australian, worked as a secretary-typist in the Secretariat of the Department of External Affairs in Sydney. Under-cover member of the Communist Party since 1943. 'K' was in contact with her personally and received interesting information from her.

(T) (7) *Miller Forbes*—born 1912, a native of Australia, deputy editor of the 'Daily Telegraph'. Expressed a desire to inform 'T' systematically concerning material prepared for the press. Both he and his wife are favourably disposed towards us.

(T) (8) *McInnes*—about 40 years of age, journalist. Has wide connections among press workers and in political and business circles. In his convictions he appears to be a man inclined to the left.

(T) (9) *Birtles B.*—about 48 years of age, prominent journalist, has contacts among writers and artists. Has travelled in Europe, knows Greece well.

(T) (10) *Maclean*—journalist, sympathetically disposed towards us, a very well informed man. In 'T's' opinion, he will give information.

G.9

(T) (11) *Olsen O.*—promised 'T' assistance in the study of the country and in obtaining information passing through the newspaper. ([°]1).

(12) *Simpson Colin*—favourably disposed towards us.

(V) (13) *Frazer*—member of parliament, former correspondent, labour supporter, very close to Evatt. Likes to drink and on such an occasion he becomes very voluble. 'A' used him for obtaining information from Evatt.

(T) (14) *Finnard*—lawyer, graduate of Sydney University, interested in questions of Marxist philosophy. Makes very harsh remarks about the labour people. Offered to give 'A' interesting information. Was friendly with Withall, director of the federal chamber of industry.

(15) *Calwell*—Minister for Information, interested in our country. Has expressed a desire to meet 'A'.

(k) (16) *Brook*—said to be a member of the Communist Party. Brother a member of the Communist Party. Stood for election to parliament. (°1)

(V) (17) *Falstein*—aged about 40, Jew, former member of parliament, noted for his leftist speeches, very much wanted to go to the Soviet Union.

(18) *McKell*—former prime minister, was on good terms with Simonov, the first U.S.S.R. representative in Australia. Asked 'A' to turn to him for assistance.

(°1) We are unable to identify the person to whom this entry refers.

G.10

(S) (19) *Westcott*—Former worker in the department of communications of the Ministry of Foreign Affairs, his work was secret. Very cautious. Was acquainted with 'Lipsky'. Resided in Manuka Circle, Canberra; tel. B.172.

(V) (20) *Fitzhardinge*—librarian of the National library, knows quite a lot and can give useful advice. Has access to the library of the parliament. Was acquainted with 'Lip'.

(K) (21) *Hibbard L. U.*—Representative of N.S.W. State in the federal council, member of the Communist Party.

(S) (22) *Gutwach, Al—dr Mihailovich,* born in Odessa, in 1923 he went to the U.S.A. and then to Australia. Had relatives in the U.S.S.R. with whom he maintains correspondence.

G.11 (°1)

Frantishka Peter, born 1911, 2/xi—Verner'nitsa, Czech, completed 8 classes of a middle school.

From 1928 to 1931 worked as a salesman in the town of Beneshov.

From 1932 to 1937 he lived in French Morocco.

In 1937 returned to Czechoslovakia.

In 1941 was conscripted into the German army. In January 1942 he voluntarily surrendered as a prisoner. In 1944 was sent into Czech territory, and gave a good account of himself.

From 1945 to 1948 he worked as director of a hotel in the Sudeten area. He was refused citizenship. He got in touch with his wife's sister living in Sydney, who asked him to come out and settle and he left in February 1949.

Wife Frantishka and son Peter.

(°1) G.11 and G.12 are written on the front and on the back respectively of the one sheet of paper. They are in Petrov's handwriting, and are particulars copied by him from a file in the M.V.D. safe at the Embassy.

G.12 (¹)

Divishek Vintsess PECHEK
Vintsesovich his wife
Frantishka Veler.
16 Holt Street, Stanmore,
Sydney, Australia.

(¹) See footnote (1) on G.11.

G.13 (1)

(1) LOT—MCLEAN F. J. First Secretary. Willingly accepted invitations and attended receptions arranged by our workers in private apartments. In his conversations he expressed dissatisfaction with the government of Menzies, with the internal regime in the Department of External Affairs—with Spender, the chief of his department. Allegedly was a member of the Communist Party, which he left at his own desire.

(2) COOK—Charles Bresland—40—Market St. 59 Peel st., Belmore.

(3) RUSSELL Norman—born 1922. b/p (²). It is alleged that whilst in the U.S.S.R. he met two diplomats of the British Embassy, visited Embassy.

(4) MONAKH—apartment. DAGINIAN (3°)

(5) MORROW—study, etc.

(6) O'BYRNE ———— ————

(1) Pages 13 to 18 inclusive of Exhibit G together form one document. All are in Petrov's handwriting.
(2) This is an abbreviation the meaning of which is 'of no party'. Cf. the description of Russell on B.14.
(3) This is Petrov's mis-spelling of 'Daghian'.

G.14

(7) Slavianin—obtrusiveness with regard to establishing contact with Pakhomov.

(8) Olia—was made use of on external lines.

(9) 'Kliment'—Novikov N. K.—Cricket House, 254 George St.

(10) 'Mefody'— ,, N. N. Photo Studio.

(11) Olga

(12) Stanley Herbert North—worked as a cipher clerk in Moscow—........................ (¹) he was in close relations with the Americans Gilmore, Powers and Crawford; together with them he visited restaurants and consumed large quantities of alcoholic drinks.

(13) Anthony Chalesnik—Resides at the address RAGNER RD.

(14) Charli—REX Claude, Ferro—transmitted valuable information to the Communists, and then they to us.

(1) One word illegible (probably 'Olymp': in which case read 'Moscow—Olymp').

G.15–16 (1)

(1) These pages contain references, numbered consecutively from 15 to 26, to persons whose names, for reasons stated in our Report, we do not publish here. We include the references in the Annexure.

G.17 (1)

(27)

(28)

(29) RUSSELL—Correspondent—Australian United (2) Press, labour supporter, member of the Government, expressed a desire to go to Russia— is of interest for study.

(30)

(31) Max STENFENS—54 Lions Rd., Romyne, Sydney, Jew, easy going, especially in an inebriated state. Is of interest as a keeper of a house.

(32) Senator MCCALLUM—Member of the Parliamentary Foreign Affairs Committee, member of the Liberal Party.

(1) For reasons stated in our Report, we do not publish here the references numbered 27, 28, and 30, but include them in the Annexure.

(2) The Russian words for 'Correspondent Australian United' are crossed out in the original.

G.18

Answers to questions. Had contact with Pakhomov.

(33) Vassilev—Kustar.

(34) Nil—John Pringle—hates the politics of the Americans; is sympathetic to communism. (1)

(35) Doctor Clive Sandy—dentist—denture maker, 38 Fletcher Street, Essendon, Victoria, W.5., Tel. FU.7166. Melbourne—on illegal workers.

(36) John Graham—Gonetz—seamens trade union, sailed in the capacity of fireman. His father resides at 18 Hindley Street, Townsville, Qld. Gonetz resides at the address 54 Day St. Sydney Tel. BU.1122.

(1) We are unable to identify the person to whom this entry refers.

Notes

Chapter 1

1. Conversations with Bialoguski, 1974, and his book, *The Petrov Story* (London: Heinemann, 1955).

2. Rebecca West, *The New Meaning of Treason* (New York: Viking Press, 1964), p. 233.

3. *National Times*. In its issues of 3–8 September and 10–15 September 1973 it published at length the results of an inquiry into the Petrov affair and its aftermath.

Chapter 2

1. L. F. Crisp, *Ben Chifley* (Melbourne: Longman, 1960), p. 360.

2. Ibid., p. 355.

3. Ibid., p. 356.

4. Ibid.

5. Ibid., p. 358.

Chapter 4

1. J. D. Pringle, *Have Pen Will Travel* (London: Chatto and Windus, 1973).

Chapter 5

1. W. J. Brown, ed., *The Petrov Conspiracy Unmasked* (Sydney: Current Books, 1957), p. 31.

2. Ibid., p. 33.

3. Ibid.

4. *Commonwealth of Australia: Parliamentary Debates* (hereafter cited as Hansard), House of Representatives, 27 May 1952, p. 808.

5. Ibid., pp. 871–72.

6. *Commonwealth of Australia: Royal Commission on Espionage, Transcript of Proceedings* (hereafter cited as Transcript), p. 2703.

7. *Have Pen Will Travel*, p. 116.

Chapter 6

1. Hansard, H. of R., 22 February 1956, pp. 164–65.

Chapter 7

1. Hansard, H. of R., 12 August 1954, p. 284.

Chapter 8

1. For a recent and thorough examination of Australian society, see A. F. Davies and S. Encel, eds., *Australian Society: A Sociological Introduction*, 2nd ed. (Melbourne: Cheshire, 1970); refer particularly to the chapter 'Urban Communities' for a discussion of the cities' importance.

2. Hansard, H. of R., 13 April 1954, pp. 326–28.

3. Hansard, H. of R., 14 April 1954, p. 372 (Evatt was reading his statement in Parliament the following day).

4. Russell H. Barrett, *Promises and Performances in Australian Politics* (Vancouver: Publications Centre, University of British Columbia, 1963), p. 81.

5. James Jupp, *Australian Party Politics* (Melbourne: Melbourne University Press, 1964), p. 20.

Chapter 9

1. *Sun-Herald*, Thursday 15 April 1954.

2. *Sydney Morning Herald* (hereafter cited as *SMH*), Thursday 15 April 1954.

3. Ibid.

4. Hansard, H. of R., 14 April 1954, p. 373.

5. *SMH*, Thursday 15 April 1954.

6. Ibid.

7. Ibid.

8. Ibid.

9. Ibid.

10. Ibid., Friday 16 April 1954.

11. Ibid., Thursday 15 April 1954.

12. Ibid., Friday 16 April 1954.
13. Ibid., Saturday 17 April 1954.
14. *Sun-Herald*, Sunday 18 April 1954.
15. *SMH*, Monday 19 April 1954.
16. Ibid.
17. Ibid., Tuesday 20 April 1954.

Chapter 10

1. *A. M. (Australian Magazine)*, 27 April 1954.
2. *The Petrov Story*, p. 219; Vladimir and Evdokia Petrov, *Empire of Fear: The Petrovs' Own Story* (New York: Praeger, 1956), p. 299.
3. *SMH*, Saturday 17 April 1954.
4. Ibid., Tuesday 20 April 1954.
5. *The Petrov Conspiracy Unmasked.*
6. *The Petrov Story*, p. 222.
7. *Empire of Fear*, p. 299.
8. This account is based mainly on the *SMH*, Tuesday 20 April 1954.

Chapter 11

1. *SMH* editorial, Saturday 10 April 1954. This editorial was published before the announcement of Petrov's defection, and was probably a reaction to the contemporary discussion of the Royal Commission led by Mr Justice Dovey into alleged police brutality in New South Wales.
2. *SMH*, Thursday 15 April 1954.
3. *Canada: Report of the Royal Commission on Espionage (1946).*
4. *SMH*, Tuesday 27 April 1954.
5. Ibid., Thursday 29 April 1954.
6. Ibid., editorial, Friday 30 April 1954.
7. Ibid., Saturday 1 May 1954.
8. George Healy, *A.L.P.: The Story of the Labor Party* (Brisbane: Jacaranda Press, 1955), p. 218.
9. *Daily Mirror*, Friday 30 April 1954.
10. *Commonwealth of Australia: Report of the Royal*

Commission on Espionage (hereafter cited as *Report*), p. 1.

Chapter 12

1. *SMH*, Tuesday 20 April 1954; see also *Western Mail,* 6 May 1954.
2. *SMH*, Saturday 24 April 1954.
3. Ibid.
4. Ibid., Tuesday 20 April 1954.
5. Ibid., Wednesday 5 May 1954.
6. Ibid.
7. Ibid., Thursday 6 May 1954.
8. Ibid., Saturday 1 May 1954.
9. Ibid., Friday 7 May 1954.
10. Ibid.
11. Ibid., editorial, Tuesday 4 May 1954.
12. Ibid., Thursday 6 May 1954.
13. Ibid., Friday 7 May 1954. Menzies was speaking in Brisbane.
14. *Promises and Performances in Australian Politics,* p. 83.
15. *SMH*, Tuesday 11 May 1954. Fadden was speaking in the seaside resort of Southport.
16. Ibid., Wednesday 12 May 1954.
17. Ibid., Tuesday 18 May 1954.
18. Ibid., Monday 19 April 1954.
19. Ibid., Tuesday 4 May 1954.
20. Ibid., Saturday 17 April 1954.
21. Ibid., Saturday 15 May 1954.
22. *Sun-Herald*, Sunday 16 May 1954.
23. *SMH*, Wednesday 5 May 1954.
24. Ibid., Tuesday 27 April 1954.
25. *Sun-Herald* editorial, Sunday 18 April 1954.
26. *SMH*, Tuesday 18 May and Wednesday 19 May 1954.
27. Ibid., Saturday 15 May 1954.
28. Ibid., Thursday 20 May 1954.
29. Ibid.
30. Ibid., Thursday 27 May 1954.

Chapter 13

1. David J. Dallin, *Soviet Espionage* (New Haven: Yale University Press, 1955), p. 14; Allen Dulles, *The Craft of Intelligence* (New York: Signet Books, 1965), pp. 83–100, 103–15; *Transcript*, p. 8.

2. *A.M.*, 13 July 1954.

3. *Transcript*, pp. 143–45.

4. Ibid., p. 32.

5. *Voice,* May 1954.

6. *Transcript*, p. 26.

7. Ibid., p. 61, paragraphs 14–19 (hereafter abbreviated in the form: *Transcript*, p. 61/*14–19*).

8. Ibid., p. 93/*495–500*.

9. Ibid., p. 210/*841*.

10. Ibid., p. 213.

11. *SMH*, Wednesday 21 April 1954.

12. *Transcript*, pp. 189/*434–39*, 225/*599–604*, 225/*619*.

13. Ibid., p. 214/*47–59*.

14. *Report*, p. 36.

15. *Transcript*, p. 250.

16. Ibid., p. 250/*595*.

17. Ibid., p. 267/*679–82*.

18. Ibid., p. 297/*998–1000*.

19. Ibid., p. 268/*732–36*.

20. Ibid., p. 309/*396*.

21. Ibid., p. 317/*1–5*.

22. Ibid., pp. 325–46.

23. Ibid., p. 321/*1–3*.

24. Ibid., pp. 120/*118–24*, 322–23.

25. Ibid., pp. A–N (after p. 317).

Chapter 14

1. Hansard, H. of R., 11 August 1954, pp. 156–62.

2. Hansard, H. of R., 12 August 1954, pp. 240–45 (Ward), 247–49 and 282–84 (Menzies), 284–86 (Evatt).

3. Hansard, Senate, 12 August 1954, pp. 208–16.

4. *Transcript*, p. 815/*19–20*. For Dalziel's extraordinary

telegram to Menzies on 14 July 1954, suggesting that both he and the prime minister submit themselves for judgment to the courts of the Presbyterian Church, see *Transcript*, p. 816/*68*.

5. Albert Thomas Grundeman (1925–57). For his association with Dr Evatt, see *Transcript*, pp. 309/*405*, 431, 446/*930*, 2638/*239*.

6. *SMH*, Tuesday 17 August 1954.

7. *Transcript*, p. 422/*418–24*.

8. Ibid., p. 429/*98*.

9. Ibid., p. 501/*867*.

10. Ibid., pp. 830–31.

11. *Report*, p. 273.

12. *Transcript*, p. 478/*862–65*.

13. Ibid., p. 1055/*586*.

14. Ibid., p. 505.

15. Ibid., p. 509 ff.

16. Ibid., p. 461/*121*, and *SMH*, Friday 11 September 1954.

17. Ibid., p. 418/*239–43*.

18. Ibid., p. 499/*770–88*.

19. Ibid., p. 609/*48–66*.

20. Ibid., p. 591/*507–10*.

21. Ibid., pp. 590–92.

22. Ibid., p. 428/*54*.

23. Ibid., pp. 591 ff, 604/*1148*, 605/*1183–84*.

24. Ibid., p. 731/*111*.

25. Ibid., pp. 661/*1171–76*, 687/*849*.

26. Ibid., pp. 681–85.

27. Ibid., pp. 688–89.

28. Ibid., pp. A–N (after p. 317).

29. Ibid., p. A.

30. *SMH*, Saturday 5 September 1954.

31. *Sun-Herald*, Sunday 6 September 1954.

32. *The Petrov Conspiracy Unmasked*, pp. 224–29.

33. *Transcript*, p. 732/*124*.

34. Ibid., p. 727/*19*.

35. *SMH*, Tuesday 8 September 1954.

36. *Transcript*, p. 733/*169*.

37. Ibid., pp. 781–810.

38. Ibid., p. 947/*33*.

39. *The Petrov Story*, pp. 99–101, 151, 172, 174, 188; see also *Transcript*, pp. 260–61, 2257/*787–94*.

40. *Transcript*, p. 1246/*492–93*.

41. The interim report appears as Appendix 2 to the *Report*, pp. 418–29.

Chapter 15

1. *Report*, pp. 59–60.

2. *Transcript*, p. 1028/*890*.

3. *Report*, p. 11/*31*.

4. Ibid., p. 192.

5. Ibid., p. 207.

6. Ibid., pp. 331–35.

7. *Transcript*, pp. 1251–52; see also *Empire of Fear*, pp. 266–67.

8. *Report*, pp. 411–12.

9. Ibid., p. 241.

10. Ibid., pp. 241–50.

11. *Transcript*, p. 2441/*19*.

12. Ibid., pp. 1334/*338*, 1395/*428*.

13. Ibid., p. 2488/*433*.

14. Ibid., pp. 2477–97.

15. *Report*, p. 299/*20*.

16. *The Petrov Conspiracy Unmasked*, p. 230; *Transcript*, pp. C–D (after p. 317).

17. *Transcript*, p. C/*82* (after p. 317).

18. Hansard, H. of R., 13 June 1956, p. 3118.

19. For the evidence and various arguments, see *Transcript*, pp. 2157/*93*, 2166–68, 2173/*640–47*, 2197/*585–86*, 2199/*684–94*, 2265/*12–13*, 2299/*183*, 2321/*24–36*, 2369/*25*. For Petrov counting the money, see *Transcript*, pp. 2117/*327–28*, 2166.

20. *Report*, pp. 70–72.

21. Ibid., pp. 224, 831.

22. Ibid., pp. 63–65.

23. Ibid., p. 301/*29*.

Chapter 16

1. *Soviet Espionage*, pp. 503–07.
2. *The Craft of Intelligence*, p. 132.
3. A brief discussion of this 'growing cooperation' appears in *The Craft of Intelligence*, pp. 54–55.
4. *Transcript*, pp. 734–41.
5. *Empire of Fear*, p. 269.
6. *Transcript*, p. 753/*230*.

Chapter 17

1. Bialoguski does not mention his relationship to the McMaughs in his book; see *The Petrov Story*, p. 161, and *Empire of Fear*, p. 286.
2. *The Petrov Story*, pp. 159–62.
3. *Transcript*, p. 737/*298–300*.
4. *Empire of Fear*, p. 88.
5. *The Petrov Story*, pp. 165, 170; *Empire of Fear*, p. 286.
6. *The Petrov Story*, p. 169.
7. *Daily Telegraph*, 5 and 8 June 1955.
8. *Transcript*, p. 739/*340*; *The Petrov Story*, p. 177; *Empire of Fear*, p. 287.
9. *The Petrov Story*, pp. 181–86. At this meeting on 31 January, Mrs Petrov said that she and her husband would be going back to the Soviet Union 'about March or April'; thus her statement tended to corroborate the date Petrov had already set for his defection, 5 April.
10. *Transcript*, p. 948/*53*.
11. *The Petrov Story*, p. 189; *Transcript*, p. 739/*359*. Bialoguski tape-recorded the conversation.
12. *The Petrov Story*, p. 191. Petrov's activities this day seem designed to frustrate the meeting with Richards. When he did not show up at the appointed time, Bialoguski contacted him. He said he had 'been delayed' and postponed the meeting.
13. *Transcript*, p. 1028/*890*.
14. *The Petrov Story*, p. 191.
15. *Transcript*, p. 741/*404*; *Empire of Fear*, pp. 288–89; *The Petrov Story*, p. 192.

16. 'In the West, whenever this happens, and when the motives of the diplomat appear to be *bona fide*, the requested protection and material assistance needed until the diplomat can find a new livelihood in his new home are usually granted' (*The Craft of Intelligence*, p. 131).

17. *The Craft of Intelligence*, p. 200.

18. *Transcript*, p. 747/71.

19. *Transcript*, p. 748/98–99; *The Petrov Story*, pp. 200–01; *Empire of Fear*, p. 290. After Richards had left, Petrov named the exact date of his defection, 3 April. He said his successor would be arriving that day.

20. For descriptions of this meeting and the questions asked of Petrov by Richards, see *Transcript*, p. 749/127–31, and *Empire of Fear*, pp. 290–91.

21. *Empire of Fear*, p. 291.

22. *Transcript*, p. 1028/890.

23. Ibid., p. 745/24 ff.

24. Ibid., pp. 136–37.

25. Some of these conversations may have been tape-recorded, but no transcripts have ever been released; see *Report*, p. 30/81.

26. *Transcript*, p. 747/82; *Empire of Fear*, p. 291. Petrov 'was extremely agitated on that night' (*Transcript*, p. 753/229).

27. Depending on the source, the raiders were First Secretary Vislykh, and Ambassador Generalov or the minor official Christoborodov; see *Transcript*, p. 752/221, *The Petrov Story*, p. 204, and *Empire of Fear*, p. 292. The desks of Kislytsin and Platkais were also raided, and a paper was found out of place in the latter's.

28. *Empire of Fear*, p. 294.

29. *Transcript*, p. 752/219–25.

30. For Petrov's and Richards' activities on 2 April, see *Transcript*, p. 754/300, *Empire of Fear*, pp. 295–96, and *The Petrov Story*, pp. 203–04. Petrov tells how, while hurrying to catch his plane, he nearly bumped into Menzies, who was returning from an election tour of Western Australia.

31. Accounts of the activities of 3 April are found in

Empire of Fear, p. 297, *The Petrov Story*, p. 205, and *Transcript*, p. 755/*330*.

32. The Petrovs' 'relations were not without tension. Mrs Petrov was much more adaptable than her husband, and socially he sometimes got on her nerves. In the home, too, it was frequently apparent that he exasperated her by some of his mannerisms. Petrov's tendency to exaggerate these deficiencies to annoy his wife did not help the situation.' (*The Petrov Story*, p. 171.)

33. *The Petrov Story*, pp. 194–202.

Chapter 18

1. Moscow Letter A-8 of 27 September 1952; *Report*, p. 363.

2. *The Craft of Intelligence*, p. 47.

3. *Transcript*, pp. 783–84, and *Report*, p. 389. The woman, Mrs Kazanova, wanted to make arrangements for her will, and to be visited by a relative from Russia. The Moscow Letter raises the possibility of sending 'an illegal worker, under the guise of a relative of Kazanova' to Australia.

4. *Transcript*, p. 21.

5. *The Craft of Intelligence*, p. 81.

6. *The New Meaning of Treason*, p. 154.

7. Sadovnikov's cipher clerk, Gubanov, left Australia on 5 March 1951; Sadovnikov himself left on 18 April 1951; see *Transcript*, pp. 90/*310*, 156/*658*.

8. *Transcript*, p. 1752/*103*.

9. *The Petrov Conspiracy Unmasked*, p. 170. Dr Charles Monticone for twenty years carried out all handwriting investigations for the New South Wales police force.

10. Ibid., pp. 65–66; *Report*, pp. 125/*426*, 132/*461*.

11. *The Petrov Story*, pp. 58, 96.

12. According to an ASIO statement in the *Report*, pp. 119–20, Petrov claimed he got this information from Pakhomov, and in *Empire of Fear*, p. 269, he says he got it from Kislytsin.

13. *Transcript*, pp. 2533–34. Clayton also denied ever

going to the Russian Social Club or Australia–Soviet House; see *Transcript*, p. 2503/*1141–49*.

14. For the many questions on this topic, see *Transcript*, pp. 2486/*348*, 2487/*410* (re. Miss Bernie), and 2536–39 (incl. George Legge). Clayton denied ever meeting Miss Barnett (*Transcript*, p. 2484/*262–64*). Miss Barnett could find no resemblance between Clayton and the man she saw outside Rose's home in 1950; see *Transcript*, pp. 1355, 1357/*281–97*, 2544/*504–19*.

15. Both the Petrovs and Bialoguski mention the Klodnitskys, who seem to have been very active in Communist circles; see *Empire of Fear*, p. 261, *The Petrov Story*, pp. 42-43, 53, 62, and *Transcript*, p. 2683/*46–50*.

16. *Report*, p. 409.

17. Ibid., p. 182/*652*.

18. Sydney Max Falstein (b. 30 May 1914), Labor MHR for Watson (NSW) 1940–49.

19. *Report*, p. 299/*20*.

20. *The Petrov Conspiracy Unmasked*, pp. 234–35.

21. *Report*, p. 428/*53*.

22. It is important to appreciate that in Canberra Windeyer had said Document J was only thirty-seven pages in length; it is most unlikely that Lockwood did not know this. See *Transcript*, p. 2603/*165*.

23. *Transcript*, p. 1044/*181*.

24. Ibid., p. 955/*372*.

25. Ibid., p. 194/*73*.

26. Ibid., p. 1027/*848–49*; *Report*, p. 393.

27. *Report*, p. 393.

28. *Transcript*, p. 535/*1039*.

29. *The Craft of Intelligence*, p. 199.

30. *Transcript*, p. 1073/*86*.

31. Ibid., p. 1073/*106–13*.

32. Ibid., p. 559/*701* (Insp. Rogers), p. 1002/*1326–53* (Miss Rook).

33. On pages J-35 and J-25; see *Transcript*, p. 829/*709*.

34. *Transcript*, p. 1077/*246*.

35. Ibid., p. 1058/*700*.

36. Ibid., p. 1059/*716–18*.
37. Ibid., pp. 197/*215–17*, 1127/*784*.
38. Ibid., p. 419/*286*.
39. Ibid., p. 418/*239–43*.
40. Ibid., p. 1055/*567*.
41. Ibid., p. 1042/*123*.
42. *SMH*, Friday 11 September 1954.

Chapter 19

1. *Transcript,* p. 722/*37*.
2. *Royal Commission into the Communist Party in Victoria: Report*, p. 7.
3. *Transcript*, p. 2315/*713*.
4. *Report*, p. 61/*177*.
5. *Transcript*, p. 6.
6. *The Petrov Story*, p. 238.
7. *Transcript*, p. 1591/*281*.
8. Ibid., p. 2634/*73*.
9. Ibid., p. 1659/*118–20*.
10. *Report*, p. 99.
11. *Transcript*, p. 918/*91–93*.
12. Ibid., pp. 262/*442–55*, 877/*1121–22*.
13. Ibid., p. 6.
14. *Report*, pp. 66–67.
15. *Transcript*, p. 1979/*80–83*.
16. Quoted in *The Petrov Conspiracy Unmasked*, p. 132.
17. Ibid.
18. *Transcript*, p. 187/*375*.
19. Ibid., p. 113/*390*.
20. Ibid., p. 127/*310–15*.

Chapter 20

1. *National Times*, 10–15 September 1973.
2. Menzies, as he showed then and in his original appointment of the Royal Commissioners, was thoroughly versed in the necessity for delicacy in negotiations with the judiciary. In the early 1930s the leadership of the conservative Australian government had determined that it was time for Menzies to

ascend from the Victorian Legislative Assembly, where he was attorney-general, to the Australian Parliament. Latham, the Australian attorney-general, held the safe conservative seat of Kooyong and was prepared to cede it to Menzies, provided he was rewarded by being appointed chief justice of Australia. The trouble was that there was already a chief justice, Sir Frank Gavan Duffy, and he had no reason to step down. Menzies fixed that by appointing Gavan Duffy's son to the Victorian Supreme Court. Latham resigned, as did Menzies, and Menzies then took Latham's seat. Gavan Duffy held on, to Latham's chagrin, but resigned after being created a privy councillor in 1936. Latham finally assumed his rightful place.

Chapter 21

1. *National Times*, 3–8 June 1973.

Bibliography

Official sources

Commonwealth of Australia: Parliamentary Debates (Hansard), House of Representatives, 1953–57.

Commonwealth of Australia: Parliamentary Debates (Hansard), Senate, 1953–57.

Commonwealth of Australia: Report of the Royal Commission on Espionage. Sydney: Government Printing Office, 1955.

Commonwealth of Australia: Royal Commission on Espionage, Transcript of Proceedings. 9 vols., 2796 pp.

Memoirs

Bialoguski, Michael. *The Petrov Story.* London: Heinemann, 1955.

Petrov, Vladimir, and Petrov, Evdokia. *Empire of Fear: The Petrovs' Own Story.* New York: Praeger, 1956.

Secondary sources

Barrett, Russell H. *Promises and Performances in Australian Politics.* Vancouver: Publications Centre, University of British Columbia, 1963.

Barron, John. *KGB: The Secret Work of Soviet Secret Agents.* London: Hodder and Stoughton, 1974.

Brown, W. J., ed. *The Petrov Conspiracy Unmasked.* Sydney: Current Books, 1957.

Crisp, L. F. *The Australian Federal Labor Party, 1901–1951.* Melbourne: Longman, 1955.

———. *Ben Chifley.* Melbourne: Longman, 1960.

Dallin, David J. *Soviet Espionage.* New Haven: Yale University Press, 1955.

Davies, A. F., and Encel, S., eds. *Australian Society: A Sociological Introduction.* 2nd ed. Melbourne: Cheshire, 1970.

Deriabin, Peter, and Gibney, Frank. *The Secret World.* New York: Doubleday, 1959.

Dulles, Allen. *The Craft of Intelligence*. New York: Signet Books, 1965.

Ellis, Ulrich. *A History of the Australian Country Party*. Melbourne: Melbourne University Press, 1963.

Gouzenko, Igor. *The Iron Curtain*. New York: Dutton, 1948.

Healy, George. *A.L.P.: The Story of the Labor Party*. Brisbane: Jacaranda Press, 1955.

Jupp, James. *Australian Party Politics*. Melbourne: Melbourne University Press, 1964.

Khokhlov, Nikolai. *In the Name of Conscience*. New York: David McKay, 1959.

Kurzman, Dan. *Subversion of Innocents*. New York: Random House, 1963.

Moorehead, Alan. *The Traitors*. New York: Dell, 1965.

Philby, H. A. R. *My Silent War*. London: MacGibbon and Kee, 1968.

Pringle, John Douglas. *Have Pen Will Travel*. London: Chatto and Windus, 1973.

Reynolds, P. L. *The Democratic Labor Party*. Brisbane: Jacaranda Press, 1974.

Santamaria, B. A. *The Price of Freedom*. Melbourne: Campion Press, 1964.

Webb, Leicester. *Communism and Democracy in Australia: A Survey of the 1951 Referendum*. New York: Praeger, 1955.

West, Katharine. *Power in the Liberal Party*. Melbourne: Cheshire, 1966.

West, Rebecca. *The New Meaning of Treason*. New York: Viking Press, 1964.

Whitington, Don. *The Rulers: Fifteen Years of the Liberals*. Sydney: Angus and Robertson, 1964.

———. *Ring the Bells: A Dictionary of Australian Federal Politics*. Melbourne: Georgian House, 1956.

Wolin, Simon, and Slusser, Robert M. *The Soviet Secret Police*. New York: Praeger, 1957.

Newspapers

Nation Review, 13–19 September 1974.

National Times, 3–8 September and 10–15 September 1973.

New York Times, April–May 1954.

Sydney Morning Herald, and its Sunday paper, the *Sun-Herald*, 1954–55.

Articles (published in Australia)

A. M. (*Australian Magazine*), 27 April 1954; 20 April 1954; 6, 13, 20 July 1954.

Australian Quarterly, June 1954.

Canberra Letter, 16 June 1954.

Canberra Survey, January 1954.

Current Notes (Department of External Affairs), April 1954.

Daily Telegraph, articles by Mrs Patricia Bialoguski, 1–11 June 1955.

Inside Canberra, 29 April 1954, 3 June 1954.

Operation Petrov, T. M. Wixted & Co., Public Forum, Sydney—Pamphlet 28. First issued 27 October 1966.

Pix, 1 May 1954.

Voice, May and December 1954.

Western Mail, 6 May 1954.

Articles (published outside Australia)

British Yearbook of International Law, vol. XXV, 'Espionage and Immunity: Some Recent Problems and Developments'.

National Republic (Boston), April 1956.

The People (UK), article by Petrov, 18 September 1955.

Reporter (New York), 24 March 1955.

Saturday Evening Post, serialized article by Bialoguski, 6 August–10 September 1955.

Time and Tide (London), 1 October 1955, 10 March 1956.

Index